PSYCHOLOGY

Anjanie McCarthy

Fanshawe College

Pearson Canada Inc., 26 Prince Andrew Place, North York, Ontario M3C 2H4.

9780134771236

1 18

Library and Archives Canada Cataloguing in Publication

McCarthy, Anjanie, 1976-, author
    Psychology / Anjanie McCarthy (Fanshawe College).

ISBN 978-0-13-477123-6 (spiral bound)

    1. Psychology—Textbooks.   2. Textbooks.   I. Title.

BF121.M15 2018   150   C2017-906424-X

Contents

Pearson FlexText

Essential Employability Skills

Top skills employers seek:

Success in any sector is dependent upon more than core academic knowledge or technical and occupational skills. Employers need critical thinkers, problem solvers, and leaders to tackle the challenges of today's workplace. Employees with successful career paths learn to communicate effectively, engage appropriately with others, and be self-reliant. Effective career readiness and employability strategies develop the whole learner and incorporate personal and social capabilities; critical thinking and problem-solving skills; and academic and occupational knowledge.

That is what Pearson FlexText is all about.

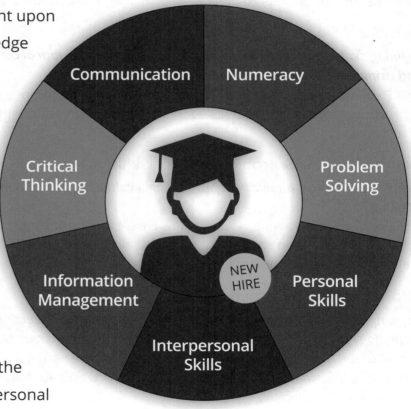

For more information on Pearson's commitment to employability, visit **pearsoned.com/employability**.

Pearson FlexText helps bridge the skills gap and helps students and instructors make the most of valuable face-to-face class time.

We created this resource to help students achieve academic success while also developing the key skills that hiring managers value in candidates.

Communication Skills

Defining skill areas: reading, writing, speaking, listening, presenting, and visual literacy

Students may not be developing their reading skills because they do not have access to course materials – either by choice or by circumstance. FlexTexts are affordable and accessible. FlexTexts include learning objectives and chapter summaries in combination with concise discussions of key topics to support reading comprehension, and provide individual and group activities that afford students the opportunity to practice their writing and communication skills.

Numeracy Skills

Defining skill areas: understanding and applying mathematical concepts and reasoning, analyzing and using mathematical data, and conceptualizing

This FlexText is designed to be an in-class activity workbook, one that allows faculty to provide instructional support to students as they apply mathematical and statistical analysis across a range of activities.

Critical Thinking & Problem-Solving Skills

Defining skill areas: analyzing, synthesizing, evaluating, decision making, creativity, and innovative thinking

The exercises and activities found in this FlexText are not simply factual, recall, or "skill and drill" activities. They engage students at different levels of Bloom's Taxonomy to help students develop critical thinking and problem-solving skills.

Information Management Skills

Defining skill areas: gathering and managing information, selecting and using appropriate tools and technology for a task or project, computer literacy, and internet skills

Not all of the exercises in a FlexText are pen-and-paper activities. Many require students to engage with online information and assets to help them investigate how to analyze and solve an array of problems and challenges.

Interpersonal Skills

Defining skill areas: teamwork, relationship management, conflict resolution, leadership, and networking

FlexText is designed to be brought into class. It can help to facilitate group work and collaborative problem solving, and activities can be implemented in ways that help students to develop their interpersonal skills.

Personal Skills

Defining skill areas: managing self, managing change, being flexible and adaptable, engaging in reflexive practice, and demonstrating personal responsibility

Making the decision to purchase course materials and actively engage with course content is one of the first steps toward demonstrating personal responsibility for success in school. The page layout of a FlexText also encourages note taking and promotes the development of strong study skills.

1 Research Methods

LEARNING OBJECTIVES

L01 Describe six possible mistakes that can occur in research

L02 Explain the eight steps of the scientific method

L03 Summarize the strengths and weaknesses of descriptive methods used in research

L04 Compare and contrast the correlational and experimental approaches to research

LEARN...

Psychology is the scientific study of mind and behaviour, and like all other sciences it is founded on empiricism. Empiricism is the view that information that is observed and collected by us is true, valid, and reliable. The process of gathering information in this way is called research and it is the best way for us to learn about the unknown. But, there are mistakes that can be made in research. For example, Measurement Bias can occur if research tools or methods are not valid (measures what it is meant to measure) and reliable (consistently produces the same results for a specific participant every time it is used), or Observer Bias can occur if a researcher can only see what she/he expects to see when observing others. To address these and other potential biases and errors in research, the Scientific Method is used. The Scientific Method outlines the key steps a researcher should take when engaging in research: Identify the problem, Conduct background research, Formulate a hypothesis, Test the hypothesis, Analyze results, and Report results. There are several methods that researchers can use to observe behaviour. Descriptive methods allow researchers to gather information on a topic without focusing on the relationships that may exists between factors. Descriptive methods include Naturalistic Observation (watching animals or humans behave in their normal environment), Laboratory Observation (watching animals or humans behave in a laboratory setting), Case Study (gathering information from one individual or a small group of individuals), and Survey (asking participants a series of questions about a topic). If researchers want to examine the relationship between two factors, they can use either a correlational or an experimental approach. Both correlational and experimental approaches examine the relationship between variables. The correlational approach will tell us the strength and direction of a relationship but cannot tell us if one variable causes the other. The experiment is the only approach that allows us to examine cause-and-effect relationships between variables. Each research approach has its strengths and weaknesses. For example, the strength of a case study is that it allows for the collection of a lot of detailed information, but its weakness is that the information collected is likely not applicable to others.

Psychology Is a Science

L01 Describe six possible mistakes that can occur in research

When we hear the word "science", disciplines like biology, physics, and chemistry may pop into our minds, but **psychology**, the study of mind and behaviour, is also a science (Baird & McCarthy, 2014). Psychology and other sciences are founded on **empiricism**, which is the view that information that is observed and collected by us is true, valid, and reliable, and as such, it can best help us to understand the unknown. The process of gathering information in this way is called **research**. But, there are mistakes that can be made in research. What are some potential mistakes that researchers can make?

- **Population Error:** It can occur when we incorrectly choose the population of people we want to observe for our study. If a researcher is not examining the correct group of people for a specific behaviour, event, belief, etc., then the information gathered is not useful, and instead provides inaccurate information about a topic.

- **Sample Error:** It can occur when we run a study using participants who have been incorrectly selected from a correct population. Given that it is not always possible to include the entire population of interest in a study, addressing sample error is important to ensure that information gathered accurately reflects the larger population. In research, the sample must be **representative** of the larger population we are interested in examining. To be representative of the population, a sample must be similar in make up in all key demographics, such as age, education, and gender to the population. When a sample is representative of a population, the information gathered from the sample can be **generalized** to the population. This means that we can say the behaviours seen in the sample are what we would see in the larger population of interest.

- **Measurement Bias:** It can occur when we use tools or methods to gather information that are not valid and reliable. A tool is **valid**, if it measures what it is supposed to measure. A tool is **reliable** if, under the same conditions, it gives the same results for a specific participant every time it is used. In research, using a tool that is not valid or reliable will lead to incorrect information on a topic.

- **Observer Bias:** It occurs when we see what we expect to see. The observer bias is dangerous because it causes us to miss information on a topic while focusing only or primarily on information that is consistent with our beliefs about a topic. In research, the observer bias can lead to an incomplete and inaccurate explanation for why and how something happens.

- **Hindsight Bias:** It is the false belief that you always knew something. We experience hindsight bias only after an event has occurred. When we look at the event, it is easy for us to believe that we always knew or predicted it was going to happen. The danger of hindsight bias is that researchers may miss key information, or may incorrectly categorize information as common sense, or may develop preconceptions about how and why something happens.

- **False Consensus Effect:** It is the false belief that people share our beliefs and behaviours. The false consensus effect can lead to the incorrect and dangerous belief that people think and behave as we do, and in research it can lead to an inability to recognize individual differences in key psychological processes such as motivation, learning, social interactions, and mental health.

These are just some of the biases and errors that can occur in research. Mistakes can differ depending on the type of research method used. While it is not possible to eliminate all mistakes, the scientific method is a helpful and necessary guide for researchers (Baird & McCarthy, 2014).

 # Practice...

1. _____ is the view that information that is observed and collected by us is true, valid, and reliable.
   a. Observation
   b. Empiricism
   c. Population
   d. Generalization

2. To study aggressive behaviours in girls, a researcher conducts a study at an all-boys school. The researcher has made what type of mistake?
   a. Sampling error
   b. Hindsight bias
   c. Observer bias
   d. Population error

3. The researcher from Question 2 finds that participants in his study (conducted at the all-boys school) commit two to three aggressive acts an hour. From these results, the researcher writes a paper stating that girls are just as aggressive as boys. The researcher has made what type of mistake?
   a. Sampling error
   b. Hindsight bias
   c. Observer bias
   d. Population error

4. A tool is _____, if it measures what it is intended to measure.
   a. reliable
   b. representative
   c. valid
   d. generalizable

5. A researcher examines ice cream preferences and finds that more people prefer chocolate to strawberry ice cream. Upon seeing these results, the research states, "I knew it!" The researcher has made what type of mistake?
   a. Hindsight bias
   b. Measurement bias
   c. Observer bias
   d. False consensus bias

 Apply…

1. **Mistakes in Research**

   Provide an example for each of the six research mistakes discussed in this chapter.

   • Population Error

   _____

   _____

   _____

   _____

   _____

   _____

   • Sample Error

   _____

   _____

   _____

   _____

   _____

   _____

   _____

   • Measurement Error

   _____

   _____

   _____

   _____

   _____

   _____

   • Observer Bias

   _____

   _____

   _____

   _____

   _____

   _____

to be continued

Apply...

continued

- Hindsight Bias

_____
_____
_____
_____
_____
_____
_____

- False Consensus Bias

_____
_____
_____
_____
_____
_____
_____

2. **Population versus Sample**

- What is the difference between a research population and a research sample?

_____
_____
_____
_____
_____
_____
_____

- Why do we need to use samples to conduct research?

_____
_____
_____
_____
_____
_____
_____

The Scientific Method

 Explain the eight steps of the scientific method

The **scientific method** was developed to help researchers address and limit mistakes (previously discussed) that can occur while conducting research. All sciences use the scientific method. The steps of the scientific method are outlined below.

The scientific method:

1. Identify the problem

2. Conduct background research

3. Formulate a hypothesis

4. Test the hypothesis

5. Analyze data

6. Interpret data

7. Publish results

8. Retest

- **Step 1:** Researchers must identify the topic, issue, behaviour, action, belief, etc. that they are interested in examining.

- **Step 2:** Researchers look up all the information that has been published by other researchers on the topic. This is sometimes referred to as a **literature review**. Researchers will look up this information in **peer-reviewed journals**. Peer-reviewed journals are an accepted and trustworthy source of information because they contain the work of researchers that have been judged by peers in their field as appropriately and unbiasedly presenting significant findings on a topic.

- **Step 3:** Researchers use the information they have gathered and summarized from their literature review to develop a plausible explanation for the topic they are interested in studying. Specifically, researchers will develop a **hypothesis**, which can be thought of as an educated guess or explanation for why or how something happens. A hypothesis must be specific and simple enough so that it can be tested in a study, such as an experiment. The goal then of a hypothesis is to be useful in explaining something we do not fully understand. A hypothesis is not "true" or "false." It is best to think of a hypothesis as either being supported or not supported by evidence. A hypothesis that is supported by evidence is useful in explaining something so that we understand it better than we did before. A hypothesis is not absolute, and may not be supported if context or population changes.

- **Step 4:** Researchers develop a study to test whether their hypothesis is supported by evidence. There are different approaches that a researcher may use to see if their hypothesis explains why or how something happens. These approaches or methodologies will be discussed further in this chapter.

- **Steps 5 and 6:** After researchers complete their study, they must then examine or analyze their results. The type of information or data collected during a study will determine the type of analyzes researchers will use, and based on these results researchers will discover whether their hypothesis is supported or not supported. If the results do not support the hypothesis, researchers should think again about their topic and attempt to develop a new hypothesis (Step 3) that may explain what is happening. When this is done, researchers must then complete Steps 4, 5, and 6 to see if their new hypothesis is supported by the information, which they have collected in their study.

- **Step 7:** When researchers analyze their study results and find that they support their hypothesis, then they must complete Step 7, which involves writing a scientific paper to be published in a peer-reviewed journal. These papers are referred to as **empirical articles,** which identify them as presenting information gathered through the scientific method.

- **Step 8:** Once researchers have published their findings, it is important for other researchers to replicate the study to see if they get the same results. It is also important to build on the research findings to identify any limitations to the findings. In this way, researchers develop new questions that they can explore through the scientific method.

Figure 1 illustrates how the scientific method works to stimulate empirical investigations.

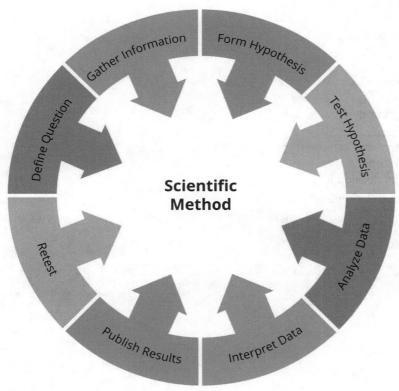

FIGURE 1 Steps in the scientific method.

Keith Bell/Shutterstock

Practice...

1. What is the correct order of steps in the scientific method?
   a. Identify the problem, Formulate a hypothesis, Conduct background research, Test the hypothesis, Analyze your results, Report your results
   b. Conduct background research, Formulate a hypothesis, Identify the problem, Test the hypothesis, Analyze your results, Report your results
   c. Formulate a hypothesis, Conduct background research, Identify the problem, Test the hypothesis, Analyze your results, Report your results
   d. Identify the problem, Conduct background research, Formulate a hypothesis, Test the hypothesis, Analyze your results, Report your results

2. The goal of the scientific method is to _____.
   a. identify a discipline as a science
   b. prove a hypothesis is true
   c. to decrease potential bias
   d. to increase measurement error

3. When researchers conduct background research on a topic, they will _____.
   a. read empirical papers to learn what other researchers have found on a topic
   b. use peer-reviewed journals to develop a possible explanation for why something happens
   c. use various methods to examine a topic
   d. write a paper to be published

4. A researcher analyzes the results of a study and finds that the hypothesis is not supported. The researcher should now _____.
   a. run the study again to make sure the results are correct
   b. rethink the original hypothesis and develop a new hypothesis
   c. conduct a literature review to see what other researchers have found
   d. use different ways to analyze the results of the study until the hypothesis is supported

5. A hypothesis _____.
   a. is an educated guess
   b. can be true
   c. can never be revised
   d. is absolute

 **Apply...**

1. **Identifying the Hypothesis**

    Access peer-reviewed journals and choose one empirical/research paper for this assignment. Read the empirical paper you have chosen and identify the hypothesis.

    The hypothesis of the study is:

    _____

    _____

    _____

    _____

    _____

    _____

    _____

    _____

    _____

    _____

    _____

    _____

    _____

    Read the rest of the paper.

    Was the hypothesis supported in the study? How do you know it was supported/not supported in the study?

    _____

    _____

    _____

    _____

    _____

    _____

    _____

    _____

    _____

    _____

    _____

    _____

to be continued

 **Apply...**

continued

2. **Developing a Hypothesis**

Individually, in pairs, or in small groups, think of a behaviour that you are interested in (for example, bullying, smoking cigarettes, volunteering at a food bank, having a baby) and develop a hypothesis that attempts to explain why people engage in this behaviour.

Hypothesis:

_____

_____

_____

_____

_____

_____

_____

_____

_____

_____

_____

_____

_____

_____

Next, share your hypotheses with the class for whole class discussions on what makes a strong and testable hypothesis.

_____

_____

_____

_____

_____

_____

_____

_____

_____

_____

_____

_____

_____

Descriptive Methods

L03 Summarize the strengths and weaknesses of descriptive methods used in research

There are several methods that researchers can use to observe behaviour. **Descriptive methods** allow researchers to gather information on a topic without focusing on the relationships that may exists between factors. There are other research methods that focus on relationships (discussed in the next topic). The descriptive methods used in research are discussed below (Baird & McCarthy, 2014).

- **Naturalistic Observation:** In naturalistic observation, researchers watch how animals or humans behave in their normal environment. The major advantage or strength of naturalistic observation is that it provides a realistic picture of behaviour. There are three disadvantages or limitations of naturalistic observation.

    First, the **observer effect** is the tendency of people or animals to change their behaviour when they know they are being observed. To decrease observer bias, **participant observation** is used. In participant observation, the observer becomes a participant in the group being observed. In this way, the group gets used to having this person around and is more likely to behave as they normally would.

    Second, the **observer bias**, discussed previously, is the tendency of observers to see what they expect to see. To decrease observer bias, **blind observers** are used. Blind observers are people who do not know what the research question is and as such, they do not have any expectations or preconceptions of what they will see while observing participants.

    Third, each naturalistic setting is unique and as such, observations may not be generalizable to other settings.

- **Laboratory Observation:** In laboratory observation, researchers watch how animals or humans behave in a laboratory setting. The major advantages or strengths of laboratory observation are that it allows researchers to have greater control over the environment in which they observe participants and that it allows the use of specialized equipment. The disadvantage or limitation of laboratory observation is that the artificial situation that a lab presents may result in artificial behaviour by participants.

- **Case Study:** In a case study, researchers gather information from one individual (or a small group of individuals). The major advantage or strength of a case study is that it allows for the collection of a lot of detailed information. The disadvantage or limitation of a case study is that the information collected is likely not applicable to others.

- **Survey:** Researchers use surveys to ask participants a series of questions about a topic. The major advantages or strengths of a survey are that a researcher can collect data from large numbers of people, and it allows researchers to study behaviours that participants may otherwise hide from others. There are two disadvantages or limitations of surveys.

First, it is critical that the sample used is representative of the population of interest otherwise the data collected will not reflect what is happening in general. Using **random sampling**, where research participants are randomly selected from the population of interest, increases the likelihood that the research sample will be representative of the population.

Second, participants may not always answer survey questions accurately or honestly. Participants may lie on their survey answers or may answer questions based on what they believe to be true, but is in fact inaccurate.

Practice...

1. _____ is the tendency of people or animals to change their behaviour when they know they are being observed and is a limitation of _____.
   a. Observer effect, laboratory observation
   b. Observer effect, naturalistic observation
   c. Observer bias, laboratory observation
   d. Observer bias, naturalistic observation

2. Blind observers are used to decrease _____.
   a. the need for random sampling
   b. the artificial nature of labs
   c. observer bias
   d. participant dishonesty

3. The advantage of a case study is that it allows _____.
   a. for the collection of a lot of detailed information
   b. researchers to study behaviours that participants may otherwise hide
   c. the observer to become friends with the participants
   d. for random sampling from the population of interest

4. For survey results to be meaningful, _____.
   a. the sample must include all members of the population of interest
   b. the sample must be representative of the population of interest
   c. participant observation must be used
   d. specialized lab equipment must be used

 # Apply...

1. **Designing a Descriptive Study**

   Individually, in pairs, or small groups, come up with a research question that can be addressed using descriptive research methods. Develop a corresponding hypothesis. Choose one of the descriptive research methods discussed to address your research question, and provide an explanation for your choice.

   Research Question:

   _____

   _____

   _____

   _____

   _____

   _____

   _____

   _____

   _____

   Hypothesis:

   _____

   _____

   _____

   _____

   _____

   _____

   _____

   _____

   _____

   Descriptive method used and rationale for this choice:

   _____

   _____

   _____

   _____

   _____

   _____

   _____

   _____

to be continued

continued

2. **Strengths and Limitations of Descriptive Research Methods**

   In this chapter, we discussed the strengths and limitations of specific descriptive research methods.

   • Discuss the overall strengths and limitations of descriptive research methods.

   _____

   _____

   _____

   _____

   _____

   • How do descriptive research methods help us to understand others?

   _____

   _____

   _____

   _____

   _____

   • What types of information can we collect?

   _____

   _____

   _____

   _____

   _____

   • What types of research questions cannot be answered using descriptive research methods?

   _____

   _____

   _____

   _____

   _____

   • In what ways can researchers use the information gathered through descriptive research methods?

   _____

   _____

   _____

   _____

   _____

Exploring Relationships: Correlational and Experimental Designs

LO4   Compare and contrast the correlational and experimental approaches to research

Researchers who want to examine the relationship between two factors, or variables, can use either a correlational or an experimental approach.

- **Correlation** tells us if two variables are related. We look at the **correlation coefficient (*r*)**, to find out the direction of a relationship and the strength of the relationship between two variables. The correlation coefficient ranges from −1.00 to +1.00.

    The **number** of the correlation coefficient tells us the strength of a relationship. The closer the number is to −1.00 or +1.00 the stronger the relationship between the variables. A correlation coefficient of 0.0 indicates no relationship between variables. A correlation coefficient of −1.00 or +1.00 indicates a perfect relationship (Figures 2A to C). Perfect correlations are very rare.

    The **sign** of the correlational coefficient tells us the direction of the relationship. In a **positive correlation**, the variables are related in the **same** direction. As one variable increases, the other variable increases, and as one variable decreases, the other variable decreases. In a **negative correlation**, variables are related in **opposite** directions. As one variable increases, the other variable decreases.

    The strength of a correlational approach is that we can learn how two variables are related.

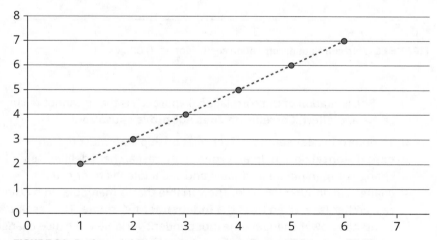

FIGURE 2A Perfect positive correlation; correlation coefficient = +1.00.

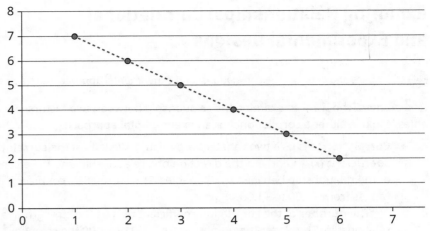

FIGURE 2B Perfect negative correlation; correlation coefficient = −1.00.

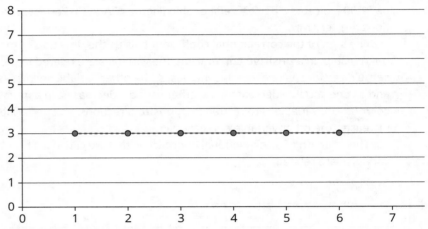

FIGURE 2C Zero correlation; correlation coefficient = 0.00.

The limitation of the correlational approach is that it cannot tell us cause-and-effect. **Correlation does not prove causation!**

- To determine **cause-and-effect** relationships, we must use an **experimental** design. In an experiment, researchers deliberately change or manipulate a variable and see if it leads to or causes changes in another variable. The variable that is manipulated by the researcher is referred to as the **independent variable**. The researcher wants to know if changing the independent variable will cause changes in another variable, the **dependent variable**. The researcher measures changes in the dependent variable that result from changes in the independent variable.

    There are several ways that researchers can design an experiment. One of the most common approaches is to have an **experimental group** and a **control group**. Participants in the experimental group receive the independent variable, while participants in the control group do not. With a design like this, researchers can compare measures of the dependent variable when the independent variable is present (experimental group) compared to absent (control group). The presence/absence of the independent variable must be the only difference between groups in an experiment. Specifically, the participants must be similar across groups to ensure that any changes found between groups are due to the presence versus absence of the independent variable, and not to some pre-existing differences between groups. To minimize differences across groups, **random assignment** of participants to groups is used.

The strength of the experiment is that it addresses cause-and-effect relationships. There are two main limitations of the experiment. First, the **placebo effect** occurs when changes in the dependent variable are not actually the result of changes in the independent variable, but rather are the result of participant expectations that a change will happen. To address the possibility of a placebo effect, a **single-blind study** is used. In a single-blind study, participants do not know if they are in the experimental group or the control group. Second, the **experimenter effect** occurs when a researcher's expectations unintentionally influence the results of a study. To address the possibility of an experimenter effect, a **double-blind study** is used. In a double-blind study, neither the experimenter nor the research participants know if the participants are in the experimental or control group. This approach also decreases the placebo effect.

 # Practice...

1. Which correlational coefficient indicates the **strongest** relationship between two variables?
   a. 0.6
   b. −0.8
   c. −0.4
   d. 0.3

2. Which correlational coefficient indicates the **weakest** relationship between two variables?
   a. 0.6
   b. −0.8
   c. −0.4
   d. 0.3

3. Which correlational coefficient indicates the **strongest positive** relationship between two variables?
   a. 0.6
   b. −0.8
   c. −0.4
   d. 0.3

4. A negative correlation indicates _____.
   a. that two variables are not related
   b. a perfect correlation
   c. that two variables are related in opposite directions
   d. a correlational coefficient with a positive (+) sign

5. The experiment differs from a correlational study in which of the following ways?
   a. An experiment looks at the relationship between two variables but a correlational study does not.
   b. An experiment tells us about the causal relationship between two variables but a correlational study does not.
   c. A correlational study tells us about the causal relationship between two variables but an experiment does not.
   d. A correlational study requires the manipulation of an independent variable but an experiment does not.

Apply...

1. **Identifying an Experiment**

   Access peer-reviewed journals and choose one empirical paper that presents an experiment. Read the paper and answer the following questions, which will help you identify key aspects of an experiment.

   What is the hypothesis?

   _____

   _____

   _____

   _____

   _____

   _____

   What is the independent variable?

   _____

   _____

   _____

   _____

   _____

   _____

   What is the dependent variable?

   _____

   _____

   _____

   _____

   _____

   _____

   What groups or conditions did the participants belong to (for example, control, experimental)?

   _____

   _____

   _____

   _____

   _____

to be continued

 **Apply...**

continued

2. **Designing an Experiment**

    Individually, in pairs, or small groups, come up with a research question that can be addressed using an experiment. Develop a corresponding hypothesis. Answer the following questions about your experiment.

    What is the research question?

    _____

    _____

    _____

    What is the hypothesis?

    _____

    _____

    _____

    What is the independent variable?

    _____

    _____

    _____

    What is the dependent variable?

    _____

    _____

    _____

    What groups or conditions did the participants belong to (for example, control, experimental)?

    _____

    _____

    _____

    Share your hypotheses with the class for whole class discussions on what makes a good experimental design.

    _____

    _____

    _____

    _____

KNOW...

Learning Objectives

1. Six possible mistakes that can occur in research include:
   - **Population Error:** Choosing the incorrect population for our study, which can lead to the collection of inaccurate information about a topic.
   - **Sample Error:** Using a sample that is not representative of the population of interest, which can lead to results that cannot be generalized.
   - **Measurement Bias:** Using tools or methods to gather information that are not valid and reliable, which can lead to incorrect information on a topic.
   - **Observer Bias:** When we see what we expect to see, which can lead to an incomplete and inaccurate explanation for why and how something happens.
   - **Hindsight Bias:** The false belief that you always knew something, which can lead to preconceptions about how and why something happens.
   - **False Consensus Effect:** The belief that people share our beliefs and behaviours, which can lead to an inability to recognize individual differences.

2. The scientific method:
   - **Identify the Problem:** Researchers must identify the topic, issue, behaviour, action, belief, etc. that they are interested in examining.
   - **Conduct Background Research:** Researchers conduct a literature review to find out what is known about the topic.
   - **Formulate a Hypothesis:** Based on the information in the literature review, researchers develop an educated guess or explanation for why or how something happens. The hypothesis must be testable.
   - **Test the Hypothesis:** Researchers develop a study to test whether their hypothesis is supported by evidence.
   - **Analyze Results:** Researchers examine or analyze their results. The type of information or data collected during a study will determine the type of analyzes researchers will use, and based on the results researchers will discover whether their hypothesis is supported or not supported.
   - **Report Results:** Researchers will write a scientific paper to be published in a peer-reviewed journal.

3. Strengths and weaknesses of descriptive methods used in research are summarized in Table 1.1.

TABLE 1.1   Strengths and weaknesses of descriptive methods.

Method	Strengths	Weaknesses
Naturalistic observation	• Provides a realistic picture of behaviour	• Observer Effect • Observer bias
Laboratory observation	• Greater control over the environment • Use of specialized equipment	• Possible artificial behaviour by participants
Case study	• Collection of a lot of detailed information	• Information collected is likely not applicable to others
Survey	• Can collect data from large numbers of people • Study behaviour otherwise concealed	• Sample must be representative of population or results are not useful • Inaccurate or deceptive responses are possible

4. Both correlational and experimental approaches examine the relationship between variables. The correlational approach will tell us the strength and direction of a relationship but cannot tell us if one variable causes the other. The experiment is the only approach that allows us to examine cause-and-effect relationships between variables.

Key Terms

Psychology: The study of mind and behaviour.

Empiricism: The view that information that is observed and collected by us is true, valid, and reliable, and as such, it can best help us understand the unknown.

Research: The process of gathering information in ways consistent with empiricism.

Population Error: Choosing the incorrect population for our study.

Sample Error: Using a sample that is not representative of the population of interest.

Measurement Bias: Using tools or methods to gather information that are not valid and reliable.

Observer Bias: When we see what we expect to see.

Hindsight Bias: The false belief that you always knew something.

False Consensus Effect: The belief that people share our beliefs and behaviours.

Sample Error: Using participants who have been incorrectly selected from a correct population.

Representative Sample: A selection of individuals from the larger population of interest, who are similar in make up in all key demographics, such as age, education, and gender to the population.

Generalized or Generalizable: The ability to apply information about a sample to the population of interest.

Valid: Measures what it is supposed to measure.

Reliable: Produces the same results for a specific participant every time it is used under the same conditions.

Scientific Method: A method or protocol to help researchers address and limit biases and errors that can occur while conducting research.

Literature Review: Reading research papers on a topic in order to learn what has previously been done and found on a topic.

Peer-Reviewed Journals: A collection of research papers that have been judged by peers in their field as appropriately and unbiasedly presenting significant findings on a topic.

Empirical Articles: Research papers usually published in peer-reviewed journals.

Hypothesis: An educated guess or explanation for why or how something happens.

Descriptive Methods: An approach to gather information on a topic without focusing on the relationships that may exists between factors.

Naturalistic Observation: Watching how animals or humans behave in their normal environment.

Observer Effect: The tendency of people or animals to change their behaviour when they know they are being observed.

Participant Observation: The observer becomes a participant in the group being observed in order to reduce observer effect.

Blind Observer: People who do not know what the research question is which decreases observer bias.

Laboratory Observation: Watching how animals or humans behave in a laboratory setting.

Case Study: Gathering information from one individual (or a small group of individuals).

Survey: Asking participants a series of questions about a topic.

Random Sampling: Participants are randomly selected from the population of interest, increases the likelihood that the research sample will be representative of the population.

Correlation: The relationship between two variables.

Correlation Coefficient (*r*): The statistical value of a correlation that indicates the direction and strength of a relationship between two variables.

Positive Correlation: Two variables are related in the same direction.

Negative Correlation: Two variables are related in the opposite direction.

Experiment: A research approach that examines causal relationships.

Independent Variable: The variable that is manipulated by the researcher.

Dependent Variable: The variable that is measured by the researcher.

Experimental Group: Group that receives the independent variable.

Control Group: Group that does not receive the independent variable.

Random Assignment: A method of placing participants in groups to minimize pre-existing differences across groups.

Placebo Effect: Changes in the dependent variable are the result of participant expectations that a change will happen.

Single-Blind Study: Participants do not know if they are in the experimental group or the control group leading to decreased placebo effect.

Experimenter Effect: Researcher's expectations unintentionally influence the results of a study.

Double-Blind Study: Neither the experimenter nor the research participants know if the participants are in the experimental or control group leading to decreases in experimenter bias and placebo effect.

Answers to Practice

Psychology Is a Science
1. b   2. a   3. d   4. c   5. a

The Scientific Method
1. d   2. c   3. a   4. b   5. a

Descriptive Methods
1. b   2. c   3. a   4. b

Exploring Relationships: Correlational and Experimental Designs
1. b   2. d   3. a   4. c   5. b

Reference

Baird, A., & McCarthy, A. (2014). *THINK psychology* (2nd Canadian Edition). Don Mills, ON: Pearson Education, Inc.; pp. 16–29.

2 Human Brain

LEARNING OBJECTIVES

L01 Name each lobe of the human brain and list the primary functions of each lobe

L02 List the three types of neurons and identify the parts of a neuron

L03 Explain the steps that occur during neural communication

L04 Describe some key brain structures, and the "use it or lose it" principle of brain development

LEARN...

Humans have a complex nervous system that is specialized, efficient, and adaptable. The purpose of the nervous system is to convey messages throughout our body. We can divide our nervous system into two parts: The Central Nervous System which consists of our brain and spinal cord and is the largest part of our nervous system, and the Peripheral Nervous System which controls and communicates to limbs and organs. This chapter focuses on the brain. The human brain is complex and yet relatively small compared to the rest of our bodies. The cells in the brain, called neurons, are involved in everything that we do! As we develop, neurons grow and organize themselves into an efficient system that controls both internal mental processes (such as thinking and remembering) and external behaviours (such as walking and smiling). Different areas, parts, or regions of the brain regulate different functions. Our cerebral cortex can be divided into four lobes, each of which "specializes" in specific functions and activities. The frontal lobes are involved in executive functions like planning, organizing, problem solving, and decision making. The temporal lobes are involved in hearing, and understanding speech, and they house the limbic-reward system. The occipital lobes are responsible for vision, integration of colour, size, and movement, and making sense of visual stimuli. The parietal lobes are responsible for sensory processing. Our brain is filled with neurons. Neurons act as communicators for our nervous system and are responsible for the passage of effective and correct messages to different parts of our body and central nervous system. When neurons are processing messages within itself the messages take an electrical form, but when those messages need to be passed on to other neurons the message is converted to chemical messages. Neurotransmitters are chemical messengers that carry messages between neurons. The general and simplified process of neural communication can be summarized in the following steps: A neuron receives a message that needs to be passed on to another neuron. The neurotransmitter that holds that message travels down the axon of the first neuron until it reaches the end of the axon and is released into the gap that exists between neurons. The neurotransmitter binds to receptor sites on the dendrites of the other neuron and the message is passed on. We will take a quick look at some of the other parts of our brain, such as the limbic system, that will be discussed in greater detail in later chapters.

Parts of the Human Brain: Lobes

L01 Name each lobe of the human brain and list the primary functions of each lobe

Humans have a complex nervous system that is specialized, efficient, and adaptable. The purpose of the nervous system is to convey messages throughout our body. We can divide our nervous system into two parts:

- **Central Nervous System:** Consists of our brain and spinal cord and is the largest part of our nervous system.
- **Peripheral Nervous System:** Controls and communicates to limbs and organs, divided into **somatic nervous system**, which controls our conscious actions and gathers sensory information, and **autonomic nervous system**, which controls automatic or unconscious acts.

This chapter discusses the human brain.

The human brain is complex and yet relatively small compared to the rest of our bodies. The cells in the brain, called **neurons,** are involved in everything that we do! As we develop, neurons grow and organize themselves into an efficient system that controls both internal mental processes (such as thinking and remembering) and external behaviours (such as walking and smiling). All our internal and external activities are controlled by our brain and our brain is constantly changing and adapting to our experiences. In fact, the brain that you had when you started reading this chapter is not the brain you will have after you have read this chapter. Our brain changes in response to everything we do, say, learn, attempt, and so on. In this chapter, we will learn about the human brain.

Different areas, parts, or regions of the brain regulate different functions. Our cerebral cortex can be divided into four lobes, each of which "specializes" in specific functions and activities.

Key functions of each lobe are listed below.

- **Frontal Lobes:** Each frontal lobe is located in the front of our brain, and it plays a role in personality, judgment, reasoning, problem solving, and rational decision making; it allows us to think through problems in a logical, systemic manner, and to understand immediate and possible future consequences; it controls impulsivity, aggression, ability to organize thoughts, and plan for the future.
- **Temporal Lobes:** Each temporal lobe is located on the side of our brain close to our ears, and it is responsible for hearing, understanding speech, forming an integrated sense of self, sorting new information, and short-term memory; it houses the limbic-reward system (amygdala, hippocampus, nucleus accumbens, and ventral tegmental area; discussed further in the chapter on Consciousness).

   The limbic system regulates our emotions and motivations, such as fear, anger, and pleasure. Our experience of pleasure is the result of the activation of a specialized circuit of neurons in the limbic area called the **reward system**. We will discuss the reward circuit in more detail in the chapter on Consciousness.

- **Occipital Lobes:** Each occipital lobe is located at the back of our brain, and it is responsible for vision, integration on colour, size, and movement, making sense of visual stimuli.

- **Parietal Lobes:** Each parietal lobe is located on the side of our brain closer to the top, and it is responsible for processing somatosensory information obtained through touch, temperature, body position, and pain; it houses Wernicke's area which is involved in understanding spoken language (Figure 1).

The lobes of the brain do not develop at the same rate. For example, the temporal lobe, and the limbic-reward circuit in particular, matures when we are around 18–19 years of age, but the frontal lobe does not fully develop until we are in our mid-20s. The Prefrontal Cortex (PFC), which is located at the very front of the frontal lobe, is one of the last areas of our brain to fully develop. The PFC is responsible for more accurate and efficient approaches to problem solving and decision making, and better impulse control. This difference in development means that adolescents have a more developed limbic-reward system compared to their frontal lobe. We will discuss the implications of this later in this chapter.

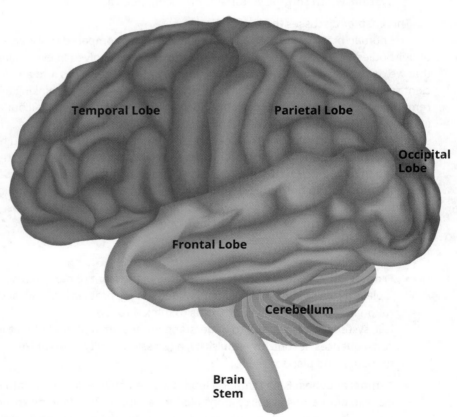

FIGURE 1 Brain anatomy.

Yoko Design/Shutterstock

Practice...

1. The largest part of the human nervous system is the _____ nervous system.
   a. peripheral
   b. autonomic
   c. sympathetic
   d. central

2. Conscious control of our body's functions is handled by the _____ nervous system, while unconscious (unaware) body functions are controlled by the _____ nervous system.
   a. sympathetic; parasympathetic
   b. peripheral; central
   c. somatic; autonomic
   d. volitional; automatic

3. The occipital lobe of the cerebral cortex, located at the bottom of the back of your brain, is responsible for processing input from which of your sensory systems?
   a. Vision
   b. Hearing
   c. Smell
   d. Touch

4. The reward system is located in the _____ lobe, which is also responsible for processing _____ information.
   a. temporal, visual
   b. temporal, auditory
   c. frontal, visual
   d. frontal, auditory

5. The last part of our brain to fully develop is the:
   a. prefrontal cortex.
   b. limbic system.
   c. parietal lobe.
   d. occipital lobe.

 **Apply...**

1. Drawing the brain

   Look up the human brain online and find an image of it. Draw or copy the image in space below. Label the lobes of the brain and list the main functions of each lobe.

to be continued

 **Apply...**

continued

2. Do we only use 10% of our brain?

Perhaps you have heard someone say that we only use 10% of our brain. Is this true? Using peer-reviewed journals find empirical evidence to answer this question. Summarize research findings and provide an answer to the question, "Do we only use 10% of our brain?" Remember to cite the resources you have used to support your answer.

_____

_____

_____

_____

_____

_____

_____

_____

_____

_____

_____

_____

_____

_____

_____

_____

_____

_____

_____

_____

_____

_____

_____

_____

_____

_____

_____

Neurons: Types and Structure

L02 List the three types of neurons and identify the parts of a neuron

As previously noted, our brain is filled with neurons. Neurons act as communicators for our nervous system and are responsible for the passage of effective and correct messages to different parts of our body and central nervous system.

There are three general categories of neurons:

1. **Sensory Neurons:** They carry information from sense organs to the brain for processing.

2. **Motor Neurons:** They carry signals from the brain to our muscles, organs, tendons, etc.

3. **Interneurons:** They act as the connectors between sensory and motor neurons.

Most of the neurons we have are interneurons. They integrate information, facilitate communication between sensory and motor neurons, and help us to understand the world around us—a process referred to as sensation and perception, which will be discussed in chapter of the same name. There are about 100 billion interneurons all of which are located in the central nervous system (Baird & McCarthy, 2014). Neurons are specialized in the messages they receive and pass on. Their specialization depends not only on the type of neuron they are but also on where in the brain they are located. You will learn more about localized functions of neurons in the chapter on Sensation and Perception.

What does a neuron look like?

Each neuron consists of a cell body, axon, and dendrite.

- **Cell Body:** The control centre of the neuron, contains the nucleus, receives information from dendrites.
- **Axon:** An electricity conducting fibre that carries information away from the cell body; most axons are covered by a **myelin sheath**, which is a waxy covering that serves to speed and strengthen the signals the neuron is passing on to other neurons; the myelin sheath does not fully cover the axon but has spaces in it, called **nodes of Ranvier**.
- **Dendrite:** Receives messages from other neurons; their branches contain receptor sites for neurotransmitters (Figure 2).

Neurons do not touch other neurons. Instead there is a gap between the axon terminal, the very end of the axon, of one neuron and the dendrites of another neuron. This is referred to as a **synapse** or synaptic cleft. In our next units in the chapter, we will discuss how neurons communicate.

By the time we are born, we have almost all our neurons. How do these neurons stay alive? Glial cells, of which there are 10 times more than there are neurons, are responsible for supporting neurons by keeping them in place, creating the myelin sheath, providing nutrition, and removing waste. Although the neuron receives most of the attention, it is important to remember that they would not be able to do their job without the glial cells.

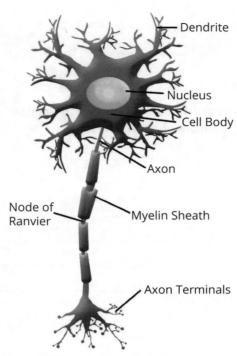

FIGURE 2 Structure of a neuron.

Ducu59us/Shutterstock

 Practice...

1. The three components of neurons
    are _____.
    a. vesicles, terminal buttons, and synapses
    b. myelin, nodes, and axon terminals
    c. cell body, axon, and dendrites
    d. hindbrain, midbrain, and forebrain

2. _____ have branches similar to a tree?
    a. Dendrites
    b. Axons
    c. Nuclei
    d. Cell bodies

3. Which of the following will allow for the fastest
    transmission of a neural signal?
    a. Unmyelinated dendrites
    b. Myelinated axons
    c. Shorter axons
    d. Multiple dendrites

4. _____ neurons carry signals from the
    brain to our muscles.
    a. All
    b. Inter
    c. Motor
    d. Sensory

5. _____ neurons are the most abundant.
    a. Motion
    b. Inter
    c. Motor
    d. Sensory

 # Apply...

1. The Myelin Sheath

   Research two disorders caused by damage or loss of myelin. You may use the internet, peer-reviewed journals, textbooks, etc. Answer the following questions about each disorder.

   • Disorder 1: _____

   How common is the disorder?

   _____
   _____
   _____
   _____
   _____
   _____

   How is the disorder treated?

   _____
   _____
   _____
   _____
   _____
   _____

   • Disorder 2: _____

   How common is the disorder?

   _____
   _____
   _____
   _____
   _____
   _____

   How is the disorder treated?

   _____
   _____
   _____
   _____
   _____

to be continued

 # Apply...

continued

2. The Neuron

    Draw a neuron in the space provided and label the cell body, dendrites, axon, axon terminal, myelin sheath, and synapse.

Neural Communication

LO3 Explain the steps that occur during neural communication

Now that you know the parts of a neuron and their function, we can discuss how neurons communicate with one another.

Setting the Stage

In order to understand how neurons communicate, we need to first understand what is happening when neurons are not communicating with one another—when they are at rest.

- Neurons only communicate, referred to as **firing**, when necessary. A neuron fires only when a specific threshold is reached.

- All other times, neurons are at rest.

- When neurons are at rest, they are negatively charged. Neurons are filled with particles that have an electrical charge. These are called ions. Some ions are positively charged (for example, potassium and sodium) and some are negatively charged (for example, chloride and protein).

- When the neuron is at rest, it contains more negatively charged ions than it does positively charged ions.

- When at rest, neurons have an electrical charge of −70 mv. We say that it has a resting potential of −70 mv.
- The environment around the neuron is positively charged.
- So, there is a difference in electrical charge between the inside and outside of the neuron.
- At the nodes of Ranvier, there are channels that open and close. When the channels are open, they allow ions from inside the neuron to exit into the surrounding environment, and they allow ions from the surrounding environment (which has a high concentration of positively charged sodium ions) to enter the neuron. When this happens, the charge inside the neuron changes.
- As previously noted, neurons do not touch. This means that they must find a way to communicate messages across the gap that separates axon terminals and receptors on dendrites.
- Neurons use chemical messages known as **neurotransmitters** to pass messages across the synapse, also referred to as the synaptic cleft.
- Each neuron creates and stores neurotransmitter in their cell body in small sacs called **vesicles**.
- The neuron that sends the signal is called the **pre-synaptic neuron.** The neuron that receives the signal is called the **post-synaptic neuron.**
- The pre-synaptic neuron receives a message. Sometimes this message is **inhibitory**, meaning that it tells the neuron that the signal does not need to be passed on. Other times the message is **excitatory**, meaning that it tells the neuron to pass on the message to another neuron.

This is what happens when a neuron receives an excitatory message.

Steps in Neural Communication

1. The receipt of an excitatory message causes the pre-synaptic neuron to release vesicles filled with neurotransmitter.

2. As the neurotransmitter travels down the axon, it jumps from one node of Ranvier to another.

3. This causes the ion channels to open. Sodium ion channels open quickly. Potassium ion channels are slower to open.

4. Sodium ions rush into the neuron changing its electrical charge from negative to positive. Now the neuron has a higher concentration of positively charged ions. The neuron becomes depolarized. If the neuron reaches a threshold, it creates an **action potential**, which is an electrical current or impulse that travels down the axon to the axon terminal.

5. The creation, release, or firing of an action potential is an all-or-none process. This means that once a neuron's threshold is reached, it will fire an action potential in full force.

6. The action potential works its way down the axon until it gets to the axon terminal.

7. As the action potential travels down the axon, the potassium ion channels begin to open in the areas that have been passed. This causes some of the potassium ions to leave the neuron. Sodium ion channels begin to close. Potassium ion channels stay open. These activities create a

hyperpolarization in the neuron where its charge becomes even more negative than its resting potential. Eventually, with the help of ion pumps, the neuron recovers and returns to its resting potential.

8. When it reaches the axon terminal, neurotransmitter molecules are released into the synapse. The neurotransmitter is a chemical messenger that transports the message from the pre-synaptic neuron to the post-synaptic neuron. The empty vesicles, that previously transported the neurotransmitters to the axon terminal, travel back to the cell body where they are used again.

9. The neurotransmitter will bind to receptor cells on the dendrites of the post-synaptic neuron. Neurotransmitters and receptors are specifically made for each other, like a lock and key. Neurotransmitters bind to receptors that are specifically shaped to fit them. Different neurotransmitters have different shapes.

10. When the receptors bind the neurotransmitter molecules, the post-synaptic neuron converts the chemical message back to an electrical message which is processed in its nucleus. Again, this message could be inhibitory or excitatory. If it is excitatory, the process outlined above begins again in this subsequent neuron. Once the message is passed on, neurotransmitters separate from their receptors.

11. It is important that enough neurotransmitter is released to accurately pass on a message to another neuron; however, if too much neurotransmitter remains in the synapse, it can pass on a message too many times. After some time has passed, the pre-synaptic neuron begins a **reuptake** process in which neurotransmitter molecules that are in the synapse are deactivated, broken down into its chemical components, and taken back into the pre-synaptic neuron. In this way, neurons engage in the process of recycling (Figure 3).

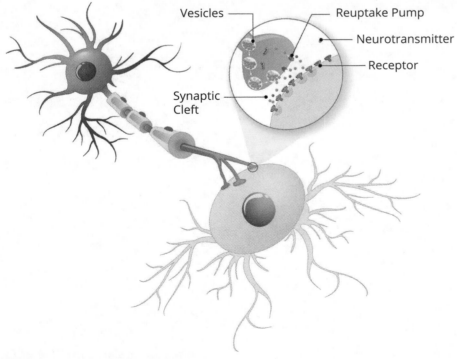

FIGURE 3 Neural communication.

Designua/Shutterstock

Practice...

1. A neuron fires only when a certain _____ is reached.
   a. threshold
   b. sensory minimum
   c. motor minimum
   d. absolute difference

2. When one neuron sends a message to another neuron instructing it not to fire, this process is known as _____.
   a. restriction
   b. inhibition
   c. sensory degradation
   d. catalytic conversion

3. When you walk up to a light switch, you might notice that it has two positions—"On" and "Off". If you lift the switch enough, the light turns on. If you do not, the light stays off. This is very similar to the _____ principle of the human neuron.
   a. on/off
   b. inhibition-stimulation
   c. all-or-none
   d. dendritic limitation

4. The electrical charge of the neuron during its _____ potential is negative, while the electrical charge of the neuron during its _____ potential is positive.
   a. anionic; cationic
   b. resting; action
   c. dormant; stimulated
   d. action; resting

5. Activity or communication within a neuron is _____, but it is _____ between neurons.
   a. electrical, electrical
   b. chemical, chemical
   c. chemical, electrical
   d. electrical, chemical

 **Apply…**

1. Neurotransmitters

   Most of us have heard about neurotransmitters. We may even know about neurotransmitters like dopamine or serotonin. For this activity, look up the different types of neurotransmitters that we have and what each one does. Create a table or point-form list with your findings.

   _____

   _____

   _____

   _____

   _____

   _____

   _____

   _____

   _____

   _____

   _____

   _____

   _____

   _____

   _____

   _____

   _____

   _____

   _____

   _____

   _____

   _____

   _____

   _____

   _____

   _____

   _____

   to be continued

Apply...

continued

2. Agonist and antagonist

Look up neural agonist and antagonist. You may use the internet, peer-reviewed journals, textbooks, etc. Define each term and provide an example of each.

_____

_____

_____

_____

_____

_____

_____

_____

_____

_____

_____

_____

_____

Key Brain Structures

LO4 Describe some key brain structures, and the "use it or lose it" principle of brain development

We started this chapter with a discussion of the four lobes of the brain that make up the cerebral cortex (also referred to as the neocortex to indicate that it is the newest part of our brain to develop through evolution). While these four lobes tell us a lot about the types of things our brain does, it is only part of the story. Our brain is responsible for many things ranging from keeping us alive, to interpreting the world around us, to the creation of emotional expressions. We will discuss many of these parts of our brain in future chapters. Let us take a quick look at some key brain structures. Their locations in the brain are illustrated in the diagrams below.

1. **The brain stem and subcortical structures: Keeps us alive!** (it is considered to be the oldest part of our brain) (Figure 4).

   - Medulla—breathing and heart rate

   - Pons—sleep, dreaming, coordination

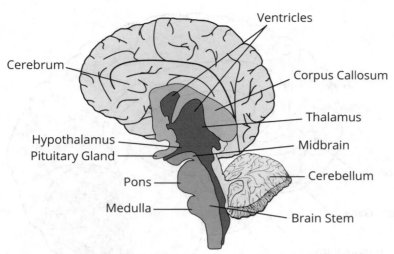

FIGURE 4 Brain anatomy including brain stem and subcortical structures.

Ducu59us/Shutterstock

- Thalamus—consciousness, sensory processing
- Cerebellum—coordination, balance
- Basal ganglia—learning, motor control, processing emotions

2. **Limbic system: Social, emotional, and cognitive processes** (it is considered to be a newer part of our brain) (Figure 5)
    - Amygdala—unconscious emotional responses, learning
    - Hypothalamus—circadian cycles, regulation of biological needs
    - Hippocampus—learning, memory

We learned in our first unit in this chapter that different parts of our brain develop at different rates and are completed at different ages. In addition, we know that we have almost all our neurons from birth, so how does our brain continue to grow? Two things happen: neurons make new connections after birth, and glial cells continue to divide and multiply. Neural connections form when we learn.

We undergo three significant periods of brain growth that result from the creation of new neural connections—*in utero*, birth to 3 years (early years), and pre-adolescence. These periods consist of two basic stages—growth spurts/overproduction of neurons and pruning. Overproduction results in a significant increase in the number of neurons and synapses. After the overproduction of neural connections, a pruning process follows in which the brain prunes and organizes its neural pathways. The brain works towards being efficient, and it will only keep the neural connections that are used. Our brain will prune away neural connections that we do not use—the "use it or lose it" principle. Thus, it is important that as toddlers and children we engage in activities that strengthen neural connections. We can strengthen neural connections by practicing behaviours we have learned, discussing, or recalling information stored in our memory, etc.

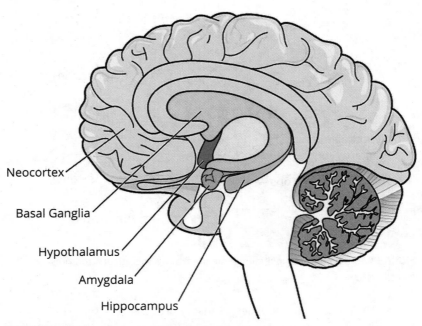

Neocortex

Basal Ganglia

Hypothalamus

Amygdala

Hippocampus

FIGURE 5 Brain anatomy including the limbic system.
Blamb/Shutterstock

 Practice...

1. Which of the following is **not** associated with the brainstem?
   a. Cerebellum
   b. Pons
   c. Medulla
   d. Limbic system

2. The _____ is a part of the brain that regulates cardiac and respiratory function.
   a. pons
   b. amygdala
   c. hippocampus
   d. medulla

3. Which structure (or set of structures) in the human brain is/are most responsible for experiencing emotions?
   a. The limbic system
   b. The brainstem
   c. The basal ganglia
   d. The cerebral cortex

4. Which of the following does **not** explain how our brain grows after birth?
   a. "Use it or lose it" principle
   b. Creation of neural connections
   c. Glial cells divide
   d. All of the above are ways that our brains grow after birth

5. Mary is not good at math, but she has acquired basic math skills. Mary no longer wants to take math at school. Based on the principle of "use it or lose it", the best advice that you can give Mary is to continue to take math and to practice her math skills so that the neural connections for math are strengthened.
   a. True
   b. False

 **Apply...**

1. The triune brain

    Paul MacLean proposed the "triune brain." Research the triune brain. What can we learn from this model about how our brain works?

    _____

    _____

    _____

    _____

    _____

    _____

    _____

    _____

    _____

    _____

    _____

    _____

    _____

    _____

    _____

    _____

    _____

    _____

    _____

    _____

    _____

    _____

    _____

    _____

    _____

    _____

    _____

    _____

    _____

to be continued

continued

2. The "Use It or Lose It" principle and technology

   Discuss what you see as the impact of technology on the "use it or lose it" principle of brain development and specialization.

   _____

   _____

   _____

   _____

   _____

   _____

   _____

   _____

   _____

   _____

   _____

   _____

   _____

   _____

   _____

   _____

   _____

   _____

   _____

   _____

   _____

   _____

   _____

   _____

   _____

   _____

   _____

   _____

   _____

KNOW...

Learning Objectives

1. **Lobes of the Human Brain and their Primary Functions**
   - **Frontal Lobes:** Executive functions like planning, organizing, problem solving, and decision making
   - **Temporal Lobes:** Hearing, understanding speech, and houses the limbic-reward system
   - **Occipital Lobes:** Vision, integration on colour, size, and movement, and making sense of visual stimuli
   - **Parietal Lobes:** Sensory processing

2. **Three Types of Neurons and Parts of a Neuron**
   1. **Sensory Neurons:** Carry information from sense organs to the brain for processing
   2. **Motor Neurons:** Carry signals from the brain to our muscles, organs, tendons, etc.
   3. **Interneurons:** Act as the connectors between sensory and motor neurons
   - **Cell Body:** The control centre of the neuron, contains the nucleus, receives information from dendrites
   - **Axon:** An electricity conducting fibre that carries information away from the cell body
   - **Dendrite:** Receives messages from other neurons; their branches contain receptor sites for neurotransmitters

3. **Steps that Occur during Neural Communication**
   1. Post-synaptic neuron receives an excitatory message and releases vesicles of neurotransmitter
   2. As the neurotransmitter travels down the axon, it jumps from one node of Ranvier to another, opening ion channels, and causing the neuron to depolarize.
   3. The resulting action potential works its way down the axon until it gets to the axon terminal.
   4. When it reaches the axon terminal, neurotransmitter molecules are released into the synapse.
   5. Neurotransmitter binds to receptor cells on the dendrites of the post-synaptic neuron.
   6. Chemical message is converted back to an electrical message that the neuron processes.
   7. Pre-synaptic neuron engages in reuptake and returns to its resting potential.

4. **Key Brain Structures, and the "Use It or Lose It" Principle of Brain Development**

- Medulla: Breathing and heart rate
- Pons: Sleep, dreaming, coordination
- Thalamus: Consciousness, sensory processing
- Cerebellum: Coordination, balance
- Basal ganglia: Learning, motor control, processing emotions
- Amygdala: Unconscious emotional responses, learning
- Hypothalamus: Circadian cycles, regulation of biological needs
- Hippocampus: Learning, memory
- "Use It or lose It" approach: During the pruning stages of brain development, our brain will remove weakened, or under used neural connections. The brain does this so that it can be efficient.

Key Terms

Central Nervous System: Consists of our brain and spinal cord.

Peripheral Nervous System: Controls and communicates to limbs and organs.

Somatic Nervous System: Part of the peripheral nervous system that controls our conscious actions.

Autonomic Nervous System: Part of the peripheral nervous system that controls automatic or unconscious acts.

Cell Body: The control centre of the neuron, contains the nucleus, receives information from dendrites.

Axon: An electricity conducting fibre that carries information away from the cell body.

Myelin Sheath: Insulates the axon and serves to speed and strengthen the signals the neuron is passing on to other neurons.

Nodes of Ranvier: Spaces in myelin sheath where action potential jumps.

Dendrite: Receives messages from other neurons; their branches contain receptor sites for neurotransmitters.

Synapse: Space between the axon of one neuron and the dendrites of another neuron.

Neurotransmitters: Chemical messengers.

Pre-synaptic Neuron: The neuron that sends the signal.

Post-synaptic neuron: The neuron that receives the signal.

Inhibitory Message: Tells the neuron that the signal does not need to be passed on.

Excitatory Message: Tells the neuron to pass on the message to another neuron.

Action Potential: Electrical current or impulse that travels down the axon to the axon terminal and leads to the release of neurotransmitter into the synapse.

Reuptake: Process in which neurotransmitter molecules that are in the synapse are deactivated, broken down into its chemical components, and taken back into the pre-synaptic neuron.

Answers to Practice

Parts of the Human Brain: Lobes
1. d   2. c   3. a   4. b   5. a

Neurons: Types and Structure
1. c   2. a   3. b   4. c   5. b

Neural Communication
1. a   2. b   3. c   4. b   5. d

Key Brain Structures
1. d   2. d   3. a   4. d   5. a

Reference

Baird, A., & McCarthy, A. (2014). *THINK psychology* (2nd Canadian Edition). Don Mills, ON: Pearson Education, Inc.; pp. 34–45.

3 Sensation and Perception

LEARNING OBJECTIVES

LO1 Describe sensation and perception

LO2 Define absolute and difference thresholds

LO3 List the steps associated with visual processing

LO4 List the steps associated with auditory processing

LO5 Explain olfaction, gustation, and somesthetic and cutaneous senses

LEARN...

In this chapter, we discuss the processes of sensation and perception. Through these processes, we learn about what is happening in the world around us. Our five senses—sight, smell, touch, hearing, and taste—are the staring points for sensory systems that allow us to collect information from the outside world. Our ability to detect external stimuli and to transform this information into neural signals is referred to as sensation. Sensation is a signal-detection process. Our ability to detect information in the outside world is critical for our survival, yet we are not perfect at it. We are limited by sensory thresholds. Our absolute threshold is the smallest amount of external energy needed for us to detect a stimulus half of the time it is present. Our difference threshold is the smallest difference between two stimuli that can be detected 50% of the time. Each of our sensory systems responds to specific external stimuli. Our visual sensory system responds to light waves between 700 nm (perceived as the colour red) and 400 nm (perceived as the colour violet). For vision, the process starts with light entering our eye through our pupils, then that physical energy travels through the eye to retina which is at the back of the eye. The retina contains rods, which help us to see in low light, and cones, which allow us to see colour. From the retina, the physical energy is converted to neural signals that are sent to the occipital lobe where it is processed. That processing of neural signals gives us the perception or understanding of what we have seen. A similar process occurs with sound. Our outer ears collect and funnel sound waves down into the inner ear, where receptors receive the signals. The physical energy of the sound is then converted to neural signals that are sent to the temporal lobe. It is here that we process the neural signals and perceive the sounds we heard. Our perception of sound tells us many things including how loud it is, its pitch, and its location. While our visual and auditory sensory processes respond to physical energy, it is chemical molecules that activate our processes for smell and taste. Our olfactory or smell receptors are located at the top of our nasal cavity, and our gustatory or taste receptors can be found on our taste buds on our tongues. Our fifth sense combines awareness and feedback from our body and skin.

Sensation and Perception

L01 Describe sensation and perception

How do we learn about, understand, and respond to the world around us? Our **sensory systems** allow us to detect and interpret all the stimuli in the outside world. Through our sense organs, like eyes, ears, and skin, information from the world around us is passed onto specific regions of our brain where they are processed. This allows us to make sense of the world around us and to react appropriately. For example, we LOOK with your eyes, but we SEE with your brain. This process is referred to as sensation and perception. **Sensation** refers to our detection of external stimuli and the transformation of that physical energy into neural signals. **Perception** is the process where these neural signals are processed, organized, and interpreted by our brain. It is the "What is this? What does this mean? part of the process.

Why do we need sensation and perception? The simple answer is that we need it to survive. In order to detect and respond to life-threatening events in the world, we must first be able to detect that there is danger (sensation), and then understand and respond to that danger (perception) in a way that keeps us safe. Sensation and perception are so important that all animals have specialized sensory systems based on their specific behaviours and environments. In humans and animals, sensation can be thought of as a stimulus-detection process. The goal of sensation is to accurately detect the presence or absence of a stimulus and to pass on that information to our brain. But, our ability to detect external stimuli is not perfect, and we, as with all animals, are limited by our sense organs' abilities to collect this information. These limitations are determined by each sense organ's **sensory threshold**. Each species has different sensory thresholds. The study of how much sensory stimulation is required for us to detect external stimuli and how that information is experienced is studied through **psychophysics.** We will discuss sensory thresholds later in this chapter.

So, we know that we need sensation and perception to survive, but what exactly happens in this process? Sensation occurs when a receptor cell or cells are activated in one of our five sense organs (eyes, ears, skin, nose, and tongue). Each sense organ has specialized sensory neurons that pass on information from the receptor cells to the brain. In order to pass on this information, it must be changed from physical energy, such as light and sound, into electrical energy that the brain can process—this is called **transduction.** Each receptor cell is specialized to respond to specific sensory information, and in general, the strength of the stimuli impacts the speed of activation. More intense stimuli will lead to quicker activation, and therefore quicker detection of a stimulus. However, if a stimulus is constantly present and does not change in intensity, our sensory receptor cells get used to the stimuli (habituates) and they no longer respond to it—they ignore the stimuli. This is called **sensory adaptation** (Baird & McCarthy, 2014). An example of sensory adaptation is when you forget to empty your garbage and leave for a week's vacation. When you return your nose "lights up" with the foul smell of garbage, but after a few minutes you no longer notice the smell. Sensory adaptation is necessary for us to navigate the world—without it we would be constantly aware of all the background stimuli in our lives.

Now that we have discussed the basic principles of sensation, we can explore some key aspects of perception. Remember that perception is our interpretation of sensory information. Theories that attempt to explain perception include:

- **Top-down Processing:** The way perception is influenced by our beliefs, expectations, and previous experiences. This can lead to the development of a **perceptual set**, which is a mental predisposition to perceive things in a certain way.

- **Gestalt Principles:** Our perception is governed by the law of pragnaz—we organize information into its simplest form. The elements of pragnaz are:

  ◊ Proximity: We perceive items that are close together as belonging together

  ◊ Similarity: We perceive items that are similar in shape, size, or colour, as belonging to a pattern

  ◊ Closure: We perceive images as complete, and will "fill in the blanks" of incomplete images

  ◊ Continuity: We perceive intersecting lines as part of a continuous pattern

  ◊ Symmetry: We perceive two shapes that are not connected, but are symmetrical, as being a single object

  ◊ Common fate: We perceive objects that move together in the same direction as being part of the same object

Gestalt principles also attempt to explain why and how we are able to differentiate between an object and its background or surroundings. This is called the figure–ground relationship, and holds for all our senses (Figure 1).

What rules do you think you are following when you look at the images below?

Object Recognition

View-Dependent: Previously seen objects form a template that we use to compare future images.

View-Independent: Recognition of images results from our visual system's ability to identify the combination of parts that make up the image.

Ideally, we are able to receive accurate information on which to base our judgments or perceptions. However, sometimes our perceptions are incorrect because our interpretation of sensory information is inaccurate. For example, we may say that "our eyes are playing tricks" when we think we see something

FIGURE 1 Gestalt principles—the law of pragnaz.
Peter Hermes Furian/Shutterstock

FIGURE 2 Reversible figure: a goblet or two heads?
Imagewriter/Shutterstock

that is not really there, such what we experience when we look at reversible figures or illusions.

What do you see first when you look at Figure 2?

In addition to illusions, perception can also vary across individuals. For example, some people experience **synaesthesia,** which occurs when sensory information is processed in an incorrect part of the brain. The most common form of synaesthesia is letter/digit colour synaesthesia. In this situation, letters/digits are perceived as colours.

 Practice…

1. _____ is the process through which we detect physical energy from the environment and convert that energy to neural signals.
   a. Sensation
   b. Perception
   c. Detection
   d. Transduction

2. _____ is to reception as _____ is to interpretation.
   a. Transduction; sensation
   b. Perception; transduction
   c. Sensation; perception
   d. Perception; sensation

3. When you arrive at your friend's house, you notice the sound her air conditioner makes, but after spending some time there, you no longer notice it. This is called _____.
   a. perceptual adaptation
   b. sensory adaptation
   c. sensory systems
   d. transduction

4. All of the following are Gestalt principles of perception, EXCEPT _____.
   a. proximity
   b. closure
   c. continuity
   d. perceptual set

Apply...

1. **Sensation and Perception in Real Life**

   You are at a party. You hear a familiar voice. You look over and see the person. Describe the processes that will happen as you determine whether you know this person or not. Start with the initial stimuli and end with your final decision.

   _____
   _____
   _____
   _____
   _____
   _____
   _____
   _____
   _____
   _____
   _____
   _____
   _____
   _____
   _____
   _____
   _____
   _____
   _____
   _____
   _____
   _____
   _____
   _____
   _____
   _____
   _____

to be continued

Apply...

continued

Sensory Thresholds: Absolute and Difference Thresholds

L02 Define absolute and difference thresholds

We have just discussed sensory systems. Sensory systems work in a three-part process: first there is a physical stimulus, then this physical stimulus is detected by sensory receptors, and then this physiological response leads to sensory experiences, such as smell or sight. The whole process relies on our ability to accurately detect the presence of a physical stimulus. Our ability to detect physical or external stimuli depends on species-specific sensory thresholds. Sensory thresholds are broadly discussed in terms of:

- **Absolute Threshold:** It is the smallest amount of external energy needed for a person to detect a stimulus 50% (half) of the time. For example, it is the amount of sound needed for us to say, "I hear something." Basically, the absolute threshold is where we say—YES! I detect external energy. The lower our absolute threshold the higher our sensitivity, or ability to detect external energy. But our absolute threshold is not perfect and can fluctuate based on factors such as fatigue, importance of stimulus, and expectation. For example, when we are tired we have higher absolute thresholds, which means that we need higher levels of external energy to detect a stimulus. In other words, it helps to explain how we can detect specific stimuli among "noise" in the environment. To study this ability, researchers ask participants to indicate if they perceived a stimulus (for example, heard a tone) under two conditions: Stimulus Present and Stimulus Absent. Participant responses are then categorized as Hit, Miss, False Alarm, or Correct Rejection. The table below shows how participant responses are scored. Ideally, we would want to score high in the HIT and CORRECT REJECTION categories as this would indicate a high level of sensitivity to external stimuli and thus an efficient and accurate sensory system (Table 3.1).

- **Difference threshold,** also known as the **Just Noticeable Difference** (JND), is the smallest *difference* between two stimuli that can be detected 50% of the time. We use Ernst Weber's Law to determine the JND. The JND is proportional to the magnitude of the stimulus for which comparison is being made. This proportion is called Weber Fraction and tells us the amount of change needed to make a difference. For example, if you were to carry a 2 kg package, adding 1 additional gram will not make a difference, but if you were carrying 20 grams, 1 gram will make a difference (Baird & McCarthy, 2014).

TABLE 3.1   Possible responses when a stimulus is present or absent.

	Respond "Absent"	Respond "Present"
Stimulus Present	MISS	HIT
Stimulus Absent	CORRECT REJECTION	FALSE ALARM

Practice...

1. The _____ threshold is the smallest amount of energy needed for a person to detect the presence of a stimulus 50% of the time.
   a. just noticeable
   b. difference
   c. absolute
   d. sensory

2. Which of the following would be the best example of the just noticeable difference?
   a. Just for fun, Jordan sometimes adds an extra 10 kg to the free weights his friend Will is lifting in the gym. Will always comments that the weights feel heavier but tries to lift them anyway just to show Jordan how strong he is.
   b. Just for fun, Jordan sometimes adds an extra 5 kg to the free weights his friend Will is lifting in the gym. Half the time Will comments that the weights feel heavier but the other half of the time he does not notice the change in weight.
   c. Just for fun, Jordan sometimes adds an extra 5 kg to the free weights his friend Will is lifting in the gym. Will never comments that the weights feel heavier and simply lifts them as though nothing has changed.

   d. Just for fun, Jordan sometimes adds an extra 10 kg to the free weights his friend Will is lifting in the gym. Once in a while, Will comments that the weights feel a little heavier than normal but chalks it up to muscle fatigue.

3. Failure to detect a sensory stimulus when one is present is known as a _____.
   a. hit
   b. miss
   c. correct rejection
   d. false alarm

4. The _____ our absolute threshold the _____ our sensitivity.
   a. lower, greater
   b. higher, greater
   c. lower, lower
   d. higher, higher

5. Our ability to detect external stimuli depends on _____ sensory thresholds.
   a. perceptual
   b. species-generalized
   c. hierarchical
   d. species-specific

Apply...

1. **Absolute Thresholds**

   - Define Absolute Threshold.

   _____

   _____

   _____

   - Find the absolute thresholds for humans for our five senses. You may use the internet, books, journal articles, etc. Cite your sources.

     ◊ Audition

   _____

   _____

   _____

   Source(s) used to locate absolute thresholds:

     ◊ Vision

   _____

   _____

   _____

   Source(s) used to locate absolute thresholds:

     ◊ Olfaction

   _____

   _____

   _____

   Source(s) used to locate absolute thresholds:

     ◊ Gustation

   _____

   _____

   _____

   Source(s) used to locate absolute thresholds:

     ◊ Somesthetic/Cutaneous

   _____

   _____

   _____

   Source(s) used to locate absolute thresholds:

   _____

to be continued

 # Apply...

continued

2. **Difference Thresholds**

- Define Difference Threshold.

_____

_____

_____

- Find the difference thresholds for humans for our five senses. You may use the internet, books, journal articles, etc. Cite your sources.

  ◊ Audition

_____

_____

_____

Source(s) used to locate difference thresholds:

  ◊ Vision

_____

_____

_____

Source(s) used to locate difference thresholds:

  ◊ Olfaction

_____

_____

_____

Source(s) used to locate difference thresholds:

  ◊ Gustation

_____

_____

_____

Source(s) used to locate difference thresholds:

  ◊ Somesthetic/Cutaneous

_____

_____

_____

Source(s) used to locate difference thresholds:

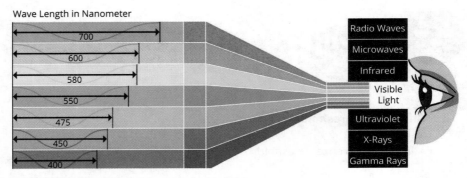

Wave Length in Nanometer

FIGURE 3 Visible light spectrum for humans.
Udaix/Shutterstock

Vision

L03 List the steps associated with visual processing

The sense organ associated with vision is the eye. As humans, we perceive a small part of electromagnetic (EM) spectrum. Specifically, we see light waves that measure between 700 nm (perceived as the colour red) and 400 nm (perceived as the colour violet). Figure 3 shows the visible light spectrum.

How does light from this spectrum lead us to see? In brief, the process starts with light entering our eye through our pupils, then that physical energy travels through the eye to the retina which is at the back of the eye. The retina contains rods, which help us to see in low light, and cones, which allow us to see colour. From the retina, the physical energy is converted to neural signals that are sent to the occipital lobe where it is processed. That processing of neural signals gives us the perception or understanding of what we have seen.

Figure 4 shows some key parts of the eye.

A key part of the visual process is **visual accommodation**, where the lens changes shape in order for us to properly focus on an object. When this happens, the image is accurately projected onto the retina. The images are projected upside-down, but when the receptor cells on the retina transduce the light energy into neural signals they send these signals to the brain in their up-right form. People who are not able to accurately project light energy onto the retina will have difficulty with visual processes. For older individuals, they may experience **presbyopia**, which is a hardening of the lens leading to a decrease in its ability to change shape for focusing. Other individuals may

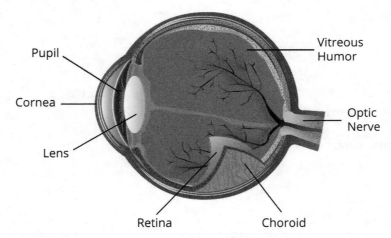

FIGURE 4 Parts of the human eye.
GraphicsRF/Shutterstock

experience myopia (short-sightedness) or hyperopia (far-sightedness) (Baird & McCarthy, 2014).

- **Myopia:** Difficulty seeing far away objects; eyeball is longer—back to front; lens focuses light in front of retina
- **Hyperopia:** Difficulty seeing close-up objects; eyeball is too short; lens focuses light behind retina

Once the optic nerve sends visual information to the brain, and to the occipital lobe specifically, we begin the process of interpreting or perceiving the meaning of that visual information. One of the things that we perceive is colour. The photoreceptors located in the retina play a role in colour perception. The two types of photoreceptors, each named for their shape, that are found in the retina are:

- **Cones:** For colour and detail; function best in high illumination; concentrated in centre of retina; fovea (in centre of retina) contains only cones
- **Rods:** Function best in low illumination; 500 times more sensitive to light than cones; found mostly in periphery of retina—though everywhere in retina except fovea

In order for rods and cones to be activated, the visual information passes through a series of other cells until it reaches them. Figure 5 shows the order in which light travels towards the back of the retina.

The rods and cones have neural connections with bipolar cells. Cones have a "single line" connection (one to one), while many rods connect to single bipolar cell. Bipolar cells have neural connections with ganglion cells, and the axons of ganglion cells form the optic nerve. A "blind spot" is created where the optic nerve exits from the eye. From the optic nerve, neurotransmitters (neural signals) carry

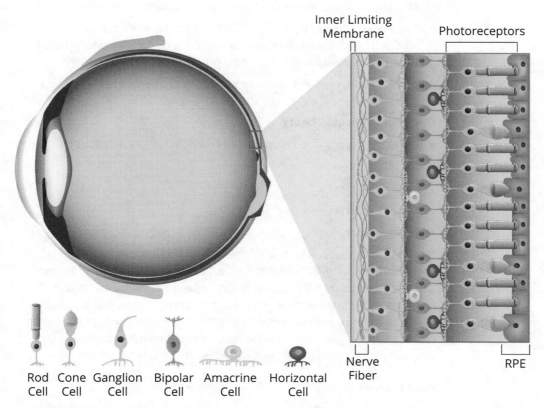

FIGURE 5 Retinal cells involved in vision.
Designua/Shutterstock

the visual information to be processed. The amount of light taken in by the eye determines the rate of neurotransmitter release:

Increased light into eye = increased rate of neurotransmitter release
    = stronger signal to be processed.

Because we have rods and cones we are said to have a dual visual system—we can see in both high- and low-light conditions. Through a process called dark adaptation, we become better able to see in low-light situations over time. When we have limited or low lights, the rods and cones adapt differently. During dark adaptation, cone sensitivity reaches its maximum after 10 minutes in low light, while rods reach their full sensitivity after 30 minutes. It is rods that allow us to see in limited light, as they are much more sensitive to light than cones, being able to detect light intensities that are 1/10 000 as strong as those before dark adaptation. Interestingly, rods are not sensitive to red light and as such they remain dark adapted in red light. The use of red light is common on submarines, and by astronomers and pilots (Baird & McCarthy, 2014).

Unlike rods, cones function best in higher light. The cones gather information that allow us to see colour. There are three theories that attempt to explain how we see colour.

Theories of Colour Vision

1. **Trichromatic Theory**
   - Three types of color receptors in retina
   - Cones most sensitive to blue, green, red wavelengths
   - Visual system combines activity from these cells
   - Colours are perceived by additive mixture of impulses; we combine or add different wavelengths of light to create different colours
   - If all wavelengths of light are equally activated a white colour is produced. In subtractive colour mixing, each colour's wavelengths are absorbed by the other wavelengths producing a black colour
   - Cannot explain red-green colour blindness or afterimages

2. **Opponent-Process Theory**
   - Three cone types, each responds to two different wavelengths
     ◊ Red or green
     ◊ Blue or yellow
     ◊ Black or white
   - Explains afterimages

   Staring at a certain colour causes neural processes to become fatigued. When we look away from that colour, a "rebound" effect occurs, during which the receptors will respond to the opposite colour's wavelength. For example, if you stare at the colour red, the receptors that respond to the wavelength for red will become tired. When we look away from the colour red, we will see green because the receptors are now responding to the wavelength for green (the opponent colour for red).

3. **Dual Process Theory**
   - Current view of colour vision
   - Combines trichromatic and opponent-process theories

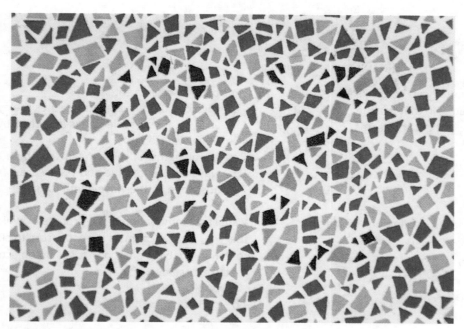

FIGURE 6 Example of a test for red-green colour blindness.
HUAJI/Shutterstock

- Three types of cones sensitive to short (blue), medium (green), and long (red) wavelengths stimulate opponent-process reactions.
- Opponent processes occur in ganglion cells, neurons in relay stations, and visual cortex.

Humans can be:

- **Trichromats:** Normal colour vision
- **Dichromats:** Deficient in one system (red-green is most common)
- **Monochromat:** Sensitive to black-white only

In Figure 6, people with red-green colour blindness may not be able to see number 62.

In our discussion of visual processing, we ended with the retina sending neural impulses to the brain. Let us pick up the process from that point now. Neural impulses travel next to the primary visual cortex, which is located in the occipital lobe. The primary visual cortex contains **feature detectors**. Feature detectors are neurons that respond to specific types of visual stimuli. For example, we have feature detectors that are activated by bars, others to edges, others to colour, others to movement, and so on. A unified image or images are created through the parallel processing of multiple feature detectors, so that we get a complete image of what is happening in the outside world (Baird & McCarthy, 2014). We can see colour, movement, shape, distance, and so on simultaneously. This information is sent to the visual association cortex where we interpret the information in terms of our memories, knowledge, and context. After this process is complete, we have perceived—attached meaning to—the visual information we have received.

Practice...

1. The _____ of your eye is sort of like a movie screen at a cinema, in that it is the part of the eye onto which light gets projected.
   a. fovea
   b. cornea
   c. retina
   d. lens

2. Which type of photoreceptors allows us to see colors?
   a. Cones
   b. Rods
   c. Ganglion cells
   d. Bipolar cells

3. When light enters the human eye, what is the correct order of structures through which that light passes?
   a. Cornea, lens, pupil
   b. Sclera, cornea, lens
   c. Pupil, lens, cornea
   d. Cornea, pupil, lens

4. The colour black is created when _____.
   a. each colour's wavelength reaches the eye
   b. each colour's wavelength is absorbed by other wavelengths
   c. wavelengths for red and blue combine
   d. wavelengths for blue and yellow are absorbed by the wavelength for green

5. Visual accommodation is the process by which the _____ adjusts in shape from thick to thin to enable a person to focus on objects that are close by or far away.
   a. pupil
   b. cornea
   c. lens
   d. fovea

 # Apply...

1. **How Can the Blind See?**

    Research Brian Borowski. What can we learn about the connection between vision and audition from his story?

    _____

    _____

    _____

    _____

    _____

    _____

    _____

    _____

    _____

    _____

    _____

    _____

    _____

    _____

    _____

    _____

    _____

    _____

    _____

    _____

    _____

    _____

    _____

    _____

    _____

    _____

    _____

    _____

    _____

    _____

to be continued

Apply...

continued

2. **Label the Parts of the Eye and List Their Functions.**

_____
_____
_____
_____
_____
_____
_____
_____
_____
_____
_____
_____
_____
_____
_____
_____
_____
_____
_____
_____
_____
_____
_____

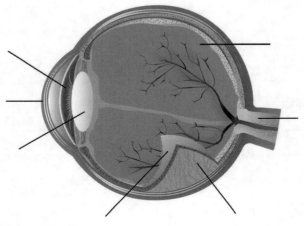

Pearson Education

Audition

LO4 List the steps associated with auditory processing

The sense organ associated with hearing is the ear. We process sound by taking in sound waves which are then converted to neural impulses that are processed in the auditory cortex which is located in the temporal lobe.

The following parts are the ear are involved in auditory processing:

- **Outer Ear:** Pinna (part you use for earrings and sunglasses); sound enters auditory canal, causes eardrum (tympanic membrane) to vibrate

- **Middle Ear:** Vibration causes malleus, incus, and stapes (three tiny bones) to vibrate; amplifies sound more than 30X; causes oval window to move in and out

- **Inner Ear:** Contains the cochlea; contains the basilar membrane which contains hair cells which are our sound receptors; the hair cells have neural connections with the auditory nerve that sends signals to the thalamus which in turn sends signals to the auditory cortex in the temporal lobe

Figure 7 outlines the key parts of the ear involved in auditory processing.

The Process of Hearing

1. The outer ear collects sound waves and then funnels the sound waves around us. Sound waves have two characteristics:

   - **Frequency:** Number of sound wave cycles (Hz) per second; related to the pitch; the greater the number of cycles per second, the higher the sound

   - **Amplitude:** Amount of compression and expansion of sound waves; the bigger the wave, or the greater the expansion of the wave, the louder the

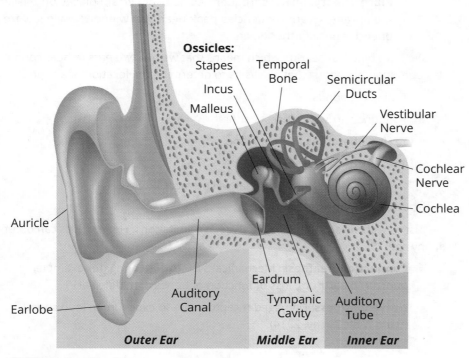

FIGURE 7 Human ear anatomy.

sound we perceive; measured in Decibels (dB); dB follow a logarithmic scale—each increase of 10 = 10-fold increase in loudness; some examples are: restaurant = 50 dB; rock band = 120 dB; jet = 140 dB.

2. Sound waves travel to the eardrum.

3. When the sound reaches the eardrum it causes it to vibrate, this results in the hammer, anvil, and stirrup hitting one another thereby passing on the vibrations to the oval window.

4. The vibrations then move from the oval window to the cochlea in the inner ear.

5. The resulting vibrations in the cochlea cause the fluid within it to move causing movement in the basilar membrane.

6. Hair cells in the basilar membrane activate receptor cells and the auditory message is sent to the auditory cortex where it is processed and perception occurs.

Auditory processing involves the perception of both loudness and pitch.

- **Loudness:** High amplitude waves result in higher firing rate of neurons and a greater release of neurotransmitter; certain neurons fire only to specific amplitudes.
- **Pitch:** There are two theories that attempt to explain how we process the frequency of sound waves.
  ◊ **Frequency Theory:** Nerve impulses "match" frequency of wave (for example, 1000 Hz = 1000 impulses/second); does not work for frequencies above 4000 Hz
  ◊ **Place Theory:** Specific frequencies peak at certain places on basilar membrane—high frequencies peak near oval window, while low frequencies peak farther down.

We have binaural hearing which means that we use two ears to hear sound. It is our binaural hearing that allows us to determine the location of a sound:

- Timing of sounds
  ◊ Sounds arrive at closest ear first
  ◊ Use differences in arrival time
- Intensity of sounds
  ◊ Sound arriving at closest ear will be more intense
  ◊ Use differences in intensities

Just as with vision, audition can also have limitations. Hearing loss can occur at any age:

- **Conduction Deafness:** Mechanical system of hearing (for example, punctured eardrum, loss of function of bones of middle ear)
- **Nerve Deafness:** Damaged receptors due to exposure to loud sounds (Baird & McCarthy, 2014).

Practice...

1. The pitch produced by a violin is related to the _____.
   a. number of wavelengths that occur each second
   b. compression of each wavelength
   c. conduction deafness
   d. binaural hearing

2. Which of the following structures is not a part of the outer ear?
   a. The pinna
   b. The ear canal
   c. The cochlea
   d. The eardrum

3. What is the name of the membrane that runs the length of the cochlea and has auditory receptors (in the form of hair cells) on its surface?
   a. The membrane of Corti
   b. The oval membrane
   c. The cochlear membrane
   d. The basilar membrane

4. According to _____, high frequencies peak near the oval window, while low frequencies peak farther down.
   a. Frequency theory
   b. Place theory
   c. Amplitude theory
   d. Loudness theory

Apply...

1. **What Is the Role of Hearing in Speech Development?**

   Research the role of hearing in speech development. Write a summary of the key information that we should know on this topic.

   _____
   _____
   _____
   _____
   _____
   _____
   _____
   _____
   _____
   _____
   _____
   _____
   _____
   _____
   _____
   _____
   _____
   _____
   _____
   _____
   _____
   _____
   _____
   _____
   _____
   _____
   _____
   _____
   _____
   _____
   _____

to be continued

Apply...

continued

2. **Label the Parts of the Ear and List Their Functions**

_____
_____
_____
_____
_____
_____
_____
_____
_____
_____
_____
_____
_____
_____
_____
_____
_____
_____

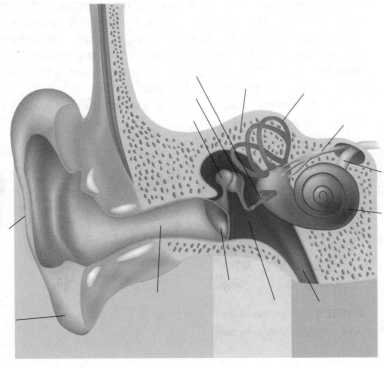

Pearson Education

Other Senses: Olfaction, Gustation, and Somesthetic and Cutaneous Senses

 Explain olfaction, gustation, and somesthetic and cutaneous senses

Smell, also known as olfaction, and taste, also known as gustation, are chemical senses because each processes molecules of a substance, and not a form of energy like seeing and hearing do.

Smelling/Olfaction

Molecules are carried in the air and when we inhale those molecules travel up through our nose to the top of our nasal cavities. The nasal cavities contain 10 million receptor cells. Odour molecules "lock" into certain receptor sites. Different combinations of olfactory receptor cells are activated by different odours, which allows us to detect over 10 000 smells. The receptor cells send messages to the olfactory bulb in the brain and then on to different parts of the brain. Just as with vision and hearing, our ability to detect smells can be less than perfect. For example, our ability to detect odours peaks in early adulthood, women have better odour detection abilities than men, and certain disorders such as Parkinson's disease can negatively impact our odour detecting abilities.

Most often, we are aware when we smell an odour, but there are some chemical substances that enter our olfactory system and are processed without us knowing. These substances, found in natural body scents, are called **pheromones,** and they can trigger sexual arousal or aggressive behaviour in others (Baird & McCarthy, 2014).

Taste/Gustation

Our taste buds are the receptors for chemical substances that we put in our mouth. We have about 9000 taste buds grouped in different regions on our tongue that are located on edges and back of tongue. Our taste buds respond to five basic qualities—sweet, sour, salty, bitter, and umami (Figure 8). Each taste bud has 60–100 receptor cells. We are constantly replacing taste buds, roughly every 10 days (Baird & McCarthy, 2014).

Our fifth sense is often referred to as touch, but it is actually a combination of multiple senses:

Sweet   Salty   Sour   Bitter   Umami

FIGURE 8 Taste areas of the human tongue.

Peter Hermes Furian/Shutterstock

Body/Somesthetic Senses

- Sense of Kinesthesis: Feedback about muscles and joint position; receptors are found in the nerve endings in muscles, joints, and tendons

- Vestibular Sense: Balance and spatial orientation of body; receptors are found in the inner ear; the three semicircular canals contain receptors for head movements

Skin/Cutaneous Senses

- Sensitive to four tactile sensations: Pressure, pain, warmth, and cold

- Skin is the largest organ in body: Contains a variety of receptor structures

- Pain and temperature: Free nerve ending receptors beneath skin's surface

- Touch and pressure: Nerve fibres at base of hair follicles send messages to somatosensory cortex

 # Practice...

1. Which of the following human sensory systems does not rely on the presence of microscopic hairs, or cilia, for the reception of sensory information?
    a. Gustation
    b. Audition
    c. Vision
    d. Olfaction

2. Which of the following is not one of the "skin senses"?
    a. Pain
    b. Touch
    c. Pressure
    d. Movement

3. The semicircular canals and vestibular sacs are parts of our vestibular system that help our body to maintain balance. In which part of the body are these functions located?
    a. The eyes
    b. The ears
    c. The skin
    d. The nose

4. Humans are able to detect over _____ smells.
    a. 50 000
    b. 25 000
    c. 10 000
    d. 5000

5. Receptor cells for gustation are found on our _____.
    a. tongue
    b. leg
    c. scalp
    d. muscles

Apply...

1. **Super-Taster**

   • What is a super-taster? Research this answer using the internet, books, journal articles, etc.

   _____

   _____

   _____

   _____

   _____

   _____

   _____

   _____

   _____

   _____

   _____

   _____

   _____

   _____

   • Imagine you are a super-taster and have been hired as a food consultant. What food would you choose to consult on and taste-test for as a job? Why?

   _____

   _____

   _____

   _____

   _____

   _____

   _____

   _____

   _____

   _____

   _____

   _____

to be continued

 **Apply...**

continued

2. **Somesthetic and Cutaneous Senses**

   Take a 5–10 minute walk. As you are walking, think about all the body and skin sensations you are experiencing. List these experiences and categorize these as either somesthetic or cutaneous. You can use the table below to record your experiences.

Somesthetic	Cutaneous

to be continued

 **Apply...**

continued

3. **Cortical Homunculus**

• What is a cortical homunculus?

_____

_____

_____

_____

_____

_____

_____

_____

_____

• What parts of the body do you think take up the most space on a cortical homunculus? Why?

_____

_____

_____

_____

_____

_____

_____

_____

_____

• How might a cortical homunculus be different for professional athletes?

_____

_____

_____

_____

_____

_____

_____

_____

_____

KNOW...

Learning Objectives

1. Sensation and perception:
   Sensation and perception is the process through which we make sense of the world around us. Sense organs collect information about the sights, smells, sounds, tastes, and tactile stimuli in the outside world. This information is then passed on to the brain where it is organized and interpreted. Sensation refers to our detection of external stimuli and the transformation of that physical energy into neural signals. Perception is the process where these neural signals are processed, organized, and interpreted by our brain. It is the "What is this? What does this mean? part of the process.

2. Absolute and difference thresholds
   - **Absolute Threshold:** The Smallest amount of external energy needed for a person to detect a stimulus 50% (half) of the time.
   - **Difference Threshold or Just Noticeable Difference (JND):** The smallest difference between two stimuli that can be detected 50% of the time.

3. Steps Associated with Visual Processing
   1. Light enters eye through cornea and pupil.
   2. Iris changes size of pupil depending on the amount of light (more light = smaller pupil).
   3. Lens changes size to bring object into focus.
   4. The image is project, inverted on the retina.
   5. Photoreceptors (rods and cones) on the retina receive the visual information.
   6. In day-light or high-light conditions, cones are more active, while rods are more active in low-light conditions.
   7. The optic nerve sends the visual information to the visual cortex in the occipital lobe.
   8. Feature detectors respond to the neural signals.
   9. A unified image or images are created through the parallel processing of multiple feature detectors, so that we get a complete image of what is happening in the outside world.
   10. Neural signals are then sent to the visual association cortex where we interpret the information in terms of our memories, knowledge, and context.
   11. We have now perceived—attached meaning to—the visual information we have received.

4. Steps Associated with Auditory Processing
   1. The outer ear collects sound waves and then funnels the sound waves around us. Sound waves have two characteristics: frequency and amplitude.

2. Sound waves travel to the eardrum.

3. When the sound reaches the eardrum it causes it to vibrate, this results in the hammer, anvil, and stirrup to hitting one another thereby passing on the vibrations to the oval window.

4. Vibrations then move from the oval window to the cochlea in the inner ear.

5. The resulting vibrations in the cochlea cause the fluid within it to move causing movement in the basilar membrane.

6. Hair cells in the basilar membrane activate receptor cells and the auditory message is sent to the auditory cortex where it is processed and perception occurs.

5. Olfaction, Gustation, and Somesthetic and Cutaneous Senses

- **Smelling/Olfaction:** Molecules are carried in the air and when we inhale those molecules travel up through our nose to the top of our nasal cavities. The nasal cavities contain receptor cells that send messages to the olfactory bulb in the brain and then on to different parts of the brain.

- **Taste/Gustation:** Our taste buds are the receptors for chemical substances that we put in our mouth. Our taste buds respond to five basic qualities—sweet, sour, salty, bitter, and umami.

Our fifth sense is often referred to as touch, but it is actually a combination of multiple senses:

- **Body/Somesthetic and Skin/Cutaneous Senses:** Make up our fifth sense. Somesthetic involves kinesthesis sense (muscle and joint position) and vestibular sense (balance and spatial orientation of body). Skin/cutaneous senses allow us to feel tactile sensations (pressure, pain, warmth, and cold).

Key Terms

Sensory Systems: Responsible for how we detect and interpret stimuli in the outside world.

Sensation: Our detection of external stimuli and the transformation of that physical energy into neural signals.

Perception: Neural signals from sense organs are processed, organized, and interpreted by our brain.

Sensory Threshold: The amount or level of stimulus needed for us to detect and collect sensory information about the stimulus.

Psychophysics: The study of how much sensory stimulation is required for us to detect external stimuli and how that information is experienced.

Transduction: The process of changing/transforming physical energy into electrical energy.

Sensory Adaptation: Sensory receptor cells get used to a stimulus that is constantly present and no longer responds to it.

Perceptual Set: Mental predisposition to perceive things a certain way.

View-Dependent: The theory that previously seen objects form a template that we use to compare future images.

View-Independent: The theory that recognition of images results from our visual system's ability to identify the combination of parts that make up the image.

Synaesthesia: A condition in which sensory information is processed in an incorrect part of the brain.

Absolute Threshold: The smallest amount of external energy needed for a person to detect a stimulus 50% (half) of the time.

Difference Threshold or Just Noticeable Difference (JND): The smallest difference between two stimuli that can be detected 50% of the time.

Visual Accommodation: Lens of the eye changes shape to better focus on an object.

Presbyopia: Hardening of the lens of the eye leading to a decrease in its ability to change shape for focusing.

Myopia or Near-Sightedness: Difficulty seeing far away objects; eyeball is longer—back to front; lens focuses light in front of retina.

Hyperopia or Far-Sightedness: Difficulty seeing close-up objects; eyeball is too short; lens focuses light behind retina.

Feature Detectors: Neurons that respond to specific types of visual stimuli.

Frequency: Number of sound wave cycles (Hz) per second.

Amplitude: Amount of compression and expansion of sound waves.

Pheromones: Chemicals found in body scents that can trigger sexual arousal or aggressive behaviour in others.

Answers to Practice

Sensation and Perception
1. a   2. c   3. b   4. d

Sensory Thresholds: Absolute and Difference Thresholds
1. c   2. b   3. b   4. a   5. d

Vision
1. c   2. a   3. d   4. b   5. c

Audition
1. a   2. c   3. d   4. b

Other Senses: Olfaction, Gustation, and Somesthetic and Cutaneous Senses
1. d   2. b   3. b   4. c   5. a

Reference

Baird, A., & McCarthy, A. (2014). *THINK psychology* (2nd Canadian Edition). Don Mills, ON: Pearson Education, Inc.; pp. 50–63.

4 Genetics and Evolution

LEARNING OBJECTIVES

LO1 Determine the probability of genetic transmission of single-gene traits using a Punnett square

LO2 Discuss how behavioural genetics can examine the contribution of genetics on our behaviour

LO3 Describe key evolutionary changes in humans

LO4 List three evolutionary adaptations of humans

LEARN...

Have you ever wondered what you have inherited from your parent? In this chapter, we discuss genetics and evolution. Genetic transmission occurs when genes, sections of DNA, are passed on to offspring during sexual reproduction. This forms our genome, which is our complete set of instructions for our growth and development. Our specific genetic make-up is referred to as our genotype. It is our genotype that is inherited from our parents. Our phenotype is the physical expression of our genotype, and the part that we see when we look at ourselves and others. The formation of our phenotype relies on the ways genes combine in our genotype. We can use a Punnett square to illustrate how genes can be passed on to offspring. In this chapter, we will also discuss the use of twin studies to examine the relative influences of genetics and environmental factors on who we are, how we behave, and how we engage in mental processes. We then explore the role of evolution in human survival and adaptation. The key to evolutionary change is mutation—a change in an individual's DNA that is passed on to future generations. Through evolution from our oldest ancestors, the Australopithecus family to our more recent predecessors of the Hominid family, we have developed the ability to walk on two legs, to form groups, to develop language and facial expressions, and to engage in higher order mental processes. One of the most significant evolutionary changes is our increased brain capacity—which increased from 380 cc, some 4 million years ago, to 1350 cc 300 000 years ago. Our brain capacity remains unchanged today. Evolutionary adaptations have led us to develop strategies for mating and parenting systems, such as monogamy and polygamy, to develop a need to belong to groups, to help others, and to protect our resources and families through the use of aggression.

Basics of Genetics

L01 Determine the probability of genetic transmission of single-gene traits using a Punnett square

Have you ever wondered what you have inherited from your parent? Have you heard people say that you have your mom or dad's smile? Have you ever wondered if personality and mental health are biologically determined? If so, then you have been thinking about the genetic transfer of traits. In this chapter, we examine genetics and how it impacts who we are. Let us start with the basics of genetic transmission.

Genetic transmission begins with **DNA**—deoxyribonucleic acid, which carries all of our genetic material. This genetic material is stored in the form of four chemical bases—adenine (A), guanine (G), cytosine (C), and thymine (T). It is the order of these bases that provide biological information about each of us. **Genes** are sections of DNA. Each of these sections contains information necessary for the production of proteins. A **chromosome** contains many genes and is found in the nuclei of all cells. In humans, we have 23 pairs of chromosomes. Collectively, this genetic material forms our **genome**, which is our complete set of instructions for our growth and development—our complete set of DNA.

Our specific genetic make-up is referred to as our **genotype**. It is our genotype that is inherited from our parents. When we discuss hereditary we are referring to the creation of a genotype.

Our **phenotype** is the physical expression, or observable part of our genotype. It is what we see when we look at ourselves and others. We cannot see our genotype just by looking in the mirror.

The formation of our phenotype relies on the ways genes combine in our genotype. **Alleles** are different forms of a gene, and are located on the same spot on a pair of chromosomes. If we have identical pairs of alleles, the gene is said to be **homozygous**. If we have non-identical pairs of alleles, it is referred to as **heterozygous**. In heterozygous allele pairs, one allele will be dominant, meaning that its genetic code will be expressed in our phenotype, while the other allele will be recessive. Recessive alleles are expressed in homozygous pairs of alleles (when we inherit two recessive alleles), but dominant alleles are expressed any time they are present. What this means is that certain traits can be present in our genotype but may not be expressed in our phenotype because the dominant form of the allele takes over. Most of our genetic expression comes from more complex combinations than simply a single pair of dominant or recessive alleles. It is, however, useful to our understanding of genetics to use the idea of dominant and recessive genes to demonstrate and understand genetic transmission in general.

We can use a Punnett square to illustrate how genes can be passed on to offspring. In a Punnett square, we can see the probability of passing on specific combination of alleles during sexual reproduction where two people contribute to the genes of an offspring. It will show you the genotypes and phenotypes possible.

Let us use the example of Cystic Fibrosis to demonstrate genetic transmission of single-gene traits. Cystic Fibrosis originates on a single recessive gene. In order for recessive genes to be expressed, both alleles must be recessive (that is, no dominate gene; homozygous for recessive gene).

Case 1

Parent 1 does not carry the gene for Cystic Fibrosis. This means that they do not have the recessive gene for Cystic Fibrosis. We will denote this as FF. The capital letters are used to indicate the dominate allele.

Parent 2 does not carry the gene for Cystic Fibrosis. This means that they do not have the recessive gene for Cystic Fibrosis. We will denote this as FF. The capital letters are used to indicate the dominate allele.

What is the probability that their child will have Cystic Fibrosis? We can use the Punnett square below to show that there is 0% probability that their child will have Cystic Fibrosis.

Parent 1

	F	F
F	FF	FF
F	FF	FF

Parent 2

Case 2

Parent 1 does not carry the gene for Cystic Fibrosis. This means that they do not have the recessive gene for Cystic Fibrosis. We will denote this as FF. The capital letters are used to indicate the dominate allele.

Parent 2 does carry the gene for Cystic Fibrosis. This means that they have the recessive gene for Cystic Fibrosis. They are heterozygous for the gene. We will denote this as Ff. The capital letters are used to indicate the dominate allele, and the lower case letter indicates the recessive gene.

What is the probability that their child will have Cystic Fibrosis? We can use the Punnett square below to show that there is 0% probability that their child will have Cystic Fibrosis.

Parent 1

	F	F
F	FF	FF
f	Ff	Ff

Parent 2

Case 3

Parent 1 does carry the gene for Cystic Fibrosis. This means that they have the recessive gene for Cystic Fibrosis. They are heterozygous for the gene. We will denote this as Ff. The capital letters are used to indicate the dominate allele, and the lower case letter indicates the recessive gene.

Parent 2 does carry the gene for Cystic Fibrosis. This means that they have the recessive gene for Cystic Fibrosis. They are heterozygous for the gene. We will denote this as Ff. The capital letters are used to indicate the dominate allele, and the lower case letter indicates the recessive gene.

What is the probability that their child will have Cystic Fibrosis? We can use the Punnett square below to show what happens when BOTH parents carry the recessive gene for Cystic Fibrosis.

Parent 1

	F	f
F	FF	Ff
f	Ff	ff

Parent 2

When both parents carry the recessive gene for cystic fibrosis, or any other recessive trait, there is a 1 in 4 or 25% likelihood that their child will inherit homozygous alleles for that trait. In case 3, there is a 25% chance that the child will have Cystic Fibrosis.

Case 4

Parent 1 does carry the gene for Cystic Fibrosis. This means that they have the recessive gene for Cystic Fibrosis. They are heterozygous for the gene. We will denote this as Ff. The capital letters are used to indicate the dominate allele, and the lower case letter indicates the recessive gene.

Parent 2 has Cystic Fibrosis. This means that they have homozygous recessive alleles for Cystic Fibrosis. We will denote this as ff.

What is the probability that their child will have Cystic Fibrosis? We can use the Punnett square below to show what happens when one parent carries the recessive gene for Cystic Fibrosis and one parent has Cystic Fibrosis.

Parent 1

	F	f
f	Ff	ff
f	Ff	ff

Parent 2

There is a 50% chance that the child will have Cystic Fibrosis.

What do you think would happen if BOTH parents had Cystic Fibrosis? You are correct—there is a 100% chance that their child will have Cystic Fibrosis.

Parent 1

	f	f
f	ff	ff
f	ff	ff

Parent 2

Practice...

1. How many chromosomes does a normal human cell have?
   a. 46
   b. 23
   c. 64
   d. 21

2. What does DNA stand for?
   a. Dominant Nucleotide Affect
   b. Dextroniactic Allele
   c. Deoxyribonucleic Acid
   d. Dormant Nickel Acid

3. Recently, many persons who were wrongfully convicted of crimes they did not commit have been exonerated using _____ testing; that is, a test that examines someone's unique genetic information.
   a. centromere
   b. DNA
   c. chromosomatic
   d. allele

4. Mikhail is an architect who designs beautiful homes. He takes a few weeks to draw up a blueprint, and then this plan is given to a contractor who builds the home based on the blueprint. Genetically speaking, the blueprint created by Mikhail is a _____, while the house built by the contractor is a _____.
   a. phenotype; genotype
   b. genotype; phenotype
   c. chromosome; genome
   d. centromere; chromatid

5. Genes located in the same position on the pair of chromosomes in a unit of heredity are known as _____.
   a. alleles
   b. heterozygotic
   c. mitotic genes
   d. Mendelian genes

 Apply...

1. Genome Canada

   Look up Genome Canada online (https://www.genomecanada.ca/). Navigate through their webpage and write a list of five projects that are currently being explored. You may select any five projects you find interesting.

   1. _____

   _____

   _____

   2. _____

   _____

   _____

   3. _____

   _____

   _____

   4. _____

   _____

   _____

   5. _____

   _____

   _____

2. Punnett square

   - *Scenario 1*: Jill and Tom are expecting their first child. Jill has dark hair and Tom is blond. They are wondering whether their child will have blonde hair. Use a Punnett square to find out what the probability is that their child will be blonde. NOTE: Dark hair is dominant.

   _____

   _____

   _____

   _____

   _____

   _____

   _____

   _____

   _____

   _____

   _____

   _____

   to be continued

Apply...

continued

- *Scenario 2*: Stephanie and Jonathon are expecting their fourth child. Both Stephanie and Jonathon have dark hair. They already have three children. Two of their children have dark hair and one has blonde hair. They are wondering whether their fourth child will have blonde hair. Use a Punnett square to find out what the probability is that their child will be blonde. NOTE: Dark hair is dominant.

_____

_____

_____

_____

_____

_____

_____

_____

_____

_____

_____

_____

_____

_____

_____

_____

_____

_____

_____

_____

_____

_____

_____

_____

_____

_____

_____

Behavioural Genetics

 Discuss how behavioural genetics can examine the contribution of genetics on our behaviour

In addition to wondering where our physical features came from, we may also wonder where our behaviour originated. We may wonder who in our genetic pool is stubborn, or artistic, or a daredevil. **Behavioural genetics** is the study of the effects of genetics on our behaviour.

Behavioural genetics uses twin studies to examine the relative influences of genetics and environmental factors on who we are, how we behave, and how we engage in mental processes.

Let's say we are interested in the genetic contribution to our intelligence. We can use twins to study how much of our intelligence is due to genetics and how much is due to environmental factors.

To do this, we would need to compare intelligence across four separate groups:

1. Identical twins (monozygotic) reared together

2. Identical twins (monozygotic) reared apart

3. Fraternal twins (dizygotic) reared together

4. Fraternal twins (dizygotic) reared apart

Identical twins or monozygotic twins occur when a single fertilized egg splits into two. They are 100% genetically identical. They have the same genotype.

Fraternal twins or dizygotic twins occur from separate and unique fertilized eggs. They are 50% genetically identical. They are no more genetically similar than any pair of siblings. They have different genotypes.

(It is also important to note that we are 50% genetically identical to each parent.)

The basic premise of our examination of the role of genetics in intelligence is the following:

*   If intelligence is the result of *only* genetics, then identical twins will have the same intelligence, regardless of being raised together or apart (100% genetics).

*   If intelligence is the result of *only* environment, then twins will have the same intelligence regardless of whether they are identical or fraternal (100% environment).

In such a study, researchers will examine **heritability**, the degree to which genetics explains the differences among individuals.

What do you think researchers have found? You will have a chance to find out in your activity for this unit.

The general goal of behavioural genetics is to be able to determine how much of who we are is due to genetics and how much is due to environment. The development of this field stems from the classic nature versus nurture debate, in which researchers and theorists debated the idea of singular causes to our behaviour and mental processes. It is now generally agreed that most of our complex behaviours and mental activities are the result of interactions between our genetics and our environment.

Practice...

1. Researchers in _____ analyze the effects of genes and environmental factors on behaviour and mental processes.
   a. the Hap Project
   b. psychobiology
   c. behavioural genetics
   d. developmental psychology

2. _____ describes the degree to which a trait is able to be passed on genetically.
   a. Chromosomality
   b. Adaptability
   c. Selective breeding
   d. Heritability

3. Identical twins are to _____ as fraternal twins are to _____.
   a. heterozygotic; homozygotic
   b. dizygotic; monozygotic
   c. homozygotic; heterozygotic
   d. monozygotic; dizygotic

4. Dizygotic twins share _____ of their genetic material.
   a. 25%
   b. 50%
   c. 75%
   d. 100%

5. Why is it that monozygotic twins share 100% of their genes?
   a. Because they are the result of two sperm cells fertilizing the same egg, and thus that egg make sure to choose only the same genes from each of the sperm cells.
   b. Because they are the result of one zygote that split into two, making a perfect replica of itself.
   c. Because they are born at the same time and thus have the same start to their phenotypical development.
   d. Because they are the result of two zygotes being formed at precisely the same time.

 **Apply...**

1. Minnesota twin study

   Research the Minnesota Twin Study and their findings for the role of genetics in intelligence and personality. You may use the internet, peer-reviewed journals, textbooks, etc.

   Write a summary of the research findings. What did you learn about the role of genetics in forming our intelligence and personality? What are the implications of these findings?

   _____

   _____

   _____

   _____

   _____

   _____

   _____

   _____

   _____

   _____

   _____

   _____

   _____

   _____

   _____

   _____

   _____

   _____

   _____

   _____

   _____

   _____

   _____

   _____

   _____

   _____

   _____

   _____

   _____

   _____

Evolution

 Describe key evolutionary changes in humans

Thus far, we have discussed the transmission of genetic material to a single off-spring. Now, we will explore what happens over thousands of years of sexual reproduction. **Evolutionary Psychology** focuses on the role of evolution in human survival and adaptation. Its goal is to examine how behaviours have evolved in response to environmental stress and change. To examine the evolution of behaviours, we must examine changes that occur in genetic transmissions within a species over long periods of time. Evolution is a slow and long process, and is studied across many generations. One aspect of genetic transmission that we have yet to discuss is **mutation**. Mutation refers to a change in an organism's DNA. Mutations are the foundation of genetic change and variability across generations of a species. When these mutations are passed on to future generations then they impact evolution. Mutations occur randomly and can positively or negatively impact an organism, or they can have no impact at all. You may be surprised how little genetic variation is needed to result in dramatic differences across species.

How Genetically Similar Are Humans to Other Animals?

- We share 96.7% of our DNA with orangutans.
- We share 97.7% of our DNA with gorillas.
- We share 98.76% of our DNA with chimpanzees.
- We share 99% of our DNA with bonobos.

As we will see the 1% difference in our genetic make-up compared to bono-bos has led to significant changes in the way we move, think, and communicate.

- Humans are part of the Hominid family.
- Hominids are characterized by:
  - ◊ manner of movement (locomotion)—upright position (bipedal).
  - ◊ a large reorganized brain.
  - ◊ diminished face and teeth.
  - ◊ use and construction of tools.

How Did Hominids Evolve into Today's Humans?

- The oldest hominids belong to the genus Australopithecus.
- *Australopithecus afarensis*, our oldest relative, lived 4–2.75 million years ago, was bipedal, and had a brain capacity of 380–450 cc.
- *Australopithecus africanus*, lived 3–1.6 million years ago, was taller than its predecessor, and had a bigger brain capacity of 400–600 cc.
- *Australopithecus robustus*, lived 2.3–1.3 million years ago, was significantly larger, and had a brain capacity of 500–600 cc.
- *Australopithecus boisei* lived 2.5–1.2 million years ago, and was similar to *Australopithecus robustus* in size.
- Then we evolved into to the genus "homo."
- *Homo habilis* (handy man) used stone tools, and had longer arms, a smaller body, and a brain capacity of 700 cc.
- *Homo erectus* lived 1.8–1 million years ago, created tools, used fire, occupied caves, and had a brain capacity of 800–1300 cc.

- *Homo sapiens*—who we are today—first came to be around 200 000–300 000 years ago. We are similar to *Homo erectus* in structure, but we have rounder heads, and bigger brain capacity (1350 cc) than our ancestors (Wicander & Monroe, 1993).

One noticeable and significant evolutionary change occurred in our brain. Specifically, our brain size increased over time. Our brain capacity remains at 1350 cc today (Wicander & Monroe, 1993). Most of the growth in our brains occurred in areas responsible for higher mental processes, such as our cerebral cortex. These changes led to the development of language, greater memory, better problem-solving abilities, and to the establishment of key milestones such as agriculture, government, and culture.

Refer back to Chapter 2 on the human brain if you are unsure about what are the functions of different parts of our brain.

 Practice...

1. _____ psychology attempts to explain the development of the human mind and behaviour by studying how adaptive behaviours helped human ancestors to survive and reproduce.
   a. Evolutionary
   b. Mendelian
   c. Darwinian
   d. Developmental

2. Bipedalism refers to an animal's ability to:
   a. use opposable thumbs.
   b. walk on two legs.
   c. use their left and right hands interchangeably.
   d. switch from focusing on their eyesight to focusing on their hearing.

3. The first of our ancestors to use tools was:
   a. *Homo erectus*.
   b. *Australopithecus boisei*.
   c. *Homo habilis*.
   d. *Australopithecus africanus*.

4. We are most closely genetically identical to:
   a. chimpanzees.
   b. gorillas.
   c. great apes.
   d. bonobos.

5. The brains of humans today are bigger than the brains of *Homo sapiens*.
   a. True
   b. False

 **Apply...**

1. Mutations

   Research mutations. You may use the internet, peer-reviewed journals, textbooks, etc.

   • Make a list of four disorders in humans that are caused by the mutation of genes.

   1. _____

   _____

   _____

   2. _____

   _____

   _____

   3. _____

   _____

   _____

   4. _____

   _____

   _____

   • What are "silent mutations"?

   _____

   _____

   _____

   _____

   _____

   _____

   _____

   _____

   _____

   • What are the benefits of mutations?

   _____

   _____

   _____

   _____

   _____

   _____

   _____

   _____

to be continued

 **Apply...**

continued

2. Bonobos

   Many of us know little about bonobos. Research bonobos. You may use the internet, peer-reviewed journals, textbooks, etc.

   How are bonobos similar and different to humans?

   _____

   _____

   _____

   _____

   _____

   _____

   _____

   _____

   _____

   _____

   _____

   _____

   _____

   _____

   _____

   _____

   _____

   _____

   _____

   _____

   _____

   _____

   _____

   _____

   _____

   _____

Evolutionary Adaptations

 LO4 List three evolutionary adaptations of humans

In addition to the evolutionary changes to our physical structure and brain size, humans have also experienced several key behavioural and social adaptations.

These adaptations have been broad, affecting all humans (such as the development of language and facial expressions) as well as domain-specific, differing across context and environmental stresses (such as decision making about the safety of food and potential environmental hazards).

All humans have evolved an innate ability to develop language. We have a preference for human faces from birth which assists us in effective communication. In your chapter on Motivation and Emotion, you will examine the universality of emotional expression. We have also evolved a need to belong to a group. In Chapter 5 on Motivation and Emotion, you will learn about Maslow's Hierarchy of Needs which includes a need to belong. Humans have evolved such that we all share some personality characteristics aimed at achieving the goals of survival and reproduction.

Our evolutionary adaptations serve to increase our survival and opportunities for reproduction.

Mating and Parental Systems

We have evolved mating systems based on the sex differences typically found in levels of parental investment. We invest much time, energy, and resources in a small number of offspring, compared to other species, which means that we tend to seek out mates who are prepared to engage in a high level of parental investment. For humans, females commonly have the higher level of parental investment and as a result tend to be more selective in choosing a mate (Trivers, 1972).

Mating systems are:

- **Monogamy:**
    ◊ One female, one male
    ◊ Two parents have equal parental investment
    ◊ Common in humans
- **Polyandry:**
    ◊ One female, multiple males
    ◊ Not common
    ◊ Females have less parental investment
- **Polygyny:**
    ◊ One male, multiple females
    ◊ Males have less parental investment; females have great parental investment
    ◊ Common in mammals

Social Adaptations: Helping

Along with the evolution of a need to belong to a group, humans developed ways of helping others. We engage in:

- **Cooperation:**
    ◊ One individual helps another
    ◊ Benefits both parties

- **Altruism:**
  ◊ One individual helps another
  ◊ Risks involved for individual who helps
  ◊ **Kin selection**—increase survival of relatives, more altruistic towards relatives
  ◊ **Reciprocal altruism**—long-term, individual who helps may receive help in the future

Social Adaptations: Aggression

From an evolutionary perspective, aggression serves to increase survival by protecting mate, offspring, territories, and food supplies. Species who engage in aggressive behaviours, such as humans, also tend to have competition for mates and hierarchies of power especially among males.

 # Practice...

1. The concept of _____ is often used to explain the stereotypical image of women as seeking out "Mr. Perfect" while trying to find a mating partner.
   a. alpha males
   b. dominant special prototypes
   c. parental investment
   d. androgyny

2. Most species of mammals are _____, which describes a pattern by which the mother invests a lot of time in parenting the young while the father's "job" is over after the female is impregnated.
   a. monogamous
   b. polygynous
   c. multifaceted
   d. hydrophilic

3. Broad human adaptations include all the following except _____.
   a. language
   b. need to belong to a group
   c. choosing safe food
   d. cooperation

4. Your neighbour asks you to help him build his deck. You agree to help. Based on your understanding of human evolutionary adaptations, your help is best defined as:
   a. reciprocal altruism.
   b. cooperation.
   c. kin selection.
   d. aggression.

Apply...

1. Development of agriculture

   Research the development of agriculture. You may use the internet, peer-reviewed journals, textbooks, etc.

   How has agriculture influenced humans?

   _____

   _____

   _____

   _____

   _____

   _____

   _____

   _____

   _____

   _____

   _____

   _____

   _____

   _____

   _____

   _____

   _____

   _____

   _____

   _____

   _____

   _____

   _____

   _____

   _____

   _____

to be continued

Apply...

continued

2. Mate selection

    • What qualities do you want your mate to have?

    _____

    _____

    _____

    _____

    _____

    _____

    _____

    _____

    _____

    _____

    _____

    _____

    _____

    _____

    • What qualities do you have that you think make you a good mate?

    _____

    _____

    _____

    _____

    _____

    _____

    _____

    _____

    _____

    _____

    _____

KNOW...

Learning Objectives

1. Probability of genetic transmission of single-gene traits using a Punnett square:

REMEMBER: Capital letters indicate dominant allele, whereas lower case letters indicate recessive allele.

Here are some common genetic interactions.

- Both parents are homozygous dominant

Parent 1

	F	F
F	FF	FF
F	FF	FF

Parent 2

- Both parents are homozygous recessive

Parent 1

	f	f
f	ff	ff
f	ff	ff

Parent 2

- Both parents are heterozygous

Parent 1

	F	f
F	FF	Ff
f	Ff	ff

Parent 2

- One parent heterozygous, one parent homozygous recessive

Both parents are homozygous dominant

Parent 1

	F	f
f	Ff	ff
f	Ff	ff

Parent 2

2. How behavioural genetics can examine the contribution of genetics on our behaviour:

Behavioural genetics is the study of the effects of genetics on our behaviour. It measures heritability, which is the degree to which genetics explains the differences among individuals. To examine this, twin studies are commonly conducted using four groups: Identical twins (monozygotic) reared together, identical twins (monozygotic) reared apart, fraternal twins (dizygotic) reared together, and fraternal twins (dizygotic) reared apart. The basic premise of our examination of the role of genetics is that if something is the result of only genetics then identical twins will be the same, regardless of being raised together or apart (100% genetics), and if something is the result of only environmental factors then twins will be the same regardless of whether they are identical or fraternal (100% environment). It is now generally agreed that most of our complex behaviours and mental activities are the result of interactions between our genetics and our environment.

3. Key evolutionary changes in humans:
   - Change to bipedal
   - Increase in size
   - Increase in brain capacity, especially in areas responsible for higher mental processes
   - Ability to use and create tools

4. Three evolutionary adaptations of humans:

You can choose any three. Here are some examples:
   - Mating and parental system
   - Altruism and cooperation
   - Aggression
   - Language
   - Facial expressions

Key Terms

DNA: Deoxyribonucleic acid, carries all of our genetic material.

Genes: Sections of DNA, contains information necessary for the production of proteins.

Chromosome: Contains many genes and is found in the nuclei of all cells.

Genome: Complete set of DNA.

Genotype: Specific genetic make-up that is inherited from our parents.

Phenotype: The physical expression, or observable part of our genotype.

Alleles: Different forms of a gene.

Homozygous: Identical pairs of alleles.

Heterozygous: Non-identical pairs of alleles.

Behavioural Genetics: The study of the effects of genetics on our behaviour.

Identical Twins or Monozygotic Twins: Twins that form when a single fertilized egg splits into two making them 100% genetically identical.

Fraternal Twins or Dizygotic Twins: Twins that form from separate and unique fertilized eggs and are 50% genetically identical.

Heritability: The degree to which genetics explains the differences among individuals.

Evolutionary Psychology: Focuses on the role of evolution in human survival and adaptation.

Mutation: Refers to a change in an organism's DNA.

Monogamy: One female, one male.

Polyandry: One female, multiple males.

Polygyny: One male, multiple females.

Cooperation: One individual helps another with benefits for both parties.

Altruism: One individual helps another with risks to the individual helping.

Kin Selection: A proposed reason for altruism in which helping others increases survival of relatives.

Reciprocal Altruism: A proposed reason for altruism in which helping others eventually leads to them helping you in the future.

Answers to Practice

Basics of Genetics
1. a   2. c   3. b   4. b   5. a

Behavioural Genetics
1. c   2. d   3. d   4. b   5. a

Evolution
1. a   2. b   3. c   4. d   5. b

Evolutionary Adaptations
1. c   2. b   3. c   4. a

References

Trivers, R. L. (1972). Parental investment and sexual selection. In B. Campbell (Ed.). *Sexual selection and the descent of man.* New York, NY: Aldine de Gruyter.

Wicander, R. & Monroe. J. S. (1993). *Historical geology: evolution of the earth and life through time.* Minneapolis, St. Paul: West Publishing Company.

5 Motivation and Emotion

LEARNING OBJECTIVES

LO1 Define motivation, motives, and instincts

LO2 Explain Drive-Reduction and Arousal Theories of Motivation

LO3 Discuss the incentive, humanistic, and self-determination approaches to motivation

LO4 Illustrate how the three components of emotional experiences are explained by the six main theories of emotion

LEARN...

The term motivation is used to describe the common, yet often difficult process, we engage in every time we start and continue to work towards a goal. Our ability to become motivated is influenced by motives, which are our needs, wants, goals, etc. Our motives may be internal, meaning that they originate inside us, or external, meaning that they originate outside of us. Personal satisfaction, pride, and a sense of accomplishment are all internal motives. Rewards, money, and praise from others are external motives. We refer to motivation as intrinsic motivation, meaning that activities are motivated by internal motives, or as extrinsic motivation, meaning that activities are motivated by external motives. Several theories attempt to explain motivation. The Instinct Approach is a theory of motivation in which our instincts motivate us to act or behave in certain ways. The Drive-Reduction Theory states that our physiological needs act as motivators for our behaviour with the goal of meeting a need and regaining homeostasis. According to the Arousal Theory, we are motivated to engage in behaviours that will keep our level of physiological arousal at an optimal level. The Incentive Approach states that we are motivated to behave or act in a certain way based on incentives. The humanistic approach outlined by Maslow's Hierarchy of Needs proposes that we act to meet our needs in a hierarchical manner ranging from those needed for survival to more complex personal needs. Finally, the Self-Determination Theory states that we strive to obtain and maintain autonomy, competence, and relatedness within our social environment. Collectively, these theories of motivation address possible causes of motivation, individual differences in motivation, and common goals we all share. In this chapter, we also discuss emotion. Emotions are our subjective reaction to a stimulus. Emotion and motivation are linked as we must like or want something for it to act as a motivator. Our basic emotions are joy, anger, and fear, and our more complex emotions include guilt, embarrassment, and pride. Every time we experience an emotion, there is a physical component, a cognitive component, and a behavioural component. The question that has been debated by researchers is how these three components all fit together to give us the subjective experience of feelings, such as happy, sad, or angry. There are six theories of emotion that are outlined in this chapter including the common sense theory and facial feedback hypothesis of emotion.

What Is Motivation?

L01 Define motivation, motives, and instincts

You have likely heard a lot about motivation. Usually, statements such as "You can do it!", "I must stay motivated!", and "Find what motivates you." are used to help us stay on track and work towards a goal. But what exactly is motivation, and why do we need it?

The term **motivation** is used to describe the common, yet often difficult process, we engage in every time we start and continue to work towards a goal.

Our ability to become motivated is influenced by **motives**, which are our needs, wants, and goals. These motives provide the energy, commonly referred to as "will power", for us to act towards meeting our needs, obtaining what we want, or achieving our goals.

Motives, will vary between individuals, and as such motivation is a unique process for each of us.

Our motives may be **internal**, meaning that they originate inside us, or **external**, meaning that they originate outside of us.

Personal satisfaction, pride, and a sense of accomplishment are all internal motives. Rewards, money, and praise from others are external motives.

We refer to motivation as **intrinsic motivation**, meaning that activities are motivated by internal motives, or as **extrinsic motivation**, meaning that activities are motivated by external motives.

It is important to remember that what motives one person may not motivate another person. The key then to motivation is finding a motive that is meaningful and significant to a person. For example, the goal to achieve a healthier weight may be driven by a desire to feel better or to look better or to prevent disease—but the exact motive that drives us to work towards achieving a healthier weight may differ across individuals. If we want to motivate a person, we must first determine what they find important, and this can differ depending on age and context.

Motivation is also complex because we do not always know or understand what motivates us. In fact, sometimes our motives are unconscious and we may not even be aware of them, while other times we are fully aware of our motives.

Let us look at some of the theories that attempt to explain motivation. We will start by examining a theory of motivation that is founded on our basic, biological need for survival: **The Instinct Approach**.

According to the Instinct approach, our **instincts** (unlearned, species-specific patterns of behaviour) motivate us to act or behave in certain ways. What do you think the goal of instincts might be? The goal is survival! For this reason, the instinct approach to motivation aims to keep us alive. In addition, all humans have the same instincts, because we share the same biologically determined species-specific patterns of behaviour. For example, according to the instinct theory, our instincts keep us away from things that could harm us, and they drive us towards things that will help us find food. However, instincts cannot explain why we see individual differences in our behaviours. For example, most of us adhere to the instinct to remain safe, but this is challenged by individuals who engage in behaviours that are potentially dangerous, such as racing cars or sky diving. Other theories of motivation attempt to explain more motives that drive our behaviours—we will explore those in the next section.

Practice...

1. _____ is the process in which we engage in goal-directed behaviour.
   a. Motivation
   b. Emotion
   c. Wanting
   d. Safety

2. A(n) _____ is an unlearned complex behaviour with a fixed pattern throughout a species.
   a. reflex
   b. hedonic action
   c. motivation
   d. instinct

3. Motives may be _____, meaning that they originate inside us, or _____, meaning that they originate outside of us.
   a. external, internal
   b. internal, external
   c. biological, physiological
   d. cognitive, physiological

4. Which of the following can be explained by the instinct approach to motivation?
   a. Working towards financial security
   b. Searching for social acceptance
   c. Studying for a test in psychology class
   d. Running out of the way of a moving car

5. One limitation of the instinct approach to motivation is that it:
   a. does not explain why humans have common motives.
   b. incorrectly identifies survival as a primary motive for humans.
   c. does not address individual differences.
   d. all of the above are limitations.

Apply...

1. **Internal versus External Motives**

   • Describe a time in your life where you experienced an internal motive.

   What was the motive?

   _____

   _____

   _____

   _____

   _____

   _____

   _____

   _____

   _____

to be continued

continued

How did it help you to direct your behaviour or actions towards a goal?

_____

_____

_____

_____

_____

_____

_____

_____

_____

_____

_____

_____

- Describe a time in your life where you experienced an external motive.

  What was the motive?

_____

_____

_____

_____

_____

_____

_____

_____

_____

_____

to be continued

 **Apply…**

continued

How did it help you to direct your behaviour or actions towards a goal?

_____

_____

_____

_____

_____

_____

_____

_____

_____

_____

_____

_____

_____

- Which type of motivator do you think is most effective in helping us to achieve a goal, internal or external? Why? What does the research in this area say?

_____

_____

_____

_____

_____

_____

_____

_____

_____

_____

_____

_____

_____

Drives and Arousal Theories of Motivation

L02 Explain Drive-Reduction and Arousal Theories of Motivation

We have just learned that instincts are one type of motive that causes us to behave in ways that aim to keep us safe and alive. Other theories of motivation attempt to explain other aspects of our behaviour. Let us take a look at these other theories.

Like the instinct theory, the **Drive-Reduction Theory** is founded on biological causes of motivation with the goal of maintaining our survival. According to the drive-reduction theory, our physiological needs act as motivators for our behaviour. Specifically, when we have a physiological need, it creates discomfort which then motivates us to act in a way that decreases our discomfort. The basic premise of the drive-reduction theory lies in the idea that when all our biological needs are met we are in balance or **homeostasis**. When we are not in balance it creates discomfort, such as a feeling of being hungry, tired, or a need to use the bathroom. This discomfort causes us to act so that we regain balance.

Drive-Reduction Theory

- A change in homeostasis creates a need to return to homeostasis by obtaining something or by behaving in some way.

- The need creates discomfort for us. This is referred to as a **drive**.

- The drive motivates us to act in a way that will address our need and restore homeostasis. Our behaviour is said to be goal-directed.

According to the drive-reduction theory, drives are not always biologically determined (referred to as **primary drives**), but can also be learned or acquired (referred to as **secondary drives**). Secondary drives include the drive to obtain money, prestige, social approval, etc.

Next, we will discuss the **Arousal Theory** of motivation. According to the arousal theory, we are motivated to engage in behaviours that will keep our level of physiological arousal (mental and physical activity) at an optimal level. The optimal level is different for all of us. We all have a level of physiological arousal at which we feel most comfortable and efficient. When this level is low, we will engage in behaviours such as curiosity, exploration, and play—we want to increase our physiological arousal. When this level is too high, we may engage in avoidance behaviour and withdraw or remove stimuli—we want to decrease our physiological arousal. The goal is to regain homeostasis.

In general, our levels of optimal arousal adhere to the **Yerkes-Dodson Law**: Moderate levels of arousal lead to better performance than do levels of arousal that are too low or too high. Specifically, performance on a task is best when arousal level is appropriate to the difficulty of the task:

- Simple tasks are performed best with a high arousal level

- Moderate tasks are performed best with a moderate arousal level

- Difficult tasks are performed best with a low arousal level

The arousal theory of motivation explains individual differences and accounts for **sensation seekers**, people who need more arousal than the average person. Sensation-seekers have a higher optimal arousal level (Baird & McCarthy, 2014).

Practice...

1. The goal of drives is to re-establish _____.
   a. social goals
   b. homeostasis
   c. self-actualization
   d. reproductive success

2. The _____ law states that in general people perform at their best when they experience a moderate level of arousal; too little arousal will not motivate their best effort, and too much arousal will interfere with their performance.
   a. Berman-Silverman
   b. Wertheimer-Werth
   c. Yerkes-Dodson
   d. Shneidman-Farberow

3. Thirst and hunger are _____ drives.
   a. primary
   b. secondary
   c. arousal
   d. moderate

4. Compared to the general population, sensation seekers are more likely to engage in all of the following activities, except:
   a. bungee jumping.
   b. eating when hungry.
   c. trying new foods.
   d. riding roller coasters.

5. According to the Arousal Theory, we are more likely to turn off the radio when driving if:
   a. we are driving home from school.
   b. we are sleepy.
   c. we are hungry.
   d. we are driving in a snow blizzard.

Apply...

1. **Sensation Seekers**

   Research sensation seekers. You may use the internet, peer-reviewed journals, textbooks, etc.

   • Based on what you have read would you consider yourself a sensation seeker? Why/Why not?

   _____

   _____

   _____

   _____

   _____

   _____

   _____

   _____

to be continued

 **Apply...**

continued

- What are the risks associated with being a sensation seeker?

_____

_____

_____

_____

_____

_____

_____

_____

_____

_____

_____

_____

_____

2. **The Yerkes-Dodson Law in Our Life**

Provide examples in which your behaviour adheres to the Yerkes-Dodson Law.

- What is a simple task that you perform in which you desire a high arousal level?

_____

_____

_____

_____

_____

_____

_____

_____

_____

_____

_____

_____

to be continued

Apply...

continued

- What is a moderate task that you perform in which you desire a moderate arousal level?

_____

_____

_____

_____

_____

_____

_____

_____

_____

_____

_____

- What is a difficult task that you perform in which you desire a low arousal level?

_____

_____

_____

_____

_____

_____

_____

_____

_____

_____

_____

Incentive, Humanistic, and Self-Determination Approaches to Motivation

L03 Discuss the incentive, humanistic, and self-determination approaches to motivation

To this point, we have focused on theories of motivation in which the motivators are internal, and often biological in nature. Next, we will look at theories that attempt to explain how we are motivated by both internal and external factors.

1. **Incentive Approach to Motivation:** This states that we are motivated to behave or act in a certain way based on **incentives**, which are things that we desire or want. Incentives come from outside or external sources. Because incentives and their motivating force vary across individuals, it is important for us to understand what is and is not an incentive to a specific person. In this way, the incentive approach to motivation accounts for individual differences.

2. **Maslow's Hierarchy of Needs:** This is a humanistic approach to motivation. According to Maslow's Hierarchy of Needs, we are driven to obtain or meet different needs that range from survival to great personal accomplishments. These needs form a hierarchy in which the needs at the bottom must be met before we can met higher order needs. In the hierarchy, we move from needs aimed at survival to broader social and psychological needs. Below is a list of the needs we must meet in order (Baird & McCarthy, 2014):

   1. Physiological Needs (food, water, shelter)
   2. Safety Needs (out of danger)
   3. Belongingness and Love Needs (acceptance, belonging to group)
   4. Esteem Needs (achievements, approval)
   5. Cognitive Needs (knowledge, exploration)
   6. Aesthetic Needs (attractiveness)
   7. Self-Actualization Needs (realize our potential, contentment)

   You can see how the motives at each stage will differ.

   Maslow's last stage of self-actualization is sometimes criticized. According to Maslow, self-actualization is difficult to achieve because we struggle to sufficiently satisfy our lower needs and as such we are unable to achieve our full human potential. Instead, Maslow states that we tend to experience **peak experiences**, which are times in our lives during which self-actualization is temporarily achieved.

3. The **Self-Determination Theory of Motivation:** This theory attempts to explain the influence of social context on our motivation. According to the theory, we strive to obtain and maintain autonomy, competence, and relatedness within our social environment, and when this happens we establish a sense of well-being. In this way, the self-determination theory accounts for both intrinsic and extrinsic motivation.

Practice...

1. Every Thursday, Yvette goes to the local grocery store and spends $5 on tickets to try to win the Super Lotto. She knows that her chance of winning is very low, but she also dreams of winning the $200 million prize. Yvette's behaviour can best be explained by the _____ theory of motivation.
    a. instinct
    b. arousal
    c. drive-reduction
    d. incentive

2. The first level of Maslow's hierarchy of needs includes _____ needs.
    a. social
    b. physiological
    c. safety
    d. esteem

3. Which of the following needs best explains why people join cults or gangs?
    a. The need for knowledge
    b. The need for belongingness
    c. The need for satisfaction
    d. The need for esteem

4. The impact of social media on our goal-directed behaviours is best addressed by which theory?
    a. Yerkes-Dodson Law
    b. Arousal Theory
    c. Self-Determination Theory
    d. Incentive Theory

5. We have now discussed several theories of motivation. From these discussions, we can conclude that _____.
    a. internal and external factors play a role in motivation
    b. internal factors, but not external factors play a role in motivation
    c. external factors, but not internal factors play a role in motivation
    d. motivation is purely driven by physiological needs

 **Apply...**

1.   **Maslow's Hierarchy of Needs**

Look up Maslow's Hierarchy of Needs online. Recreate the hierarchy in the space below.

to be continued

 **Apply…**

continued

2. **Self-Determination Theory of Motivation**

   Define and give an example from your life of the three components that make up the Self-Determination Theory of Motivation.

   - **Autonomy**

     Definition:

     _____

     _____

     _____

     _____

     _____

     _____

     _____

     _____

     Real Life Example:

     _____

     _____

     _____

     _____

     _____

     _____

     _____

     _____

   - **Competence**

     Definition:

     _____

     _____

     _____

     _____

     _____

     _____

     _____

to be continued

continued

Real Life Example:

_____
_____
_____
_____
_____
_____
_____
_____
_____

- **Relatedness**

Definition:

_____
_____
_____
_____
_____
_____
_____
_____
_____
_____

Real Life Example:

_____
_____
_____
_____
_____
_____
_____
_____
_____

Emotion

L04 Illustrate how the three components of emotional experiences are explained by the six main theories of emotion

The topics of emotion and motivation are often discussed within the same chapter in introductory Psychology textbooks. These two psychological processes are linked because:

- our emotions often act as motivators.
- for something to act as a motive we must like or want it.
- the result of goal-directed behaviour impacts our emotions.

When we discuss emotions, we are referring to our subjective reaction to a stimulus. It is basically how we "feel" about something, someone, etc. Let us examine how we experience emotions.

Our basic emotions are joy, anger, and fear, and our more complex emotions include guilt, embarrassment, and pride. Every time, we experience an emotion there is a:

1. **Physical Component:** The physiological arousal that accompanies the emotion.

2. **Cognitive Component:** The way we perceive or interpret a stimulus or situation, determines our emotions.

3. **Behavioural Component:** The outward expression of our emotions (facial expressions, gestures, body postures, and tone of voice).

The question that has been debated by researchers is how these three components all fit together to give us the subjective experience of feelings, such as happy, sad, or angry. Next, we will look at some of the main theories that attempt to explain why and how we experience emotions. The easiest way to learn and understand the differences between these theories is to look at them in simple, flow-diagram format.

Theories of Emotion

1. **Common Sense Theory of Emotion:**

   Stimulus ⟶ Emotion ⟶ Physiological Arousal

2. **James-Lange Theory of Emotion**

   Stimulus ⟶ Physiological Arousal ⟶ Emotion

3. **Cannon-Bard Theory of Emotion**

4. **Cognitive Arousal Theory of Emotion**

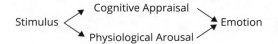

5. **Facial Feedback Hypothesis**

Stimulus ⟶ Physiological Arousal ⟶ Facial Expression ⟶ Cognitive Appraisal/Interpretation of Facial Movements ⟶ Emotion

6. **Lazarus's Cognitive Mediational Theory**

Stimulus ⟶ Cognitive Appraisal ⟶ Emotion ⟶ Physiological Arousal

 # Practice...

1. A(n) _____ refers to the subjective reaction an individual has to an object, event, person, or memory.
   a. internalization
   b. motivation
   c. cognition
   d. emotion

2. Jacquie is attempting to jump off of the high diving board for the very first time. Though she does not have a pathological fear of heights, the concept of jumping off of a 10-meter board is very stressful for her. As she walks to the edge of the board, her heart begins to pound and she gets goose bumps on her skin. These responses refer to the _____ component of an emotion.
   a. expressive behaviour
   b. physiological arousal
   c. cognitive experience
   d. affective relay

3. Which of the following book titles would be the most appropriate summary of the James-Lange theory?
   a. "I'm okay, you're okay, we're all okay!"
   b. "Sadness: Bad timing to the extreme!"
   c. "I will get angry if you irritate me!"
   d. "Why laughing makes me happy!"

4. According to the _____ theory of emotions, the mental and physiological components of emotions occur simultaneously.
   a. Cannon-Bard
   b. James-Lange
   c. Schachter and Singer two-factor
   d. Zajonc mere exposure

5. All of the following are basic emotions EXCEPT _____.
   a. joy
   b. fear
   c. pride
   d. anger

 Apply...

1. **The Universality of Emotions**

   Paul Ekman studies the universal expression of emotions. Watch the short video entitled "Emotions Revealed - KQED QUEST" (http://www.youtube.com/watch?v=-PFqzYoKkCc).

   While watching the movie, answer the following questions:

   • What emotions did Ekman identify as universal?

   _____
   _____
   _____
   _____
   _____

   • What is the purpose of emotion?

   _____
   _____
   _____
   _____
   _____

   • What evidence is cited for the genetic basis of emotion?

   _____
   _____
   _____
   _____
   _____

   • What is the Facial Action Coding System? Who uses it?

   _____
   _____
   _____
   _____
   _____
   _____

to be continued

 **Apply...**

continued

2. **The Development of Emotion**

    Research the development of emotions. You can use the internet, peer-reviewed journals, textbooks, etc.

    List the key developmental milestones in emotion (for example, how and when do we first smile?)

    _____

    _____

    _____

    _____

    _____

    _____

    _____

    _____

    _____

    _____

    _____

    _____

    _____

    _____

    _____

    _____

    _____

    _____

    _____

    _____

    _____

    _____

    _____

    _____

    _____

to be continued

 **Apply...**

continued

3. **Display Rules**

Thus far, the universal nature of emotions has been discussed; however, emotional expression varies across cultures.

Look up the term *display rules*. You can use the internet, peer-reviewed journals, textbooks, etc.

What does the term mean?

Research display rules in collectivist and individualistic cultures. You can use the internet, peer-reviewed journals, textbooks, etc.

Write a short summary of your findings.

_____

_____

_____

_____

_____

_____

_____

_____

_____

_____

_____

_____

_____

_____

_____

_____

_____

_____

_____

_____

_____

_____

_____

_____

_____

KNOW...

Learning Objectives

1. Motivation, motives, and instincts:
   - **Motivation:** The process of starting and continuing goal-directed behaviour
   - **Motives:** The stimuli that provide motivation, the reason why we act
   - **Instinct:** Unlearned, species-specific pattern of behaviour

2. Drive-reduction and arousal theories of motivation:

   Drive-Reduction Theory:
   - A change in homeostasis creates a need to return to homeostasis by obtaining something or by behaving in some way.
   - The need creates discomfort for us. This is referred to as a drive.
   - The drive motivates us to act in a way that will address our need and restore homeostasis. Our behaviour is said to be goal-directed.

   Arousal Theory:
   - We are motivated to engage in behaviours that will keep our level of physiological arousal (mental and physical activity) at an optimal level.
   - The optimal level is different for all of us. We all have a level of physiological arousal at which we feel most comfortable and efficient. When this level is low, we will engage in behaviours such as curiosity, exploration, and play. When this level is too high, we may engage in avoidance behaviour and withdraw or remove stimuli that are increasing our level of arousal.

3. Incentive, humanistic, and self-determination approaches to motivation:

   Incentive Approach to Motivation:
   - We are motivated to behave or act in a certain way based on incentives, which are things that we desire or want. Incentives come from outside or external sources. The incentive approach to motivation accounts for individual differences.

   Maslow's Hierarchy of Needs:
   - A humanistic approach to understanding motivation
   - We are driven to obtain or meet different needs that range from survival to great personal accomplishments.
   - These needs form a hierarchy in which the needs at the bottom must be met before we can met higher order needs.
   - In the hierarchy, we move from needs aimed at survival to broader social and psychological needs.

   The Self-Determination Theory of Motivation:
   - We strive to obtain and maintain autonomy, competence, and relatedness within our social environment.
   - When this happens, we establish a sense of well-being.
   - In this way, the self-determination theory accounts for both intrinsic and extrinsic motivation.

4. How the three components of emotional experiences are explained by the six main theories of emotion:

1. **Common Sense Theory of Emotion:**

   Stimulus $\longrightarrow$ Emotion $\longrightarrow$ Physiological Arousal

2. **James-Lange Theory of Emotion:**

   Stimulus $\longrightarrow$ Physiological Arousal $\longrightarrow$ Emotion

3. **Cannon-Bard Theory of Emotion:**

   Stimulus $\longrightarrow$ Brain Activity $\bigg\langle$ Physiological Arousal / Emotion

4. **Cognitive Arousal Theory of Emotion:**

   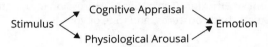

   Stimulus $\bigg\langle$ Cognitive Appraisal / Physiological Arousal $\longrightarrow$ Emotion

5. **Facial Feedback Hypothesis:**

   Stimulus $\longrightarrow$ Physiological Arousal $\longrightarrow$ Facial Expression $\longrightarrow$ Cognitive Appraisal/Interpretation of Facial Movements $\longrightarrow$ Emotion

6. **Lazarus's Cognitive Mediational Theory:**

   Stimulus $\longrightarrow$ Cognitive Appraisal $\longrightarrow$ Emotion $\longrightarrow$ Physiological Arousal

Key Terms

Motivation: The process of starting and continuing goal-directed behaviour.

Motives: The stimuli that provide motivation, the reason why we act.

Internal Motives: Motives or reasons for actions that originate inside us, such as pride.

External Motives: Motives or reasons for actions that originate inside us, such as money.

Intrinsic Motivation: Activities are motivated by internal motives.

Extrinsic Motivation: Activities are motivated by external motives.

The Instinct Approach: A theory of motivation in which our instincts motivate us to act or behave in certain ways.

Instinct: Unlearned, species-specific pattern of behaviour.

Drive-Reduction Theory: A theory of motivation in which our physiological needs act as motivators for our behaviour with the goal of meeting a need and regaining homeostasis.

Homeostasis: A state of balance or equilibrium.

Arousal Theory: A theory of motivation in which we are motivated to engage in behaviours that will keep our level of physiological arousal at an optimal level.

Yerkes-Dodson Law: Moderate levels of arousal lead to better performance than do levels of arousal that are too low or too high.

Sensation Seekers: People who need more arousal than the average person.

Incentive Approach: A theory of motivation in which we are motivated to behave or act in a certain way based on incentives.

Incentives: Things that we desire or want.

Maslow's Hierarchy of Needs: A theory of motivation in which we act to meet our needs in a hierarchical manner ranging from those needed for survival to more complex personal needs.

Peak Experiences: Times in our lives during which self-actualization is temporarily achieved.

Self-Determination Theory: A theory of motivation in which we strive to obtain and maintain autonomy, competence, and relatedness within our social environment.

Emotions: Our subjective reaction to a stimulus.

Physical Component of Emotion: The physiological arousal that accompanies the emotion.

Cognitive Component of Emotion: The way we perceive or interpret a stimulus or situation, determines our emotions.

Behavioural Component of Emotion: The outward expression of our emotions (facial expressions, gestures, body postures, and tone of voice).

Answers to Practice

What Is Motivation?

1. a   2. d   3. b   4. d   5. c

Drives and Arousal Theories of Motivation

1. b   2. c   3. a   4. b   5. d

Incentive, Humanistic, and Self-Determination Approaches to Motivation

1. d   2. b   3. b   4. c   5. a

Emotion

1. d   2. b   3. d   4. a   5. c

Reference

Baird, A., & McCarthy, A. (2014). *THINK psychology* (2nd Canadian Edition). Don Mills, ON: Pearson Education, Inc.; pp. 122–131.

6 Consciousness

LEARNING OBJECTIVES

LO1 Define consciousness, normal waking consciousness, and altered state of consciousness

LO2 Discuss the purpose of consciousness

LO3 Describe the stages of sleep

LO4 Explain how psychoactive substances impact consciousness

LEARN...

Would you say that you are aware of what is happening around you? What about in your body? We do not usually stop to think about how aware we are about things, yet many of us have used the words conscious or consciousness. Consciousness refers to our awareness, attentiveness, and responsiveness to what is happening within our body and mind, and in the environment around us. In this chapter, we look at the different levels of consciousness: (i) Unconscious: no awareness of what is going on; (ii) Nonconsciousness: everything that occurs in our body that we do not need to be aware of; (iii) Preconscious: information we are not always aware of but can bring into consciousness; (iv) Normal waking consciousness: being alert; and (v) Altered state of consciousness: any deviation from normal waking consciousness. Consciousness is critical to our survival. We must be able to detect stimuli, gather information, and respond appropriately. However, it would be overwhelming if we were aware of everything that was happening in our bodies and mind and in the environment around us. To address this, we have restrictive abilities that allow us to pay attention to immediate and important stimuli, while at the same time still processing other information nonconsciously, preconsciously, or unconsciously if needed. Our consciousness is influenced by circadian rhythms, which are built-in, biological clocks that regulate our physiological processes over a 24-hour cycle. They regulate functions such as eating and sleeping. Sleep can be considered a natural loss of consciousness. We know that we all need sleep, yet many of us are not getting enough sleep in both quantity and quality. Lack of sufficient sleep can lead to decreased alertness and, therefore, altered consciousness. When we sleep we go through five stages of sleep. Many of us have heard of rapid eye movement (REM) sleep which is a stage of sleep in which the eyes move rapidly under the eyelids and we typically have vivid dreams. We also go through four stages of non-REM sleep. Where we are in our sleep cycle will impact our consciousness, but we can also alter our consciousness through the use of psychoactive substances, which are anything that changes the way we perceive or understand the world or ourselves. They are commonly referred to as drugs and they include both legal and illegal forms. Psychoactive substances impact consciousness by changing neural communication, either by increasing or by decreasing neural activity. Different drugs impact our consciousness in different ways. Through discussion and activities you will learn about consciousness, and some of the factors that impact it.

Consciousness

 L01 Define consciousness, normal waking consciousness, and altered state of consciousness

Although we may use the term **consciousness** to refer to being awake or even to paying attention, it is in fact more complicated than that. Consciousness refers to our awareness, attentiveness, and responsiveness to what is happening within our body and mind, and in the environment around us. It is basically, how much we know about what is going on, and our ability to react to this information.

We, intuitively perhaps, understand that certain conditions improve our consciousness while others diminish it. We understand that when we are **unconscious** we are not aware of what is going on—we are "cut-off" from the information within and around us. We also understand that when we sleep we are also unaware of what is going on. But, is sleeping the same as being unconscious? We explore this later in this chapter. As stated earlier, some of us may think that being awake and being conscious are the same thing, but is it? You will look into this relationship in your activity for this unit.

In order to discuss consciousness, it is helpful to think of it in terms of a continuum. On one end, we have unconsciousness, which we can describe as being completely without awareness of ourselves and our environment. In the middle, we have **normal waking consciousness**, which we can describe as being aware, attentive, and responsive to ourselves and our environment—we are alert. It is the state you are in right now. Most people spend most of their day in this state. When we use the word "normal" in psychology we are referring to average or typical—what we usually see among individuals. At the other end, we have heightened consciousness, which we could describe as being fully conscious or fully aware of what is happening within and around us. Any deviation from normal waking consciousness—to a state of decreased consciousness or to a heightened or improved state of consciousness—is referred to as an **altered state of consciousness**. This chapter explores some of the ways that our consciousness can be altered. Our continuum may look like Figure 1.

Can you remember a time when you were aware, attentive, and responsive to your internal physical and mental processes and aware of the environment around you? What about right this moment? Most of us move through our day without thinking about our consciousness. We are often attending to specific things, like a school project, work task, conversation, driving a car, or to observing others.

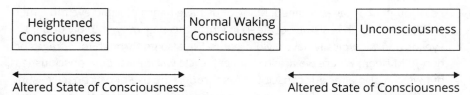

FIGURE 1 Continuum of consciousness.

Now, by this point some of you may be thinking about the fact that we are not always truly aware of everything that is happening within us or around us, yet we have knowledge about it, or we respond to it when necessary. You can think of these types of consciousness as lying on our continuum of consciousness as well. They have special terms:

- **Nonconsciousness:** All the processes that occur in our body that we do not need to monitor, regulate, or be aware of. For example, our heartbeat and breathing processes occur automatically. We are not consciously aware of them most of the time. However, we can and do become aware of these processes when there is a change in them. For example, we may become aware of our heart rate and breathing as we exercise, or we may be conscious of a full bladder (Baird & McCarthy, 2014).

- **Preconscious:** Processes and information that we are not always aware of but can bring into consciousness when we need or want to. For example, memories are not always in our normal waking consciousness, but we can recall or remember them when needed (Baird & McCarthy, 2014).

Next, we will explore some of the functions of consciousness.

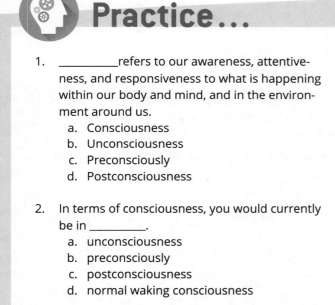

Practice...

1. _____refers to our awareness, attentiveness, and responsiveness to what is happening within our body and mind, and in the environment around us.
   a. Consciousness
   b. Unconsciousness
   c. Preconsciously
   d. Postconsciousness

2. In terms of consciousness, you would currently be in _____.
   a. unconsciousness
   b. preconsciously
   c. postconsciousness
   d. normal waking consciousness

3. Nonconscious is the same as unconscious.
   a. True
   b. False

4. In Psychology, the term "normal" is used to describe_____.
   a. typical
   b. average
   c. usually expected
   d. all of the above

5. You are in an altered state of consciousness, if _____.
   a. you recall a memory
   b. you are unconscious
   c. you deviate from normal waking consciousness
   d. you are feeling anxious

 **Apply...**

1. **Being Awake versus Being Conscious**

   Do you think being awake and being conscious are the same thing? Yes or No?

   What evidence do you have to support your position? You can use your personal experience, the internet, peer-reviewed journal articles, textbooks, etc.

   _____

   _____

   _____

   _____

   _____

   _____

   _____

   _____

   _____

   _____

   _____

   _____

2. **Consciousness Log**

   In order to better understand whether you are in normal waking consciousness or in an altered state of consciousness, you need to pay attention to your level of consciousness. To help you do this, you can document your consciousness throughout one or more days.

   For the next 2 days, keep a log of your activities and where you would place yourself on the continuum of consciousness during each of these activities.

   _____

   _____

   _____

   _____

   _____

   _____

   _____

   _____

   _____

   _____

   _____

   _____

   _____

to be continued

Apply...

continued

What Is the Purpose of Consciousness?

 Discuss the purpose of consciousness

Now that we have a general understanding of what consciousness is, we can look at its purpose. Why do we have consciousness? Why do we need to be aware of what is happening inside our bodies and minds and in the environment around us? What do you think is the reason?

Likely, you have come to realization that consciousness must play some role in our survival!

Imagine the danger we could be in if we were not aware of what was happening with our bodies or in our environment. Think about this not just for today, but through our whole evolutionary process (refer to Chapter 4 on Genetics and Evolution if you need a reminder). It is clear that we need to be aware of what is happening so that we can respond appropriately.

But, what do you think would happen if we were aware of EVERYTHING that happened in our bodies or in our external environment. Wow! That would be overwhelming indeed. It is for this reason that we have protections or safeguards that govern our consciousness. They help us to be aware of, direct our attention to, and respond to immediate, important, and potentially life-saving stimuli while other information is processed nonconsciously or even ignored as unimportant. In this way, our consciousness is *restrictive* in nature as it allows us to notice and give attention to specific information at any given time. So, how does this all fit together? How are we able to process information by choice as well as automatically? Our consciousness is multi-layered or multi-purpose in that it allows us to "maximize" information gathering so that we are processing internal and external stimuli as efficiently as possible.

We can look at two historical views or models of consciousness that have influenced how we view consciousness:

Sigmund Freud

- One of the most famous models of consciousness
- Believed that we had three levels of consciousness: Conscious, Preconscious, Unconscious
- Believed that our psyche was formed by three interacting components:
  ◊ **ID:** Completely unconscious part of who we are, comprised of our basic needs associated with survival and biological drives
  ◊ **Ego:** Mostly conscious, but some parts are preconscious and unconscious; it is the part of us that everyone sees; it serves to balance the needs of the ID and the superego
  ◊ **Superego:** Some parts are unconscious, some preconscious, and some conscious; it is the part of us that holds our ideals for morality, ethics, behaviour, etc.
- Believed that the unconscious holds socially unacceptable, "animalistic" basic desires such as drives for sex, food, and aggression.
- Concepts such as repressed memory, slip-of-the tongue, and defence mechanisms.
- Childhood plays a critical role in the development of our consciousness (Figure 2).

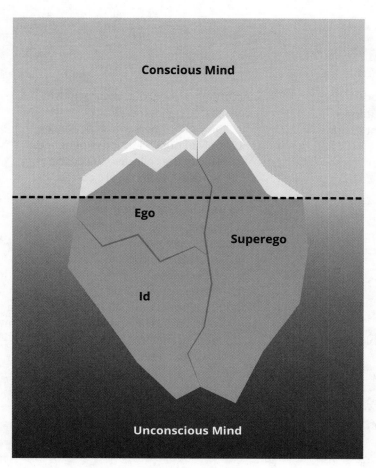

FIGURE 2 Freud's iceberg model of the psyche.
T and Z/Shutterstock

Carl Jung

- Supporter of Freud
- Our psyche is made of three main interacting parts:
  ◊ Ego: Conscious part of who we are
  ◊ Unconscious: Two parts:
    - The **personal unconscious**, which is similar to what Freud believed along with containing **complexes** which are beliefs and memories of specific concepts, derived from personal experience
    - The **collective unconscious**, which consists of our innate, shared predispositions, beliefs, and memories that all humans have because of our common evolutionary experiences
  ◊ Concepts such as archetypes
  ◊ Believe that past and future play a role in the development of consciousness

In both these models, different levels of consciousness are identified as influencing who we are and how we behave. We can see how our survival is aided and even dependent on the interactions among the different levels of consciousness. We will discuss Freud and Jung further in your chapter on Personality.

Practice...

1. Thanks to the _____ function of consciousness, we don't waste our attention on information that is not immediately relevant to our situations or salient to our own lives.
   a. bottleneck
   b. restrictive
   c. selective
   d. discriminative

2. Consciousness plays a role in _____.
   a. our survival
   b. the formation of our psyche
   c. our decision making
   d. all of the above

3. According to Freud, the ID is responsible for our _____.
   a. basic biological needs and is fully conscious
   b. moral standards and is fully conscious
   c. basic biological needs and is fully unconscious
   d. moral standards and is conscious and unconscious

4. According to Jung, our unconsciousness consists _____.
   a. only of our personal experiences
   b. only of our childhood experiences
   c. only of the collective unconscious
   d. None of the above are correct

5. The theories of consciousness proposed by Freud and Jung are similar in all of the following ways, except _____.
   a. emphasis on collective, evolutionary experiences
   b. number of interacting parts
   c. identification of childhood as playing a role in the development of consciousness
   d. identification of ego as a part of consciousness

Apply...

1. **Collective Unconscious**

   What do you think about the idea of a collective unconscious as proposed by Jung?

   _____

   _____

   _____

   _____

   _____

   _____

   _____

   to be continued

 **Apply...**

continued

Provide an example of a collective unconscious in your life.

_____
_____
_____
_____
_____
_____
_____
_____
_____

2. **Other Views of Consciousness**

- In this chapter, we identified two historical views of consciousness. There are more views of consciousness. These views may come from disciplines like psychology, neuroscience, and philosophy. Take some time to research some of the other views of consciousness. You can use the internet, peer-reviewed journals, textbooks, etc. Choose three other views and write a brief summary of each.

  ◇ View: _____
    Discipline it comes from:_____
    How does it explain consciousness?

    _____
    _____
    _____
    _____
    _____

  ◇ View: _____
    Discipline it comes from:_____
    How does it explain consciousness?

    _____
    _____
    _____
    _____
    _____
    _____

to be continued

 **Apply...**

continued

◊ View: _____
Discipline it comes from:_____
How does it explain consciousness?

_____
_____
_____
_____
_____
_____
_____
_____
_____
_____
_____
_____
_____

• Of the views you chose which one do you think best explains consciousness? Why?

_____
_____
_____
_____
_____
_____
_____
_____
_____
_____
_____
_____
_____
_____
_____
_____
_____

Altered State of Consciousness: Sleep

L03 Describe the stages of sleep

Have you noticed that you are more aware, attentive, and responsive to your internal and external worlds at different times during the day? You are not alone! In fact, we are all affected by **circadian rhythms**, which are our built-in, biological clocks that regulate our physiological processes over a 24-hour cycle. Functions such as eating and sleeping are regulated by our circadian rhythms. The suprachiasmatic nucleus, which is located within our hypothalamus, is responsible for determining when we wake up and when we fall asleep. When the time comes in our cycle for us to fall asleep, the suprachiasmatic nucleus sends a message to our pineal gland to secrete melatonin. It is melatonin that makes a person feel sleepy.

Think of the last time you felt sleepy. Where on the continuum of consciousness do you think you are when you are feeling sleepy? What about when you are asleep? In this unit, we will examine sleep and how it can impact our consciousness.

Sleep can be considered a natural loss of consciousness. We know that we all need sleep, yet many of us are not getting enough sleep in both quantity and quality.

Sleep deprivation, which is any significant loss of sleep resulting in problems in concentration and irritability, negatively impacts many areas of our life. In your activity for this unit, you will explore the impact of sleep deprivation.

Sleep is so important that our body seems to prioritize it over everything else we are doing, which can lead us to fall asleep while studying, watching a movie, or even while driving. We may also experience **microsleeps** which last only a few seconds. But, why would our bodies compel us to fall asleep, even in situations where it threatens our survival, like driving a car? We are not quite sure. There is still controversy around sleep's purpose. In general, the following theories attempt to explain why we need sleep:

- **Preservation and Protection Theory:** Sleep is an evolutionary adaptation that leads us to sleep at night and avoid predators that hunt during that time.

- **Body Restoration Theory:** Sleep allows our bodies and brain to recover from the experiences and fatigue that occur during the day.

- **Activation-Synthesis Theory:** Sleep is a side effect of neural firing during REM sleep (Baird & McCarthy, 2014).

Lack of sufficient sleep can lead to decreased alertness and, therefore, altered consciousness, difficulty regulating emotions and behaviour, difficulty learning and remembering, and health issues such as weight gain, diabetes, and heart disease (Canadian Sleep Society [CSS], 2017).

When we sleep, we go through five stages that are marked by different physiological experiences. Researchers can use electroencephalograph (EEG) to observe our brain wave activity as we go through each stage of sleep. The brain waves we show are:

- **Alpha Waves:** Brain waves that indicate a state of relaxation or light sleep

- **Theta Waves:** Brain waves indicating the early stages of sleep

- **Delta Waves:** Long, slow waves that indicate the deepest stage of sleep

Figure 3 is an example of what our brain waves may look like during different activities.

Normal Adult Brain Waves

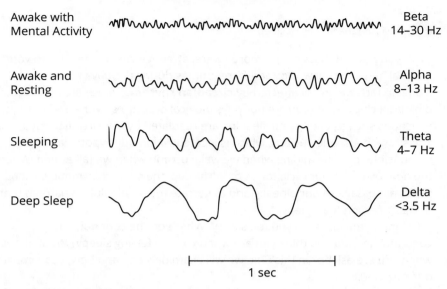

FIGURE 3 Normal brain waves EEG.

Alila Medical Media/Shutterstock

The five stages of sleep are:

- **REM (Rapid Eye Movement):** Brain waves resemble those we see when we are awake and active. Stage of sleep in which the eyes move rapidly under the eyelids and the person is typically experiencing a dream, but we now know that we can dream during any stage of sleep. We have our most vivid and emotional dreams during REM sleep, and are more likely to remember dreams that occur during this stage. You will explore dreaming in your activity for this topic.

- **NREM (Non-REM) Sleep:** Any of the stages of sleep that do not have REM.

    ◊ *Non-REM Stage One*: Light sleep, may experience hypnagogic images (vivid visual events) and hypnic jerk (knees, legs, or whole body jerks).

    ◊ *Non-REM Stage Two*: Sleep spindles (brief bursts of activity only lasting a second or two).

    ◊ *Non-REM Stages Three and Four*: Delta waves pronounced; deep sleep occurs when 50% or more of waves are delta waves.

We typically cycle through each stage each night. We usually fall asleep within 10–20 minutes and enter Non-REM Stage 1 sleep. We spend over 50% of our sleep in NON-REM Stage 2, and we experience Non-REM Stages 3 and 4 mostly in the first half of the night. We enter REM sleep four to five times during the night, with the longest periods occurring early in the morning (CSS, 2017).

If we look at the different stages of sleep, we can see how our consciousness will vary across the stages. Do you remember a time when you were asleep but were aware of what was happening around you? It is likely that you were in the early stages of sleep at that time. During deep sleep, we would experience much lower levels of consciousness; but sleeping is not the same as being unconscious. It is important to note that we can experience problems at any stage of sleep. In your activity for this topic, you will research some common sleep disorders.

Practice...

1. _____ is defined as the natural loss of consciousness.
   a. Sleep
   b. Hypnosis
   c. A coma
   d. Preconsciousness

2. How much time passes over the course of a circadian cycle?
   a. 12 hours
   b. 24 hours
   c. 14 days
   d. 28 days

3. How many stages of sleep are there in human beings?
   a. Three
   b. Four
   c. Five
   d. Six

4. What does REM stand for?
   a. Random Excitatory Memory
   b. Rapid Eye Movement
   c. Repletion of Extra Melatonin
   d. Rigorous Energetic Motion

5. Which stage of sleep is characterized by an increase in delta wave activity in the brain?
   a. REM sleep
   b. Stage 1
   c. Stage 2
   d. Stage 3

 # Apply...

1. **Why Do We Dream?**
   - There are several theories that attempt to explain why we dream. Research dreaming and write an answer to the question "Why do we dream?" using the information you have found. Include a minimum of two peer-reviewed journal articles in your answer and provide citations for all work you used.

   _____
   _____
   _____
   _____
   _____
   _____
   _____
   _____
   _____
   _____

to be continued

 **Apply...**

continued

- Dream Analysis

  Do you believe that dreams have meaning? Theorists, such as Freud, believed that dreams reveal important information. For this activity, think about a dream that you have had. Write your dream down. Using the internet research what your dream may mean. What do you think about this analysis of your dream?

  _____

  _____

  _____

  _____

  _____

  _____

  _____

  _____

  _____

  _____

  _____

  _____

  _____

  _____

  _____

  _____

  _____

  _____

  _____

  _____

  _____

  _____

  _____

  _____

  _____

to be continued

 **Apply…**

continued

2. **Sleep Disorders**
   - There are many sleep disorders. Research sleep disorders and choose four disorders that you think are most serious. Write a short explanation of each. You may use the internet, peer-reviewed journals, textbooks, etc.

     ◊ Name of Disorder: _____
       Stage of Sleep it occurs in:_____
       What happens in this disorder?

       _____

       _____

       _____

       _____

       _____

     ◊ Name of Disorder: _____
       Stage of Sleep it occurs in:_____
       What happens in this disorder?

       _____

       _____

       _____

       _____

       _____

     ◊ Name of Disorder: _____
       Stage of Sleep it occurs in:_____
       What happens in this disorder?

       _____

       _____

       _____

       _____

       _____

     ◊ Name of Disorder: _____
       Stage of Sleep it occurs in:_____
       What happens in this disorder?

       _____

       _____

       _____

       _____

to be continued

 **Apply...**

continued

- Which of the disorders that you have chosen do you think is the most dangerous? Why?

_____

_____

_____

_____

_____

_____

_____

_____

_____

_____

_____

_____

Altered State of Consciousness: Psychoactive Substances

L04 Explain how psychoactive substances impact consciousness

We know that our consciousness is impacted by our sleep/wake cycle, but we can also alter our consciousness through the use of **psychoactive substances**. A psychoactive substance is anything that changes the way we perceive or understand the world or ourselves. They are commonly referred to as drugs and they include both legal and illegal forms. Psychoactive substances change neural communication:

- **Agonists** increase neural communication (for example, mimicking a neurotransmitter)
- **Antagonists** decrease neural communication (for example, blocking receptor sites).

In Chapter 2 on the Human Brain, you were asked to research and explain agonist and antagonist as it relates to neural communication. Please review this activity, if necessary.

TABLE 6.1 The effects of psychoactive drugs on consciousness.

Classification of Psychoactive Substance	Example	Effect on Consciousness	General Effect on Neural Communication	Some Withdrawal Symptoms
Stimulants	Caffeine, Nicotine, Cocaine, Amphetamine, Methamphetamine, MDMA (ecstasy)	Increased arousal, increased alertness, increased sociability, reduced appetite, increased heart rate, respiration, and body temperature	*Agonist*—increase neural activity	Irritability, anxiety, headache, fatigue, depression
Depressants	Alcohol, Barbiturates, Rohypnol, Ketamine	Decreases anxiety, lessens inhibitions, drowsiness, relaxation, calm	*Antagonist*—decrease neural activity	Anxiety, tremors, nausea, vomiting, seizures, anxiety, heart attack, death
Opiates	Morphine, Heroin, Opium, Codeine	Pain relief, drowsiness, and sleep	*Antagonist*—decrease neural activity *Agonist*—increase neural activity	Anxiety, chills, restlessness, diarrhoea, nausea
Hallucinogens	LSD, Mescaline, Psilocybin (magic mushroom), Salvia Divinorum	Euphoria, delusions, hallucinations, euphoria	*Antagonist*—decrease neural activity	Anxiety, hyperactivity, increased arousal
Hallucinogen and Depressant	Marijuana	Relaxation, calm, increased appetite	*Antagonist*—decrease neural activity	Anxiety, hyperactivity, increased arousal, decreased appetite

From: Think Sociology 2Ce

Table 6.1 outlines main types of psychoactive substances and their impact on consciousness.

When you look at Table 6.1, it is important to note that the impact of psychoactive substances on consciousness is influenced by our starting point—where we are on the continuum of consciousness when we took the drug. For example, how many of us drink a cup of coffee or caffeinated tea when we start to feel sleepy? When we do this, the caffeine increases our neural activity and most of us will feel more alert—we have increased or improved our consciousness. But if we were already feeling anxious, when we drank our caffeinated beverage we might end up with a different outcome. Take a moment and look at Table 6.1 and ask yourself where along the continuum of consciousness someone would be if they started at normal waking consciousness and then took each of these drugs.

While you are thinking about the activity above, it may have occurred to you that the impact of a psychoactive substance, even if it belongs to the same general drug category, will depend on how powerful it is (that is, how much it changes neural communication), how much is taken, where it was taken, etc. These factors are considered when we discuss a drug's potential for addiction or dependency. **Physical dependency** on a drug occurs when we develop a tolerance (increasing amounts of the drug are need to achieve a "high") and experience withdrawal symptoms when we stop taking a drug. Table 6.1 outlines some of the withdrawal symptoms associated with certain drug categories. **Psychological dependency** on a drug occurs when we still crave the effects of a drug even after we are no longer physically dependent.

Each drug has a different potential to create within us a dependency, which is based on the following four factors:

1. **How quickly the effects of the drug are felt:** The faster we feel the effects the more addictive the drug.

2. **How long the effects of the drug last:** If a drug's effects last a long time, we do not need to take more of it as often thereby decreasing the likelihood that we will develop tolerance.

3. **How good the drugs make us feel:** The stronger the pleasurable effects of a drug the more addictive it is.

4. **The severity of withdrawal symptoms:** The more discomfort we feel after stopping a drug the more likely we are to take it again (Baird & McCarthy, 2014).

Now that we have looked at the two main ways that our consciousness is altered, it may be helpful for you to identify other methods of enhancing or decreasing consciousness, such as hypnosis or meditation. You will explore the impact of these activities on consciousness in your activities for this topic.

 # Practice...

1. Any drug that alters our consciousness is called a(n)_____.
   a. agonist
   b. antagonist
   c. illegal substance
   d. psychoactive substance

2. There are two types of psychoactive drugs, _____ and _____.
   a. legal; illegal
   b. licit; illicit
   c. passive; aggressive
   d. agonist; antagonist

3. Brad takes an agonist. Which of the following is least likely to occur?
   a. More neurotransmitters will be released in his brain.
   b. The drug might mimic a neurotransmitter.
   c. The drug might prevent neurotransmitters from binding to receptor sites.
   d. The drug might inhibit the reuptake of neurotransmitters.

4. How a drug will alter one's consciousness depends on all of the following except:
   a. where one goes after taking the drug.
   b. how much of the drug one took.
   c. where one took the drug.
   d. the method one used to take the drug.

5. Which of the following drug classifications contains both agonistic and antagonistic substances?
   a. Stimulants
   b. Depressants
   c. Opiates
   d. Hallucinogens

 **Apply...**

1. **Psychoactive Substances and Neural Activity**

    Research the following psychoactive substances and their impact on neural activity. You may use the internet, peer-reviewed journals, textbooks, etc.

    For each drug answer the following questions:

    • What neurotransmitter does it impact/change/influence?

    _____
    _____
    _____
    _____
    _____

    • What happens when the drug is taken?

    _____
    _____
    _____
    _____
    _____

    • Does the drug increase or decrease neural activity?

    _____
    _____
    _____
    _____
    _____

    • Cocaine

    _____
    _____
    _____
    _____
    _____

    • Marijuana

    _____
    _____
    _____
    _____
    _____

to be continued

 **Apply...**

continued

- Alcohol

  _____
  _____
  _____
  _____

- Heroin

  _____
  _____
  _____
  _____

- LSD

  _____
  _____
  _____
  _____

2. **Hypnosis and Meditation**

   - Hypnosis

     ◊ Have you ever been hypnotized? If so, what do you remember about that experience?

       _____
       _____
       _____

     ◊ What are your thoughts on hypnosis?

       _____
       _____
       _____

     ◊ Where on the continuum of consciousness would you be, if you were hypnotized?

       _____
       _____
       _____
       _____

to be continued

 # Apply...

continued

◊ What are some uses of hypnosis? You may need to research this answer.

_____
_____
_____
_____
_____

• Meditation

◊ Have you ever meditated? If so, what do you remember about that experience?

_____
_____
_____
_____
_____

◊ What are your thoughts on meditation?

_____
_____
_____
_____
_____

◊ Where on the continuum of consciousness would you be during meditation?

_____
_____
_____
_____
_____

◊ What are some uses of meditation? You may need to research this answer.

_____
_____
_____
_____
_____

KNOW...

Learning Objectives

1. Consciousness, unconscious, nonconsciousness, preconscious, normal waking consciousness, and altered state of consciousness:

   - **Consciousness:** Our awareness, attentiveness, and responsiveness to what is happening within our body and mind, and in the environment around us; how much we know about what is going on, and our ability to react to this information.

   - **Unconscious:** No awareness of what is going on; we are "cut-off" from the information within and around us.

   - **Nonconsciousness:** Everything that occurs in our body that we do not need to monitor, regulate, or be aware of.

   - **Preconscious:** Processes and information that we are not always be aware of but can bring into consciousness when we need or want to.

   - **Normal Waking Consciousness:** Aware, attentive, and responsive to ourselves and our environment; being alert.

   - **Altered State of Consciousness:** Any deviation from normal waking consciousness; can be decreased or heightened consciousness.

2. Purpose of consciousness:

   The main purpose of consciousness is to ensure our survival. For this reason, we have restrictive abilities that allow us to pay attention to or to be conscious of immediate and important stimuli, while at the same time still processing other information nonconsciously, preconsciously, or unconsciously if needed, or to ignore it if it is not important. It is critical to our survival that we are aware of what is happening with our bodies and mind and in our external environment. We must be able to detect stimuli, gather information, and respond appropriately.

3. Stages of sleep:

   We go through five stages of sleep:

   - REM: Brain waves resemble those we see when we are awake and active. Stage of sleep in which the eyes move rapidly under the eyelids and we experience vivid and emotional dreams. We typically have four to five REM episodes each night.

   - **NREM Sleep:** Any of the stages of sleep that do not include REM.

     ◊ *NREM Stage One*: Light sleep, may experience hypnagogic images (vivid visual events) and hypnic jerk (knees, legs, or whole body jerks).

     ◊ *NREM Stage Two*: Sleep spindles (brief bursts of activity only lasting a second or two). We spend most of our sleep in this stage.

     ◊ *NREM Stages Three and Four*: Delta waves pronounced; deep sleep occurs when 50% or more of waves are delta waves.

4. How psychoactive substances impact consciousness:

   All psychoactive substances alter our consciousness. The full impact of each drug depends on its addictive properties, and where we are when we take the drug. In general, psychoactive substances can be viewed as increasing or decreasing neural activity—this is how it impacts consciousness. In this way, we can see where on the continuum of consciousness someone would be if they were in normal waking consciousness and took a given drug. Here is what would happen:

- Drugs that act as agonists (like stimulants) will increase neural activity.
- Drugs that act as antagonists (like depressants) will increase neural activity.

Key Terms

Consciousness: Our awareness, attentiveness, and responsiveness to what is happening within our body and mind, and in the environment around us; how much we know about what is going on, and our ability to react to this information.

Unconscious: No awareness of what is going on; we are "cut-off" from the information within and around us.

Nonconsciousness: Everything that occurs in our body that we do not need to monitor, regulate, or be aware of.

Preconscious: Processes and information that we are not always be aware of but can bring into consciousness when we need or want to.

Normal Waking Consciousness: Aware, attentive, and responsive to ourselves and our environment; being alert.

Altered State of Consciousness: Any deviation from normal waking consciousness; can be decreased or heightened consciousness.

ID: Part of our psyche proposed by Freud that is completely unconscious and comprised of our basic needs associated with survival and biological drives.

Ego: Part of our psyche proposed by Freud that is mostly conscious, is seen by others, and serves to balance the needs of the ID and the superego.

Superego: Part of our psyche proposed by Freud that has parts across all levels of consciousness, and holds our ideals for morality, ethics, behaviour, etc.

Personal Unconscious: Part of our psyche proposed by Jung that contains complexes.

Complexes: Beliefs and memories of specific concepts that are derived from personal experience.

Collective Unconscious: Part of our psyche proposed by Jung that consists of our innate, shared predispositions, beliefs, and memories that all humans have due to our common evolutionary experiences.

Circadian Rhythms: Built-in, biological clocks that regulate our physiological processes over a 24-hour cycle.

Sleep Deprivation: Any significant loss of sleep resulting in problems in concentration and irritability.

Microsleeps: Unintentional periods of sleep which last only a few seconds.

Preservation and Protection Theory: Theory that proposes that sleep is an evolutionary adaptation that leads us to sleep at night and avoid predators that hunt during that time.

Body Restoration Theory: Theory that proposes that sleep allows our bodies and brain to recover from the experiences and fatigue that occur during the day.

Activation-Synthesis Theory: Theory that proposes that sleep is a side effect of neural firing during rapid eye movement sleep.

Alpha Waves: Brain waves that indicate a state of relaxation or light sleep.

Theta Waves: Brain waves indicating the early stages of sleep.

Delta Waves: Long, slow waves that indicate the deepest stage of sleep.

REM (Rapid Eye Movement): A stage of sleep in which brain waves resemble those we see when we are awake and active, and we have rapidly movement of eyes under the eyelids and we experience vivid and emotional dreams.

NREM (Non-REM) Sleep: Any of the stages of sleep that do not include REM.

Non-REM Stage One: A stage of sleep characterized as light sleep, during which we may experience hypnagogic images (vivid visual events) and hypnic jerk (knees, legs, or whole body jerks).

Non-REM Stage Two: A stage of sleep characterized in which we spend most of our time, and we have sleep spindles (brief bursts of activity only lasting a second or two).

Non-REM Stages Three and Four: A stage of sleep characterized by delta waves; when 50% or more of waves are delta waves we are in deep sleep.

Psychoactive Substance: Anything that alters our consciousness; commonly called drugs.

Agonists: Substances that increase neural communication.

Antagonists: Substances that decrease neural communication.

Physical Dependency: Physiological changes that occur when we develop a tolerance to a drug and experience withdrawal symptoms when we stop taking it.

Psychological Dependency: Cravings for the effects of a drug even after we are no longer physically dependent.

Answers to Practice

Consciousness
1. a   2. d   3. b   4. d   5. c

What Is the Purpose of Consciousness?
1. b   2. d   3. c   4. d   5. a

Altered State of Consciousness: Sleep
1. a   2. b   3. b   4. b   5. d

Altered State of Consciousness: Psychoactive Substances
1. d   2. d   3. c   4. a   5. c

References

Baird, A., & McCarthy, A. (2014). *THINK psychology* (2nd Canadian Edition). Don Mills, ON: Pearson Education, Inc.; pp. 136–147.

Canadian Sleep Society. (2017). Normal sleep. Retrieved from https://css-scs.ca/resources/brochures/normal-sleep.

7 Learning

LO1 Identify the components associated with Classical Conditioning

LO2 Discuss the use of Operant Conditioning to change behaviour

LO3 List the basic concepts associated with observational learning

LO4 Identify the parts of the brain associated with classical, operant, and observational learning

LEARN...

Right now you are actively learning in school, and in this chapter we discuss some of the ways in which we learn. When we discuss learning, we are referring to a relatively permanent change in our knowledge or behaviour. When we learn, we establish new neural connections that are strengthened every time we use or remember the information we learned. We discuss three main types of learning: Classical Conditioning, Operant Conditioning, and Observational Learning. Classical Conditioning is based on the law of association. We learn through classical conditioning by pairing a neutral stimulus with a stimulus that already elicits a response from us. The goal is for us to associate the neutral stimulus with the one it is paired with, so that the neutral stimulus will elicit the same response. Learning through classical conditioning occurs in the hippocampus and cerebellum. In Operant Conditioning, we learn through the law of effect. When we engage in behaviours for which the outcome is positive, we are more likely to continue that behaviour. Conversely, if we engage in behaviours for which we are punished we are less likely to continue that behaviour. Learning through operant conditioning occurs in the basal ganglia along with activation of the reward circuit, if reinforcement occurs. In Observational Learning, we learn by watching others. Learning through observation occurs in the frontal lobe. Once we have learned something, we never truly lose that information, but the neural connections can become weak, a process referred to as extinction. However, the information and the neural connections are still present and we are able to recover the information even after extinction. In this chapter, we apply these three types of learning to our personal experiences.

Classical Conditioning

L01 Identify the components associated with Classical Conditioning

Learning theorists think that an infant's mind is a blank slate (tabula rasa) and experience is key to the mind's development. When we talk about **learning**, we are referring to the process through which experience causes a permanent change in our knowledge or behaviour. This change may be deliberate or unintentional, beneficial or harmful, and conscious or unconscious (Hill, 2002). When we learn, we change our KNOWLEDGE or BEHAVIOUR. When we learn, we establish new neural pathways associated with that behaviour. These neural connections are strengthened every time we engage in the behaviour. So, how do we establish and maintain behaviour? How do we learn? In this chapter, we will discuss the three key ways in which we learn: Classical Conditioning, Operant Conditioning, and Observational Learning.

Classical Conditioning

- Proposed by Pavlov—foundational research "Pavlov's dogs"
- Based on the principal of ASSOCIATION
- Goal: To create a new association between two unrelated things
- Please note that the word "conditioned" simply means "learned"; you may find it helpful to keep that in mind
- Learning happens through Classical Conditioning when a previously neutral stimulus elicits a response we already have.
- The process is automatic, unintentional, and behaviour is elicited by a stimulus.

Let us look at an example of how we learn through classical conditioning.

STEP 1: Start with something that already causes an involuntary response. For example: When you see a big juicy burger (or other food you like), it causes you to salivate.

- Because the BURGER causes you to have an INVOLUNTARY response, such as SALIVATION:

  BURGER = **Unconditioned Stimulus (US)**—something that causes an involuntary response

  SALIVATION = **Unconditioned Response (UR)**—the involuntary response to an US

Step 2: Now you want something else to elicit or cause the involuntary response of salivation. For example: A bell.

- When you hear a bell it does not cause you to salivate. But now we want you to salivate when you hear the bell.
- Because the BELL does not cause you to have an INVOLUNTARY response we say that the

  BELL = **Neutral Stimulus (NS)**—something that does not cause an involuntary response

Step 3: We *condition* ourselves to associate the BELL (NS) with the big juicy BURGER (US). We do this by presenting the bell and the hamburger together many times.

- After repeated pairings, you will begin to associate the Bell (NS) with the burger (US).

- Eventually, in the absence of the US, the Bell (NS) will elicit the same involuntary response (salivation) that the burger (US) elicited.

- When this happens the Bell becomes a **Conditioned Stimulus (CS)** because we have been conditioned or taught or trained to respond to the bell in a new way. Remember: **Conditioned = Learned**.

- Now when we hear the bell (but do not see the burger) we salivate. Our response of salivating after hearing the bell is called our **Conditioned Response (CR)**. It is our **Learned Response**.

Pairing of the Unconditioned and Neutral Stimulus

There are several ways that we can present the Unconditioned Stimulus and Neutral Stimulus together so that we learn to associate the two together:

- **Delayed Conditioning:** Neutral Stimulus is presented before the Unconditioned Stimulus, and the Neutral Stimulus would remain present until the Unconditioned Stimulus is presented.

- **Trace Conditioning:** Neutral Stimulus is stopped/removed before the Unconditioned Stimulus is presented. The timing between the presentation of the NS and US must be very short in order to establish the association between the two.

- **Simultaneous Conditioning:** Neutral Stimulus is presented at the same time as the Unconditioned Stimulus. This is not effective in establishing an association.

- **Backward Conditioning:** Neutral Stimulus is presented after the Unconditioned Stimulus. This is also ineffective in establishing an association.

Thus, the best way for us to establish new associations between two unrelated things is to use delayed or trace conditioning.

Examples of Classical Conditioning in Our Lives

1. Bullying

   Bullying is an unconditioned stimulus that leads to unconditioned responses such as fear and anxiety. It is possible to establish an association between Bullying (US) and School (NS) if you are bullied at school. When this happens, the school eventually becomes a conditioned stimulus, and will elicit feelings of fear and anxiety (CR) in the absence of being bullied. It is for this reason that many children who are bullied will experience fear and anxiety simply by approaching or entering their school.

2. Food Aversion

   Have you ever eaten at a restaurant and later became ill? Even if it was not the food at the restaurant that made you ill you are likely to associate the restaurant with being ill and may not wish to return there. Food aversion, because of its ultimate goal of keeping us safe and alive, is one type of classical conditioning in which a single pairing of NS and US is often enough to establish an association.

Practice...

1. In Classical Conditioning, the _____ naturally evokes an unlearned response.
   a. conditioned stimulus
   b. conditioned reinforcer
   c. unconditioned reinforcer
   d. unconditioned stimulus

2. In classical conditioning, the _____ starts out neutral but eventually elicits a response as a result of learning.
   a. conditioned stimulus
   b. conditioned response
   c. unconditioned stimulus
   d. unconditioned response

3. Richard used to really enjoy strawberry sherbet, and when he was in Mexico, he tried frozen strawberry daiquiris. After his fourth daiquiri, he became extremely ill. Now he finds that even the sight of strawberry sherbet makes him feel queasy. What is the conditioned response in this example?
   a. The queasiness that Carson feels when he sees strawberry sherbet
   b. The sight of strawberry sherbet
   c. The strawberry daiquiris that Carson consumed
   d. The illness that followed the fourth daiquiri

4. _____ conditioning occurs when a neutral stimulus is presented before the unconditioned stimulus, and the neutral stimulus remains present until the unconditioned stimulus is presented.
   a. Backwards
   b. Trace
   c. Delayed
   d. Simultaneous

5. The word "conditioning" means:
   a. memory.
   b. learning.
   c. automatic.
   d. attention.

 **Apply...**

1. **Classical Conditioning in Our Lives**

    Remember a time in your life when you learned through Classical Conditioning. Write your learning experience in the space provided. Identify the Unconditioned Stimulus, Conditioned Stimulus, Unconditioned Response, and Conditioned Response.

    _____

    _____

    _____

    _____

    _____

    _____

    _____

    _____

    _____

    _____

    _____

    _____

    _____

    _____

    _____

    _____

    _____

    _____

    _____

    _____

    _____

    _____

    _____

    _____

    _____

    _____

    _____

    _____

to be continued

 **Apply...**

continued

2. **Autism and Classical Conditioning**

   Research autism and classical conditioning. You may use the internet, peer-reviewed journals, textbooks, etc.

   Write a summary of what you learned about autism and classical conditioning.

   _____

   _____

   _____

   _____

   _____

   _____

   _____

   _____

   _____

   _____

   _____

   _____

   _____

   _____

   _____

   _____

   _____

   _____

   _____

   _____

   _____

   _____

   _____

   _____

   _____

   _____

   _____

   _____

   _____

   _____

   _____

   _____

Operant Conditioning

LO2 Discuss the use of Operant Conditioning to change behaviour

We have previously discussed Classical Conditioning. Classical Conditioning only explains how existing behaviour might be brought about or elicited by new stimuli. It does not explain how new behaviour is acquired. In fact, most behaviour is not elicited by stimulus but is emitted or voluntarily done. We actively "operate" in our environment to produce different results. Our deliberate actions are called **Operants.** Learning that involves these operants is called **Operant Conditioning.**

Operant Conditioning

- **Based on the law of effect:** Any act that produces a satisfying outcome in a particular situation tends to be repeated in that situation (Thorndike, 1999, 1913).
- If your actions or behaviours bring you rewards then you will continue to behave/act in that way
- B.F. Skinner provided foundational work in operant conditioning
- Premise: If you want a behaviour to continue, make the outcome of the behaviour positive; if you want the behaviour to stop or to lessen, make the outcome of the behaviour negative

Let us look at an example of how operant conditioning works.

Scenario: Justin always eats cookies when he comes home from school. But, his mother does not want him to eat cookies before dinner because it ruins his appetite. His mom wants Justin to stop eating cookies before dinner.

What can she do?

To change Justin's cookie eating behaviour, his mother can use the following Behavioural Management Rules:

- Reinforce good behaviour
- Do not reinforce bad behaviour
- Punish bad behaviour

Why do these rules work?

- Reinforcements = Strengthen behaviour—Think: Reinforced Steel
- Punishment = Weakens behaviour

Steps:

1. **Reinforce good behaviour**

   When Justin does not eat cookies before dinner his mom is pleased and wants the behaviour to continue. She can use:

   ◊ **Positive Reinforcement** = REWARD—Give him something good (for example, extra technology time, praise, stickers)

   ◊ **Negative Reinforcement** = Removal of a negative stimulus (for example, no longer grounded, don't have to listen to mom nag)

   ◊ Reinforcements strengthen behaviour because the outcome of the behaviour is positive—for example, it makes a person happy

◊ There are several types of reinforcers:

■ **Primary Reinforcers:** Anything that satisfies a basic biological need, such as hunger or thirst

■ **Secondary Reinforcers:** Anything that we consider pleasurable that does not address a biological need; usually we develop these through experience

2. **Don't reinforce bad behaviour; Punish some bad behaviour**

When Justin eats cookies before dinner his mom is not pleased and wants this behaviour to stop.

She can:

- IGNORE or PUNISH Justin's behaviour

◊ **Positive or Presentation Punishment:** Give Justin an undesirable thing to do (for example, extra homework, extra chores)

◊ **Negative or Removal Punishment:** Take away something Justin likes (for example, technology, toys, parent's attention)

◊ Punishments weaken behaviour because the outcome of the behaviour is negative. For example, it makes a person unhappy.

It is generally recognized that reinforcement is more effective in bringing about changes in behaviour compared to punishment. So, let us look at the ways we can use reinforcement to establish and maintain desired behaviours. If we want to establish a behaviour, we want to reinforce it every time it occurs. This is called **continuous reinforcement**. After a behaviour is established, we should move towards **partial reinforcement**, where the behaviour is reinforced sometimes but not all the time. Table 7.1 illustrates the ways we can use partial reinforcement to maintain a desired behaviour.

TABLE 7.1 Schedules for reinforcement.

	Ratio = Number of Responses	**Interval = Time Period**
Fixed Schedule	Behaviour is reinforced after a set number of responses	Behaviour is reinforced after a set time period
Variable Schedule	Behaviour is reinforced after a varying, random number of responses	Behaviour is reinforced after a varying, random set of time periods

The use of partial reinforcement can lead to the establishment of behaviours but it will take longer than if continuous reinforcement is used. However, partial reinforcement is better at maintaining behaviour.

Working Together: Classical and Operant Conditioning

It is often the case that classical and operant conditioning work together. First, classical conditioning can be used to establish an association between two unrelated things. The behaviour exhibited by a person when this occurs can then be reinforced or punished according to the principles of operant conditioning, thereby maintaining the behaviour.

Let us look at an example of how classical conditioning and operant conditioning can work together.

Scenario: You are driving down the street and get into a car accident. Through classical conditioning, you learn to associate that specific street with the car accident. Every time you drive down that street you experience anxiety and fear. This is classical conditioning—the street is now eliciting the same response from you as the accident did.

Your friend, who travels with you frequently, notices that you are anxious and fearful when you drive down that street. Trying to help, your friend comforts you as you drive down the street. Your friend's verbal support acts as a reinforcement for your anxiety and fear. The result is that you continue to exhibit these behaviours when you drive down the street.

Now, over time if the behaviour is not reinforced, the association between the street and the accident will weaken and eventually you will be able to drive down the street without feeling anxious or fearful. This is referred to as **extinction**. Extinction is a weakening of a learned response. In classical conditioning, it occurs over time when the unconditioned stimulus is no longer paired with the neutral/conditioned stimulus. In operant conditioning, it occurs when a behaviour is no longer reinforced over time. However, we never truly completely lose what we have learned. It is more like the neural connections formed when learning weaken and may become dormant. However, we can experience **spontaneous recovery**, where we have a recurrence of a behaviour after extinction—like a reactivation of the neural pathways that formed when we learned the behaviour.

 # Practice...

1. Operant condition is based on the law of _____.
    a. association
    b. effect
    c. attention
    d. memorization

2. Which of the following is not a principle of operant conditioning?
    a. Reinforce good behaviour
    b. Do not reinforce bad behaviour
    c. Punish bad behaviour
    d. Ignore good behaviour

3. Which of the following statements about primary and secondary reinforcers is correct?
    a. Primary reinforcers are internal, while secondary reinforcers come from the environment.
    b. Primary reinforcers are associated with classical conditioning, while secondary reinforcers are associated with operant conditioning.
    c. Primary reinforcers satisfy biological needs, while secondary reinforcers depend on learning.
    d. Primary reinforcers are used first, while secondary reinforcers are used if primary reinforcers are not effective.

4. Shauna used to complete her homework right after school every day, and her parents would give her a lot of encouragement and support. Lately, her parents have not commented on Shauna's completion of her homework. Shauna no longer completes her homework right after school. Which process does this example illustrate?
    a. Extinction
    b. Avoidance
    c. Resistance
    d. Punishment

5. _____ schedule is best used, if we want to encourage the use of "please and thank-you" in toddlers?
    a. Variable-ratio
    b. Continuous reinforcement
    c. Fixed-interval
    d. Variable-interval

Apply...

1. **Operant Conditioning in Our Life**

   Remember a time in your life when you learned through Operant Conditioning. Write your learning experience in the space provided. Identify the types of reinforcement and/or punishments that were used.

   _____

   _____

   _____

   _____

   _____

   _____

   _____

   _____

   _____

   _____

   _____

   _____

   _____

   _____

   _____

   _____

   _____

   _____

   _____

   _____

   _____

   _____

   _____

   _____

   _____

   _____

   _____

   _____

   _____

   _____

   _____

   _____

   _____

   _____

to be continued

 # Apply...

continued

2. **Behaviour Modification**

Choose 1 behaviour that you see on campus that you would like to change. Using the principles of Classical and Operant Conditioning, explain how you would change this behaviour.

Observational Learning

L03 List the basic concepts associated with observational learning

Albert Bandura (1969) believed that direct reinforcement, like what is proposed by operant conditioning, could not account for all types of learning. He believed that people can learn new information and behaviours by watching other people. This type of learning is called **observational learning**, and can account for a wide variety of our behaviours.

Basic Concepts

1. **People can learn through observation**

We can learn from three types of models:

- A live model, which involves an actual individual demonstrating or acting out a behaviour.
- A verbal instructional model, which involves descriptions and explanations of a behaviour.
- A symbolic model, which involves real or fictional characters displaying behaviours in books, films, television programs, or online media.

When we learn from a model the results can vary. We can experience:

- *Acquisition*: New responses are learned by observing the model.
- *Inhibition*: A response that otherwise may be made is changed when the observer sees a model being punished.
- *Disinhibition*: A reduction in fear by observing that a model's behaviour goes unpunished in a feared activity.
- *Facilitation*: A model elicits from an observer a response that has already been learned.
- *Creativity*: Observing several models performing and then adapting a combination of characteristics or styles.

2. **Mental states are important to learning**

Bandura believed that external, environmental reinforcement was not the only factor to influence learning and behaviour. He believed that we used intrinsic reinforcement as a form of internal reward, such as pride, satisfaction, and a sense of accomplishment. Refer back to Chapter 5 on Motivation and Emotion to review the different types of motivation. He believed that intrinsic reinforcement was a very powerful motivator for learning. He called his theory a "social cognitive theory" of learning as it discussed both the cognitive aspects of learning and the impacts of social interactions and experiences. The basic premise is that we must be motivated to learn in order to learn through observation.

3. **Learning does not necessarily lead to a change in behaviour**

Observational learning demonstrates that people can learn new information without demonstrating new behaviours. Surely, you can think of some behaviours that you may see others engage in but chose not to demonstrate yourself. In addition, there are other factors that influence whether or not learning will lead to a change in behaviour:

The following steps are involved in observational learning:

- **Attention:** In order to learn, we must pay attention. Anything that detracts your attention is going to have a negative effect on observational learning.

- **Retention:** We must store the information we observed. We must also be able to retrieve that stored information.

- **Reproduction:** We must be able perform the behaviour we have observed. This may require practice.

- **Motivation:** As previously noted, we must be motivated to learn and to imitate the behaviours we have seen.

 # Practice...

1. After watching his father fold laundry, 5-year-old Micha folds the blankets on his bed. What does this example illustrate?
   a. Superstitious behaviour
   b. Observational learning
   c. Classical conditioning
   d. Positive reinforcement

2. The first step in observational learning is _____.
   a. memory consolidation
   b. reproduction
   c. attention
   d. retention

3. According to Bandura, _____ is a powerful motivator for learning.
   a. intrinsic reinforcement
   b. extrinsic reinforcement
   c. primary reinforcer
   d. negative punishment

4. _____occurs when a model elicits from an observer a response that has already been learned.
   a. Acquisition
   b. Inhibition
   c. Facilitation
   d. Creativity

5. Observational learning can occur through watching which of the following models?
   a. A live model, which involves an actual individual demonstrating or acting out a behaviour.
   b. A verbal instructional model, which involves descriptions and explanations of a behaviour.
   c. A symbolic model, which involves real or fictional characters displaying behaviours in books, films, television programs, or online media.
   d. All of the above are correct

 **Apply...**

1. **The Bobo Doll Study**

   Look up the Bobo Doll Study. Write a summary of the study and what we can learn about observational learning from it.

   _____

   _____

   _____

   _____

   _____

   _____

   _____

   _____

   _____

   _____

   _____

   _____

   _____

   _____

   _____

   _____

   _____

   _____

   _____

   _____

   _____

   _____

   _____

   _____

   _____

   _____

   _____

   _____

   _____

to be continued

 **Apply...**

continued

2. **Observational Learning in Our Life**

   Remember a time in your life when you learned through Observational Learning. Write your learning experience in the space provided. Identify the type of model used and the result of your learning.

   _____

   _____

   _____

   _____

   _____

   _____

   _____

   _____

   _____

   _____

   _____

   _____

   _____

   _____

   _____

   _____

   _____

   _____

   _____

   _____

   _____

   _____

   _____

   _____

   _____

   _____

   _____

   _____

Learning and Our Brain

LO4 Identify the parts of the brain associated with classical, operant, and observational learning

As previously noted, when we learn we are really establishing new neural connections. The more we act on the information or behaviour we have learned the stronger the neural connections will become, a process called **long-term potentiation (LTP)**. It is the process that allows us to hold onto or remember information over long periods of time. If something happens and LTP does not occur then we do not learn.

During the process of learning, our brain engages in **synaptic consolidation**, which occurs shortly after we learn something and serves to help the information move from our short-term memory to our long-term memory. **System consolidation** follows this process and is a slower process that involves reorganizing the brain so that new information can be effectivity stored in our memory. Because of these two processes, memory loss due to brain damage follows **Ribot's Law**, which states that recent memories are more affected. This is likely due to the fact that the memory consolidation processes have not occurred fully.

Depending on the type of information we have gathered, different parts of our brain are involved in the learning process:

- Sensory learning takes place in the somatosensory cortex.
- Learning through classical conditioning occurs in the hippocampus and cerebellum.
- Learning through operant conditioning occurs in the basal ganglia along with activation of the reward circuit, if reinforcement occurs.
- Learning through observation occurs in the frontal lobe.
- Emotional learning occurs in the amygdala.
- Spatial learning occurs in the hippocampus (Baird & McCarthy, 2014).

One question that often arises when we discuss learning is how we can become "smarter." If we review the key elements associated with classical, operant, and observational learning, we can see that learning requires a few common elements, such as attention, time, and consistency. In addition, being well rested and sleeping after learning are important for memory consolidation.

Practice...

1. In a very unfortunate set of events, Adriano was involved in a car collision that resulted in a head injury with resultant brain damage. According to _____ law, Adriano is going to experience greater impact on more recent memories than on remote memories.
    a. Ribot's
    b. Thorndike's
    c. Reyner's
    d. Watson's

2. Which part of the brain has been found to be most associated with operant conditioning?
    a. Basal ganglia
    b. Ascending pyramidal tracts
    c. Optic chiasm
    d. Corpus callosum

3. Which of the following parts of the brain is involved in spatial learning?
    a. The basal ganglia
    b. The amygdala
    c. The cerebellum
    d. The hippocampus

4. _____ occurs shortly after learning.
    a. Synaptic transmission
    b. Synaptic consolidation
    c. System consolidation
    d. Long-term potentiation

5. You have a test tomorrow. Your best option to ensure that you learn the necessary material is to stay up all night and cram.
    a. True
    b. False

 **Apply…**

1. **Brain Injury, Neural Plasticity, and Learning**

Research brain injury, neural plasticity, and learning. You may use the internet, peer-reviewed journals, textbooks, etc.

What does the research tell us about recovery after brain damage?

_____

_____

_____

_____

_____

_____

_____

_____

_____

_____

_____

_____

_____

_____

_____

_____

_____

_____

_____

_____

_____

_____

_____

_____

_____

_____

_____

to be continued

 **Apply...**

continued

2. **Learning Styles**

Many of us have an idea of how we like to learn best. For some of us, visual presentations are helpful while others prefer listening to information.

- What type of learning do you prefer?
- Give an example of a time when you learned something using your preferred method.
- What happens when you try to learn in a different way?

Note: If you are unsure of how you like to learn best you can find information about learning styles online.

_____

_____

_____

_____

_____

_____

_____

_____

_____

_____

_____

_____

_____

_____

_____

_____

_____

_____

_____

_____

_____

_____

_____

_____

_____

KNOW...

Learning Objectives

1. The components associated with classical conditioning:
   - Based on the law of association
   - Unconditioned stimulus elicits an automatic response.
   - Unconditioned response is the automatic response to the unconditioned stimulus.
   - Neutral stimulus does not elicit any response. We pair this with the unconditioned stimulus, using delayed or trace pairing, until the neutral stimulus elicits the same response the unconditioned stimulus does.
   - Conditioned stimulus is the learned stimulus that now elicits the same response as the unconditioned stimulus does.
   - Conditioned response is the learned response to the conditioned stimulus.

2. The use of operant conditioning to change behaviour:
   - Operant conditioning uses the law of effect to change behaviour.
   - To decrease a behaviour, we can ignore or use punishment. We want the outcome of the behaviour or its consequence to be negative so that it is less likely to continue.
   - To increase a behaviour, we can use reinforcement. We want the outcome of the behaviour to be positive so that the person is more likely to engage in the behaviour again.

3. The basic concepts associated with observational learning:
   - People can learn through observation.
   - Mental states are important to learning.
   - Learning does not necessarily lead to a change in behaviour.

4. The parts of the brain associated with classical, operant, and observational learning:
   - Learning through classical conditioning occurs in the hippocampus and cerebellum.
   - Learning through operant conditioning occurs in the basal ganglia along with activation of the reward circuit, if reinforcement occurs.
   - Learning through observation occurs in the frontal lobe.

Key Terms

Learning: The process through which experience causes a permanent change in knowledge or behaviour.

Classical Conditioning: Learning that occurs when an association is formed between two unrelated things.

Unconditioned Stimulus (US): Something that causes an involuntary response.

Unconditioned Response (UR): The involuntary response to an US.

Neutral Stimulus (NS): Something that does not cause an involuntary response.

Conditioned Stimulus (CS): Conditioned or taught to respond to previously neutral stimulus.

Conditioned Response (CR): Our learned response to the CS.

Operants: Our deliberate actions.

Operant Conditioning: Learning of deliberate actions (operants) that occurs through the use of the law of effect.

Positive Reinforcement: Giving something desirable to a person to encourage a desired behaviour to continue or increase.

Negative Reinforcement: Removal of a negative stimulus to encourage a desired behaviour to continue or increase.

Primary Reinforcers: Anything that satisfies a basic biological need.

Secondary Reinforcer: Anything that we consider pleasurable that does not address a biological need.

Positive or Presentation Punishment: Give something unwanted to a person to decrease or stop an undesirable behaviour.

Negative or Removal Punishment: Take away something wanted from a person to decrease or stop an undesirable behaviour.

Continuous Reinforcement: A schedule of reinforcement in which a desired behaviour is reinforced every time it occurs.

Partial Reinforcement: A schedule of reinforcement in which a desired behaviour is reinforced sometimes.

Extinction: A weakening of a learned response.

Spontaneous Recovery: Where we have a recurrence of a behaviour after extinction.

Observational Learning: A type of learning in which we learn new information and behaviours by watching other people.

Long-Term Potentiation (LTP): The strengthening of neural connections.

Synaptic Consolidation: Helps the information to move from our short-term memory to our long-term memory.

System Consolidation: Process that involves reorganizing the brain so that new information can be effectivity stored in our memory.

Ribot's Law: A law that states that recent memories are more affected by brain damage than older, already stored memories.

Answers to Practice

Classical Conditioning
1. d   2. a   3. a   4. c   5. b

Operant Conditioning
1. b   2. d   3. c   4. a   5. b

Observational Learning
1. b   2. c   3. a   4. c   5. d

Learning and Our Brain
1. a   2. a   3. d   4. b   5. b

References

Baird, A., & McCarthy, A. (2014). *THINK psychology* (2nd Canadian edition). Don Mills, ON: Pearson Education, Inc.; pp. 152–163.

Bandura, A. (1969). *Principles of behavior modification*. New York, NY: Holt, Rinehart & Winston.

Hill, W. F. (2002) *Learning: A survey of psychological Interpretation* (7th edition). Boston, MA: Allyn and Bacon.

Thorndike, E. (1999) [1913]. *Education psychology: Briefer course*. New York, NY: Routledge.

8 Cognition

LEARNING OBJECTIVES

LO1 Discuss some of the developmental changes that occur in our cognitive abilities

LO2 Explain three cognitive processes

LO3 Describe the main principles of major theories and tests of intelligence

LO4 List five aspects of social cognition

LEARN...

When you hear the word "cognition" what do you think of? In this chapter, we discuss cognition. Cognition refers to our mental processes, including thinking, reasoning, problem solving, and deciding. One way that we can categorize mental processes is by sorting them based on the amount of attention required for the process to occur, and whether the process happens sequentially or simultaneously. As we get older, our cognitive abilities increase. Piaget proposed that cognitive development happens in stages and that by adulthood we are able to think abstractly and to solve complex problems. The information-processing approach proposes that cognitive development is steady and gradual. This model allows us to use the model of a computer to understand cognition. Through your unit activity, you will gain knowledge about the limitations of Piaget and the Information-Processing approaches to understanding cognition. In this chapter, we discuss some cognitive processes that we engage in every day. For example, we discuss: problem solving, which is the process associated with finding a solution; reasoning, which is the process through which we organize information so that we can make decisions; and other cognitions such as attention, decision making, and intelligence. Intelligence is our capacity for cognition. Many theories attempt to explain intelligence. Some theories, such as Spearman's General Intelligence (g), propose that we have a general level of intelligence that impacts our cognitive processes, while other theories, such as Gardner's Theory of Multiple Intelligences, proposes that there are many types of intelligence (for example, Linguistic, Logical-mathematical, Spatial, and Musical). We look at other theories of intelligence and some of the ways we assess intelligence. We also discuss social cognition, which refers to the mental processes that occur in our social world. We have touched on some aspects of social cognition in previous chapters, and in this chapter, we add to our general understanding of social cognition, by looking at theory of mind, perspective taking, imaginary audience, and social intelligence. Through your unit activities, you will have a chance to learn more about problem solving, to identify strengths and weaknesses associated with testing and understanding intelligence, and to discuss the impact of technology on social cognition.

What Is Cognition?

L01 Discuss some of the developmental changes that occur in our cognitive abilities

In Chapter 7 on Learning, we discussed how behaviours develop and are changed by our environment and experience. Behavioural Psychologists believe that we must focus on behaviour because they are observable. Cognitive Psychologists, however, believe that we must focus on mental processes. They believe that to fully understand behaviour we must understand the mental processes that led to and result from behaviours. The challenge for cognitive psychologists is that they study processes that are not observable. In this chapter, we discuss cognition.

When you hear the word "cognition" what do you think of? **Cognition** includes all mental processes, such as thinking, attention, sensation, perception, reasoning, problem solving, remembering, knowing, and deciding. These processes are not observable to people looking at us, and as such researchers can only look at these processes by examining the outcomes of these processes, such as our behaviours, decisions, and reactions, or by asking us to explain our mental processes.

One way that we can categorize mental processes is by sorting them based on two factors: (i) the amount of attention required for the process to occur and (ii) whether the process happens **sequentially**, which means steps in the process occur in a specific order, or **simultaneously**, which means steps in the process all occur at the same time. Can you think of a cognitive process that requires attention and one that is more automatic? If you remember from chapters on the Human Brain (Chapter 2) and Learning (Chapter 7), attention is required for us to actively learn many things, but after this information is learned and we act upon it repeatedly, it becomes more automatic and no longer requires as much attention. Think about learning to brush your teeth as an example of this process. In Chapter 9 on Memory, we will look at this process again in terms of remembering. In addition, cognitive processes occur, as discussed in Chapter 6 on Consciousness, along a continuum of consciousness. Can you think of some cognitive processes that occur at normal waking consciousness, nonconsciousness, and precociousness?

Let us look briefly at two theories that attempt to explain cognitive development.

- **Jean Piaget's Theory of Cognitive Development:** Piaget viewed maturation (the act of getting older) as the driving force behind increased cognitive abilities. He believed that cognitive development occurs in stages, also referred to as discontinuous development. He believed that we form **schemas** (mental representations of information) based on our experiences and information we gather. When we encounter information, we engage in the process of **assimilation**—incorporating new information into an already existing schema, or **accommodation**—modifying, altering, or changing an existing schema based on new information. Table 8.1 is an outline of his developmental model.

- **Information-Processing Approach:** According to this approach cognitive development is steady and gradual, also referred to as continuous development. The approach focuses on the thinking processes that exist at all ages. The model for this approach is a computer, which allows us to break down human thinking into the separate capacities of attention, processing, and memory. We will discuss memory in more

TABLE 8.1 Piaget's stages of cognitive development.

Stage and Age Range	What can we do at this stage?
Sensorimotor Ages 0–2 years	Cognitive processes focus on the use of our senses to gather information about the world and then to respond to that information through physical or motor behaviours Develop object permanence (understanding that an object still exists even if we cannot see it)
Preoperational Ages 2–7 years	Cognitive processes focus on representing the world through symbols, such as the use of language to label and communicate Develop imagination, make-believe play
Concrete Operations Ages 7–12 years	Cognitive processes focus on more logical understanding of the world based on concrete laws Develop ability to generalize from specific experiences, conservation of mass
Formal Operations Ages 12 and up	Cognitive processes focus on more complex tasks, such as problem solving with multiple variables, thinking abstractly Develop concepts such as morality and justice

detail in Chapter 9. Recent models have moved away from the simple computer model. Key developmental changes:

◊ increase in the speed of processing information as we get older.

◊ decrease in the attention required to process information, referred to as automaticity, which increases with experience and therefore as we get older.

◊ increase in strategies used for memory (Baird & McCarthy, 2014; McMahan & Thompson, 2015).

Both theories propose ways to help us understand cognition. In your activity for this unit, you will explore some of the limitations associated with each of these theories.

Next, we will look at some key cognitive processes.

Practice...

1. Which of the following is not a cognitive process?
   a. Thinking
   b. Remembering
   c. Perceiving
   d. Running

2. Which of the following journal article titles sounds like a paper Piaget would have written?
   a. Grammar and language systems in deaf children
   b. Using a four-stage model to explain the development of thinking
   c. Using reaction time to examine the complexity of mental processes
   d. Computer simulations of human thought

3. Cognitive scientists have categorized processes into two general categories. What are these two categories?
   a. The amount of energy required and the order in which things should be done
   b. The amount of attention required and the amount of energy needed to accomplish the task(s)
   c. Whether things should be done in sequence or simultaneously and the amount of attention needed to accomplish the task(s)
   d. The amount of intelligence required and the cognitive resources needed to accomplish the task(s)

4. _____proposes that cognitive development is steady and gradual.
   a. Piaget's theory of cognitive development
   b. The information-processing approach
   c. Both (a) and (b)
   d. Neither (a) or (b)

5. As we get older, we develop increases in all of the following EXCEPT:
   a. Attention required to process information
   b. Speed at which we can process information
   c. Strategies used for memory
   d. Only (a) and (c)

 Apply...

1. **Limitations of Piaget's Theory of Cognitive Development and the Information-Processing Theory of Cognition**

    Research BOTH Piaget's theory of cognitive development and the Information-processing theory of cognition. You may use the internet, peer-reviewed journals, textbooks, etc.

    Create a list of the limitations and critiques of each theory in the space below.

    - Limitations of Piaget's theory of cognitive development:

    _____

    _____

    _____

    _____

    _____

    _____

    _____

    _____

    _____

    _____

    _____

    _____

    _____

    _____

    _____

    _____

    _____

    _____

    _____

    _____

    _____

    _____

    _____

    _____

    _____

    _____

    _____

    _____

to be continued

continued

- Limitations of Information-processing theory of cognition:

_____
_____
_____
_____
_____
_____
_____
_____
_____
_____
_____
_____
_____
_____
_____
_____
_____
_____
_____
_____
_____
_____
_____
_____
_____
_____
_____
_____
_____
_____
_____
_____

to be continued

 **Apply...**

continued

2. **Prototypes**

Define prototype. Provide what you would consider to be the prototype for each of the following categories.

Category	Prototype	Why Did You Choose that Prototype?
Fruit		
Animal		
Vehicle		
Technology		
Sport		
Disease		
Tool		

When you are finished please discuss your choices with two of your classmates.

• Did you always have the same prototype?

_____

_____

_____

_____

_____

_____

_____

_____

_____

• What factors do you think may have lead you to have the same or different prototypes?

_____

_____

_____

_____

_____

_____

_____

_____

_____

Examples of Cognitive Processes

 LO2 Explain three cognitive processes

Cognition is complex and involves many processes. Here are some examples of cognitive processes:

Concepts

- The cognitive processes involved in the formation of mental representations that allow us to group things (people, objects, events, activities, animals, etc.) together that are similar
- Help us understand, store, and use information gathered from the world around us
- Can become more complex with the creation of hierarchies of group members, and the use of **prototypes**, which are typical examples of what we would find in a category (refer to your activity for "What is Cognition?")
- **Wittgenstein's Family Resemblance Theory:** We put items together if they share certain characteristics, even if not every member of the category has similar features.
  - ◊ Example of games: Table tennis, poker, and hopscotch have very little in common, but they are united by a common thread—a family resemblance—that allows us to group them together in a single category
- **Exemplar Theory:** When we encounter information, we compare that to information we already have to determine if the new information fits into a particular category
  - ◊ Example of dogs: Category of dogs is based on all the dogs we have seen, not just a single typical or prototype of dog

Problem Solving

- The cognitive processes involved when we combine information from our current state or situation with previous information we have gathered through time, with the goal of finding a solution to a task
- Ways that we solve problems include: **Algorithms** (steps we can follow to get a solution; like a recipe); **Mental set** (pre-existing state of mind that was helpful to past problem solving); **Insight** (sudden understanding of a problem)

Reasoning

- The cognitive processes involved when we organize information into the steps needed to arrive at a result or conclusion
- Types of reasoning: **Practical reasoning** (deciding what to do, how to act); **Theoretical reasoning** (deciding what to believe, expect); **Syllogistic reasoning** (deciding if a conclusion logically follows from two or more statements that we assume to be true)

Decision Making

- The cognitive processes involved in choosing an option or outcome
- **Rational Choice Theory:** Pros versus cons analysis; choose best outcome
- **Prospect Theory:** We are more likely to make a risky decision in situations where we may lose something any way, and less likely to make a risky decision if we have already secured something positive

Attention

- The cognitive processes involved in selecting information to be processed
- **Goal-Directed Attention:** We actively choose to pay attention to something
- **Stimulus-Driven Attention:** Something in the environment grabs or catches our attention
- **Perceptual Load:** The amount of mental processing required for a task; the higher the perceptual load the more attention it requires
- **Broadbent's Filter Theory:** We use certain criteria, such as physical characteristics, to select some stimuli and ignore others; we can only attend to a few stimuli at a given time
- **Feature Integration:** We organize and categorize information from stimuli based on similarities in their features or characteristics

Multitasking

- The cognitive processes involved when we engage in more than one activity at a time; simultaneously working on more than one task
- We do not actually multitask
- We are actually switching tasks quickly which results in the use of more energy, loss time, etc.
- We are able to multitask with limited drawbacks, if the perceptual load of each task is low (Baird & McCarthy, 2014).

Now that you have a general idea of some of the cognitive processes we engage in, we can look at our capacity for cognition, also known as our intelligence.

 Practice...

1. A(n) _____ is the mental image or typical example that exhibits all of the features associated with a concept.
   a. exemplar
   b. prototype
   c. schema
   d. primary schematic

2. Banana, Olive, and Tomato. If you think of these three items, you may initially think that they have nothing in common aside from being edible products. If you look closer, however, you will find that they are all types of fruits. The way that we categorize things together based on their shared features is called the _____ theory.
   a. common attribute
   b. family resemblance
   c. shared feature
   d. unified concept

3. _____ is the act of combining current information with information stored in memory to find a solution to a task.
   a. Heuristic application
   b. Practical intelligence
   c. Exemplar seeking
   d. Problem solving

4. _____ refers to the sudden realization of the solution to a problem.
   a. Inspiration
   b. Genius
   c. Insight
   d. Unveiling

5. _____ is the cognitive process of organizing information or beliefs into a series of steps to reach conclusions.
   a. Verbalizing
   b. Centrating
   c. Reasoning
   d. Schematic processing

Apply...

1. **Breaking Down Problem Solving**

   Allen Newell and Herbert Simon (1972) proposed that we can break down the process of problem solving into our initial state, our goal state, and all states between our initial and goal states

   Spend a little time researching their model. You will see that we have learned quite a bit about problem solving from their theory.

   Think of a problem from your life and apply their general model of problem solving to it.

   - Identify the initial state, the goal state, and the states that you went through as you worked from the initial state to the goal state.

   _____

   _____

   _____

   _____

   _____

   _____

   _____

   _____

   _____

   _____

   _____

   - List the strategies, techniques, or short-cuts you used as you worked through the problem.

   _____

   _____

   _____

   _____

   _____

   _____

   _____

   _____

   _____

   _____

   _____

to be continued

 **Apply...**

continued

2. **Functional Fixedness**

Look up Norma Maier's "two-string problem" online.

- What can we learn about functional fixedness from this problem?

_____
_____
_____
_____
_____
_____
_____
_____
_____
_____
_____
_____
_____
_____
_____
_____

- How can we prevent functional fixedness?

_____
_____
_____
_____
_____
_____
_____
_____
_____
_____
_____
_____
_____
_____
_____

to be continued

Apply...

continued

3. **Inductive versus Deductive Reasoning**

Define inductive and deductive reasoning and provide an example for each.

- Inductive Reasoning

    Definition:

    _____
    _____
    _____
    _____
    _____
    _____

    Example:

    _____
    _____
    _____
    _____
    _____
    _____

- Deductive Reasoning

    Definition:

    _____
    _____
    _____
    _____
    _____
    _____

    Example:

    _____
    _____
    _____
    _____
    _____

Intelligence

L03 Describe the main principles of major theories and tests of intelligence.

Intelligence is basically our capacity for cognition. It is our ability to engage in cognitive processes, such as the ones we have previously discussed. There are several theories of intelligence. We will discuss a few of them here. Each of the theories of intelligence proposes a way to measure or quantify our cognitive abilities—these are usually called intelligence tests. Have you ever taken an intelligence test?

When we use intelligence tests to understand our cognitive abilities, we are using a **psychometric approach**. A psychometric approach uses measurements or assessments to gain knowledge about an item of interest, such as intelligence, perception, and personality.

Some tests of intelligence:

Alfred Binet Intelligence Test

- First intelligence test
- Developed test to identify children with special needs (1904)
- Developed a test for **mental age**, which refers to the cognitive level typically seen at a particular age

Stanford-Binet Intelligence Scale

- Louis Terman of Stanford University revised Binet's test
- Known as the Stanford-Binet (1916)
- Test gives an overall score called the **IQ** (intelligence quotient):

  IQ = Mental age/Chronological age × 100

- An IQ score = 100 means that a child's mental and chronological age are the same

Weschler Adult Intelligence Scale (WAIS)

- David Weschler used Stanford-Binet test to develop an intelligence test for adults (1939)
- Results used a normal curve/normal distribution rather than IQ score (Figure 1)

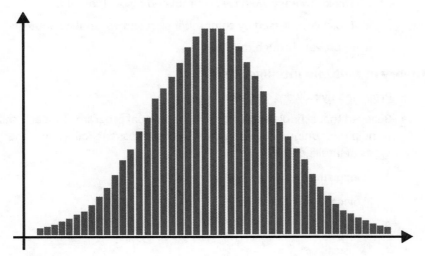

FIGURE 1 Normal distribution graph.

Shahreen/Shutterstock

- Average IQ score is 100
- When you look at the normal curve in the graph, what do you see?
  ◊ Most scores occur in the middle.
  ◊ As you move away from the middle scores, in either direction, the number of scores decreases.
  ◊ The normal curve will tell us what intelligence scores most of the population will have.
  ◊ It can help us to identify individuals with higher and lower intelligence scores than the average.
- Other widely used tests include: Wechsler Intelligence Scale for Children and Wechsler Adult Intelligence Scale

Intelligence tests have been critiqued for having several limitations. In one of your activities for this unit, you will research these limitations.

Next, we will look at some of the ways intelligence has been explained. Below are summaries of some of the most common theories or conceptualizations of intelligence. As you read each one, think about what the strengths and weaknesses of each theory are—this will be one of your exercises for this unit.

General Intelligence (g)

- Proposed by Charles Spearman
- Believed that we all have a general level of intelligence that impacts our cognitive processes

Fluid and Crystallized Intelligence

- Proposed by Raymond Cattell
- Believed that we have different and distinct types of intelligence
  ◊ **Fluid Intelligence**
    - Cognitive abilities that determine speed of analyzing, processing, and reacting to information
    - Typically assessed by performance subtests on intelligence tests
    - Peaks in early to mid-twenties
  ◊ **Crystallized Intelligence**
    - The knowledge we have accumulated through our life
    - Typically assessed by comprehension and vocabulary subtests
    - Improves through thirties

Theory of Multiple Intelligences

- Proposed by Howard Gardner
- Believed that schools should develop individual programs for each child to help their unique developmental needs across the following eight types of intelligence:
  1. Linguistic
  2. Logical-mathematical
  3. Spatial
  4. Musical
  5. Bodily-kinesthetic

6. Naturalist

7. Interpersonal

8. Intrapersonal

Triarchic Theory of Intelligence

- Proposed by Robert Sternberg
- Three aspects of intelligence:

    1. **Analytic Intelligence:** Ability to solve problem in well-defined situations with a single correct answer

    2. **Creative Intelligence:** Ability to solve problem in new situations or when novel solutions are required

    3. **Practical Intelligence:** Ability to solve problem in complicated or poorly defined situations and use solutions in real life (Baird & McCarthy, 2014)

At this point, it may seem like our cognitive processes occur in situations where other people are not around, but next we will discuss Social Cognition.

 Practice...

1. Alfred Binet developed a test to determine a child's _____.
    a. processing speed
    b. mathematics skills
    c. mental age
    d. verbal fluency

2. The formula: (Mental Age/Chronological Age) × 100 is used to determine an individual's _____.
    a. intelligence quality
    b. intelligence quartile
    c. intelligence quantity
    d. intelligence quotient

3. Henry's birth certificate says he is 10 years old. He took some tests at school which said his mental age was 15 years. What is Henry's IQ?
    a. 30
    b. 50
    c. 100
    d. 150

4. Which researcher developed an intelligence test that normed its scores according to the concept of normal distribution?
    a. David Wechsler
    b. Alfred Binet
    c. Lewis Terman
    d. Sir Francis Galton

5. One of the earliest theories of multiple types of intelligence was that of Raymond Cattell, who suggested that intelligence can be divided into two types:
    a. intrapersonal and interpersonal.
    b. fluid and crystallized.
    c. practical and creative.
    d. emotional and intellectual.

 Apply...

1. **Limitations of Intelligence Tests**

   Research intelligence tests. You may use the internet, peer-reviewed journals, textbooks, etc.

   - List the limitations of intelligence tests

   _____

   _____

   _____

   _____

   _____

   _____

   _____

   _____

   _____

   _____

   _____

   _____

   _____

   _____

   - How have these limitations been addressed by developers of intelligence tests?

   _____

   _____

   _____

   _____

   _____

   _____

   _____

   _____

   _____

   _____

   _____

   _____

to be continued

 **Apply...**

continued

2. **Strengths and Weaknesses of Various Theories of Intelligence**

Choose two theories of intelligence. List what you think are the strengths and weaknesses of each theory. After you have completed this activity, discuss your thoughts with two classmates.

Theory 1: _____

_____

_____

Strengths:

_____

_____

_____

_____

_____

Weaknesses:

_____

_____

_____

_____

_____

Theory 2: _____

_____

_____

Strengths:

_____

_____

_____

_____

_____

Weaknesses:

_____

_____

_____

_____

to be continued

 **Apply...**

continued

3. **Howard Gardner's Theory of Intelligence**

   • Do you think Howard Gardner's theory of intelligence accurately reflects our cognitive abilities? Why/Why not?

   _____

   _____

   _____

   _____

   _____

   _____

   _____

   _____

   • If you could make changes to his list of eight intelligence types, what would you add? What would you remove? Why?

   _____

   _____

   _____

   _____

   _____

   _____

   _____

   _____

   • After you have completed this activity, discuss your views with another classmate.

   _____

   _____

   _____

   _____

   _____

   _____

   _____

   _____

Social Cognition

LO4 List five aspects of social cognition

Have you heard the saying, "No man is an island"? Usually, we use this saying to make the point that none of us lives in complete isolation in which we are not affected by others and in which we do not affect others. Instead, we live in a very social world. You learned in chapters on Genetics and Evolution (Chapter 4), and on Motivation and Emotion (Chapter 5), that we have a drive to belong to a group and to be around others, and that emotions are used to convey information to others. In Chapter 7 on Learning, we discussed observational learning which is how we learn from others. Part of cognition, then, must involve detecting, processing, and acting on social information. We use the term **social cognition** to refer to the mental processes that occur in our social world—it is how we think about ourselves and others in our social interactions, relationships, groups, organizations, and so on. As discussed, we have already touched on some aspects of social cognition in previous chapters—now let's look at some additional aspects of social cognition.

Social Cognition also includes:

- **Theory of Mind:** The ability to understand that we all have mental states such as beliefs, thoughts, and emotions

- **Perspective Taking:** The ability to understand the thoughts, beliefs, emotions, desires, etc. of others, even when they are different from our own

- **Imaginary Audience:** The belief, most common in adolescents, that we are being observed by others, can lead to feelings of self-consciousness

- **Personal Fable:** The belief, most common in adolescents, that we are special and unique

- **Optimistic Bias:** Can develop from the personal fable, seen in both adults and adolescents, is the belief that we are not likely to experience bad things

- **Social Intelligence:** Our capacity to understand social situations and to react in ways that are positively perceived by group members

- **Emotional Intelligence:** Our capacity to detect and understand our emotions and the emotions of others, and the capacity to manage and reveal our emotions in ways that are socially appropriate, a part of having social intelligence

- **Reciprocal Determinism:** Proposed by Albert Bandura to explain the influences of behaviour, environment, and personal characteristics on one another, we can use this as a model to help us understand the interconnectedness of social cognitive processes, social situations, and behavioural responses to others (Figure 2) (Baird & McCarthy, 2014; McMahan & Thompson, 2015).

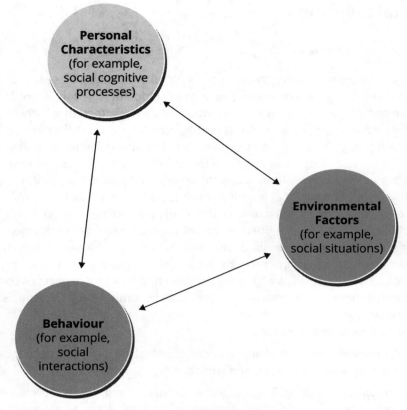

FIGURE 2 Bandura's model of reciprocal determinism.

Practice...

1. _____is the reason we assume that accidents, diseases, and other misfortunes are more likely to happen to others than ourselves.
   a. Optimistic bias
   b. Imaginary audience
   c. Emotional intelligence
   d. All of the above are reasons we assume that accidents, diseases, and other misfortunes are more likely to happen to others than ourselves.

2. A child's ability to distinguish between their own versus others' mental states is called theory of _____.
   a. schema
   b. disintegration
   c. mind
   d. egocentrism

3. Reciprocal determinism presents _____, _____, and _____as being interconnected.
   a. behaviour, social interactions, learning
   b. environment, brain size, consciousness

   c. observational learning, pride, and personal characteristics
   d. behaviour, environment, personal characteristics

4. Maddie feels that everyone is looking at her. She is self-conscious about the way she looks and acts, and feels uncomfortable around her peers. Maddie is most likely _____who holds the belief of _____.
   a. an adolescent, a personal fable
   b. an adolescent, an imaginary audience
   c. an adult, a personal fable
   d. an adult, an imaginary audience

5. Ian loves broccoli. His friend Alex hates broccoli. Ian understands that although he loves broccoli, Alex does not. Ian has developed _____.
   a. perspective taking
   b. personal fable
   c. imaginary audience
   d. reciprocal determinism

Apply...

1. **Social Cognition and Technology**

   • How do you think technology impacts social cognition?

   _____
   _____
   _____
   _____
   _____
   _____
   _____
   _____
   _____
   _____
   _____
   _____
   _____
   _____
   _____
   _____
   _____
   _____
   _____
   _____
   _____
   _____
   _____
   _____
   _____
   _____
   _____
   _____
   _____
   _____
   _____
   _____
   _____

to be continued

Apply...

continued

- Research social cognition and technology using peer-reviewed journals. Choose one peer-reviewed journal article and write a brief summary of what the researchers found. Come prepared to discuss the article with the class.

_____

_____

_____

_____

_____

_____

_____

_____

_____

_____

_____

_____

_____

_____

_____

_____

_____

_____

_____

_____

_____

_____

_____

_____

_____

_____

_____

_____

to be continued

 **Apply...**

continued

2. **Emotional Intelligence**
   - What are the benefits of having high emotional intelligence?

   _____

   _____

   _____

   _____

   _____

   _____

   _____

   _____

   _____

   _____

   _____

   _____

   _____

   - What are the drawbacks of having high emotional intelligence?

   _____

   _____

   _____

   _____

   _____

   _____

   _____

   _____

   _____

   _____

   _____

   _____

   _____

KNOW...

Learning Objectives

1. Developmental changes that occur in our cognitive abilities:

As we get older, we:

- develop object permanence, then make-believe play, then an understanding of conservation of mass and the ability to generalize from specific experiences, and to understand abstract concepts.
- increase our processing and automaticity.

2. Three cognitive processes:

Note: You can choose any three processes discussed in the chapter
Examples:

- **Problem Solving:** The cognitive processes that occur when we attempt to arrive at a solution using strategies such as algorithms, mental set, or insight
- **Reasoning:** The cognitive processes involved when we organize information so that we can make decisions, using practical, theoretical, or syllogistic strategies
- **Multitasking:** The cognitive processes when we simultaneously work on more than one task; we do not actually multitask, especially if perceptual load of tasks is high, but rather we switch quickly from one task to another

3. Main principles of major theories and tests of intelligence:

Tests:

- Alfred Binet Intelligence test: Test for mental age
- Stanford-Binet Intelligence Scale: Gives IQ; IQ = Mental age/Chronological age $\times$ 100
- Weschler Adult Intelligence Scale (WAIS): Developed for adults

Theories:

- Spearman's General Intelligence (g): We have a general level of intelligence that impacts our cognitive processes
- Cattel's Fluid and Crystallized Intelligence: Fluid Intelligence—Speed of Analyzing, Processing, and Reacting to Information; Crystallized Intelligence—Built up Knowledge
- Gardner's Theory of Multiple Intelligences: Linguistic, Logical-mathematical, Spatial, Musical, Bodily-kinesthetic, Naturalist, Interpersonal, and Intrapersonal
- Sternberg's Triarchic theory of Intelligence: Analytic intelligence, Creative intelligence, and Practical intelligence

4. Five aspects of social cognition:

Note: You can choose any five processes discussed in the chapter
Examples:

- Social intelligence
- Imaginary audience
- Perspective taking
- Optimistic bias
- Theory of Mind

Key Terms

Cognition: Internal mental processes.

Schemas: Mental representations of information based on our experiences.

Assimilation: Incorporating new information into an already existing schema.

Accommodation: Modifying, altering, or changing an existing schema based on new information.

Concepts: The cognitive processes involved in the formation of mental representations that allow us to group things (people, objects, events, activities, animals, etc.) together that are similar.

Prototype: Typical examples of what we would find in a category.

Problem Solving: The cognitive processes involved when we combine information from our current state or situation with previous information we have gathered through time, with the goal of finding a solution to a task.

Reasoning: The cognitive processes involved when we organize information into the steps needed to arrive at a result or conclusion.

Decision Making: The cognitive processes involved in choosing an option or outcome.

Attention: The cognitive processes involved in selecting information to be processed.

Multitasking: The cognitive processes involved when we engage in more than one activity at a time; simultaneously working on more than one task.

Psychometric Approach: The use of measurements or assessments to gain knowledge about an item of interest.

Mental Age: The cognitive level typically seen at a particular age.

IQ: Intelligence quotient, calculated using the formula IQ = Mental age/Chronological age × 100.

Social Cognition: The mental processes associated with what we think about ourselves and others in our social world.

Answers to Practice

What Is Cognition?
1. d   2. b   3. c   4. b   5. a

Examples of Cognitive Processes
1. b   2. b   3. d   4. c   5. c

Intelligence
1. c   2. d   3. d   4. a   5. b

Social Cognition
1. a   2. c   3. d   4. b   5. a

References

Baird, A., & McCarthy, A. (2014). *THINK psychology* (2nd Canadian edition). Don Mills, ON: Pearson Education, Inc.; pp. 152-163, 182–195.

McMahan, I., & Thompson, S. (2015). *Adolescence.* Pearson Canada Inc.

9 Memory

LO1 List the basic stages of memory

LO2 Explain sensory registers and provide two examples of sensory registers

LO3 Discuss the limitations of short-term memory and list two ways that we can address these limitations

LO4 Illustrate the key parts of each stage of memory

LEARN...

What did you eat for breakfast this morning? What did you eat for breakfast 3 days ago? Your ability to answer these questions requires you to use your memory. Memory is the name we give to our brain's system for storing and retrieving information we have collected or learned. Our memory consists of three main stages: First, information enters through our sense organs and goes to our sensory memory. If we pay attention to the information in our sensory memory then that information is converted into a form that can be stored in our memory and it moves to our short-term memory. Short-term memory is the part of our memory that holds information for immediate or short-term use. If we want information to move from short-term memory to the next part of our memory, we need to engage or "work" on this information. If this is done then the information is encoded a second time and moves to our long-term memory. Long-term memory is the part of our memory that stores information indefinitely. Once information enters our long-term memory, it has the potential to stay there forever. Storing information in our long-term memory can be unintentional, referred to as implicit memories. Information about how to do something is called procedural memory and is a type of implicit memory. Memories can also be stored intentionally or consciously, and are referred to as explicit memories. Information that is factual but not linked to our lives is called semantic memory and is an example of explicit memory. Some information will bypass short-term memory/working memory and go directly into long-term memory, such as highly emotional events or experiences, called flash-bulb memories. The last part of our memory process is retrieval, which is when we pull information from our long-term memory and send it to short-term memory so that we can use it. Our memory retrieval follows a primacy-recency effect where we are more likely to remember information that is presented first and information that is presented most recently. Memory retrieval is not perfect, and we can experience retrieval failure or forgetting. Forgetting may be due to interference, storage decay, stress, or amnesia. In your activities for this chapter, you will explore the parts of the brain that are involved with different types of memories, reflect on your own memories, and research strategies for improving memory.

What Is Memory?

L01 List the basic stages of memory

Quick—list three cognitive processes.
Were you able to complete the requested task?

If so, then you remembered what you learned in your last chapter (Cognition). If you were not able to complete the task was it because you could not remember what you read in your previous chapter? Did you forget? These processes of remembering and forgetting are all part of memory. **Memory** is the name we give to our brain's system for storing and retrieving information we have collected or learned.

How do we form memories? Below is a diagram (Figure 1) that shows the main stages that information goes through when we are forming memories. We will look at each part in more detail through this chapter.

Basic Memory Stages

In general, information enters through our sense organs (refer to Chapter 3 on Sensation and Perception), and goes to our **sensory memory**. Sensory memory is the part of our memory that stores sensory information. If we pay attention to the information in our sensory memory then that information becomes **encoded** (converted into a form that can be stored in our memory) and moves to our **short-term memory**. Short-term memory is the part of our memory that holds information for immediate or short-term use. If we do not pay attention to the information in our sensory memory then it is forgotten or lost—it is simply not processed or moved through our memory stages. You can refer to previous chapters (Chapters 7 and 8 on Learning and Cognition) for a reminder of the importance of attention. Information stays in our sensory memory for only a few seconds, but our sensory memory can hold a lot of information. Think about how much information comes in through our five senses—it is a lot indeed! Once information enters our short-term memory, it stays only for 15–30 seconds (Atkinson & Shiffrin, 1968). If we want information to move from short-term memory to the next part of our memory, we need to engage or "work" on this information. If this is done then the information is encoded a second time and moves to our **long-term memory**. Long-term memory is the part of our memory that stores information indefinitely. If we do not actively engage the information in our short-term memory then it is forgotten or lost. Unlike sensory memory, short-term memory is limited in the amount of information it can hold.

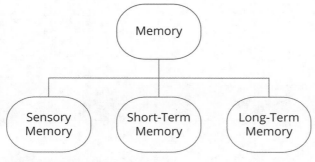

FIGURE 1 General stages of memory.

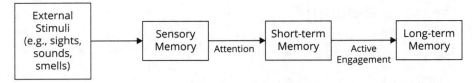

FIGURE 2 General steps in memory formation.

We will discuss this later in this chapter. Once information enters our long-term memory, it has the potential to stay there forever. If we were to illustrate the steps that information passes through to get to our long-term memory, it may look like Figure 2.

Now that we have a general idea of the stages of memory, we can look at each stage in more detail.

 **Practice...**

1. The brain's system for filing away new information and retrieving previously learned data is called _____.
   a. storage
   b. recognition
   c. recall
   d. memory

2. Which of the following is not one of the basic stages of memory?
   a. Sensory memory
   b. Working memory
   c. Immediate memory
   d. Long-term memory

3. The process of directing your attention to a specific stimulus and then converting that stimulus to a form that can be stored is called _____.
   a. attending
   b. encoding
   c. retrieval
   d. integration

4. _____ memory stores information the longest.
   a. Long term
   b. Short term
   c. Sensory
   d. Deliberate

5. Information in short-term memory lasts for up to _____ seconds.
   a. 15
   b. 20
   c. 25
   d. 30

Apply...

1. **What We Remember?**

   - Think about memories that fall into the following categories:

     ◊ Earliest memory as a child

     _____

     _____

     _____

     ◊ A happy memory

     _____

     _____

     _____

     ◊ A memory of an accomplishment

     _____

     _____

     _____

     ◊ A memory of a disappointment

     _____

     _____

     _____

   As you think about each of these memories write down your feelings, physiological reactions, level of detail in your memory, and anything else you notice.

   - What do you notice about your ability to remember? Are your memories detailed or general? What do you think is the relationship between memories and emotions?

     _____

     _____

     _____

     _____

     _____

     _____

     _____

     _____

     _____

     _____

to be continued

Apply...

continued

- Share your thoughts, ideas, and observations about memories with a classmate. In what ways are your answers to the above questions similar and different to those of your classmate?

_____

_____

_____

_____

_____

_____

_____

_____

_____

_____

_____

_____

_____

2. **Eye Witness**

- What are your thoughts about eye witness accounts?

_____

_____

_____

_____

_____

_____

_____

_____

_____

_____

_____

_____

_____

_____

to be continued

 **Apply...**

continued

- What does the research tell us about the use of eye witness accounts in trials? You will need to research this using peer-reviewed journals. Please cite your sources.

_____

_____

_____

_____

_____

_____

_____

_____

_____

_____

Sensory Memory

 Explain sensory registers and provide two examples of sensory registers

We learned in Chapter 3 (Sensation and Perception) that information about our external environment comes in through our sense organs (that is, eyes, ears, skin, tongue, nose) and is then passed on to specific parts of our brain to be processed. This sensory information can be viewed as the raw material from which we form memories. Once our sense organs collect information, this information is passed on to **sensory registers** in the brain. Sensory registers are the parts of the brain that make up the sensory memory and they can hold large amounts of information—but that information only stays in the registers for less than a second if we do not pay attention to it (Baird & McCarthy, 2014). Each sense organ has its own register. You can think of it as a specialized area that holds specific information. For example, auditory information is held in a register specific and solely for auditory information. For this reason, we can identify specific sensory memories based on the type of sensory stimuli they come from.

Some examples of sensory memory are:

- **Iconic Memory**
  - Sensory memories formed from visual information.
  - Perhaps you have heard of "photographic memory" or "eidetic memory"—the ability to store exact visual information in our memory, after viewing it for a very short time, so that we can retrieve and examine it later. The idea is that we can recall this visual information

in great detail and it would appear similar to a photograph thereby allowing us to zoom in or out or to manipulate the image as we wish. This lead to the term "photographic memory" when referring to this type of memory recall. However, the term "photographic memory" is not exactly accurate and it has not been proven that such memories—those similar to a photograph—actually occur.

◊ In reality, the use of the term "photographic memory" is incorrect. Most of us have better memory recall for visual stimuli, such as faces, but this just means that we have different abilities depending on the type of sensory memory. But, what about the term "eidetic memory"—is this accurate? The term "eidetic memory" refers to our ability to recall visual images in great detail even when we only seen them for a short time. Psychologist, Alan Searleman noted that eidetic memory only lasts a few minutes and that when images are recalled they can have errors. This holds true even for "eidetikers"—people who appear to have photographic memories because they are able to recall images in great detail (Gordon, 2013).

- **Echoic Memory**

  ◊ Sensory memories formed from auditory information

- **Haptic Memory**

  ◊ Sensory memories formed from Somesthetic and Cutaneous information

Based on these examples, you can see that specific parts of the brain are involved in the creation of sensory memories. Based on your understanding of the brain and sensation and perception, can you identify the parts of the brain that would be involved in the creation of different sensory memories (you can refer to Chapters 2 and 3 [Human Brain and Sensation and Perception] for review)? This will be one of your activities for this chapter.

If we were to create an image for sensory memory, it may look like Figure 3.

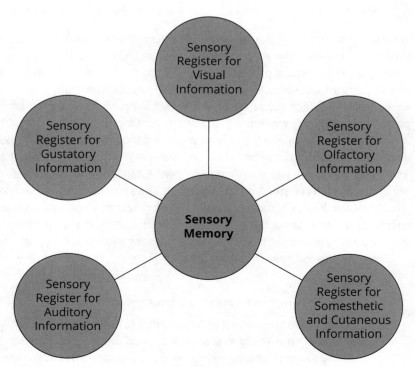

FIGURE 3 Components of sensory memory.

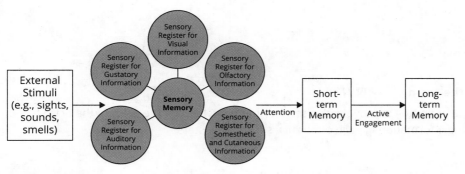

FIGURE 4 Modified stages of memory with expanded sensory memory stage.

Our modified diagram for the stages of memory would look like Figure 4.
Let's look at what happens when information moves from our sensory memory to our short-term memory. Information moves from sensory memory to short term: (i) when we turn our awareness or consciousness to the information, this is called **conscious encoding** and (ii) through **unconscious encoding**, which is unintentional and automatic.

Practice...

1. How many different kinds of sensory registers does each person have?
   a. One
   b. Three
   c. Five
   d. Seven

2. The _____ are the parts of the brain that make up sensory memory.
   a. sensory lobes
   b. sensory cortices
   c. sensory receivers
   d. sensory registers

3. If we don't pay attention to the information in our sensory registers, those data disappear within _____.
   a. ¼ second
   b. ½ second

   c. 1 second
   d. 30 seconds

4. _____ memory involves the ability to recall detailed images vividly after only a brief exposure to them.
   a. Echoic
   b. Eidetic
   c. Iconic
   d. Mirror

5. Seeing is to _____ memory as hearing is to _____ memory.
   a. iconic; echoic
   b. sensory; working
   c. atrophic; hypertrophic
   d. short term; long term

 **Apply...**

1. **Sensory Memory and the Brain**

   Research the parts of the brain that are involved in sensory memory. Identify the parts of the brain that are involved in processing information in each of our five sensory registers.

   - Memory Type:

     Part(s) of brain involved:

     _____

     _____

     _____

     _____

     _____

     _____

     _____

     _____

   - Memory Type:

     Part(s) of brain involved:

     _____

     _____

     _____

     _____

     _____

     _____

     _____

     _____

   - Memory Type:

     Part(s) of brain involved:

     _____

     _____

     _____

     _____

     _____

     _____

     _____

     _____

to be continued

 **Apply...**

continued

- Memory Type:

  Part(s) of brain involved:

  _____

  _____

  _____

  _____

  _____

  _____

- Memory Type:

  Part(s) of brain involved:

  _____

  _____

  _____

  _____

  _____

  _____

2. **Attention**

   We learned that we need to pay attention to sensory information in order for it to move to our short-term memory. This is not always easy to do. List five things that can impair our ability to attend to information in our sensory memory.

   1. _____

   _____

   _____

   _____

   _____

   2. _____

   _____

   _____

   _____

   _____

   _____

to be continued

 **Apply...**

continued

3. _____

_____

_____

_____

_____

4. _____

_____

_____

_____

5. _____

_____

_____

_____

Short-Term Memory

 Discuss the limitations of short-term memory and list two ways that we can address these limitations

What comes to mind when you hear the term "short-term memory"? Likely the word "short" stands out—and it should. Our short-term memory is not only limited in how long information is stored there but also how much information we can store. George Miller observed that on average we can hold seven plus or minus two units or items of information in our short-term memory—this is called Miller's Magic Number or Miller's Law. This means that we can hold between five and nine pieces of information in our short-term memory. This is not a lot of information. For this reason, we often use strategies that allow us to hold more information in our short-term memory. One example is **chunking**, where we break up large pieces of information into small groupings or units that are easier to remember. Can you think of an example of chunking from your life? How about a phone number? Including the area code a phone number has 10 digits which according to Miller's Law is too much for us to hold in our short-term memory—yet we often remember phone numbers? Often we do this through chunking—we break up the 10 digits into smaller grouped pieces of information. Usually, for phone numbers we break it up into the following: area code—first three numbers—last four numbers. For example, 5196502359 becomes 519-650-2359. We may even take our chunking further and organize the information as: 5-19-6-50-23-59. As long as the number of chunked items is seven plus or minus two units of information our short-term memory can store it. We may already be using chunking in other ways, such as to help us store information for grocery shopping, directions to a location, or for an upcoming test.

As previously stated, information in short-term memory will stay there for about 15–30 seconds unless we actively engage in the information. One of the most common ways that we actively engage with information in our short term is through **rote rehearsal**. We engage in rote rehearsal when we repeat information in an attempt to learn it. It can be a good strategy for holding information in our short-term memory for a longer time. Perhaps, you have used this strategy to help you remember information such as a phone number, grocery list, directions, or course material for a test. You can see how repetition of chunked material would be easier to do.

Perhaps, you have heard the term "working memory". Working memory is sometimes used to mean the same thing as short-term memory, but they are not necessarily the same thing. There are different hypothetical models that attempt to explain how working memory and short-term memory are related (Aben, Stapert, & Blokland, 2012):

- Short-term memory and working memory are the same.
- Short-term memory and working memory are independent of each other.
- Short-term memory and working memory are part of the same system, they do not transfer information to each other.
- Short-term memory and working memory work together, each transferring information to the other as needed.

Regardless of how short-term memory and working memory are conceptualized, it is important to know that this stage of memory is limited in the amount of information it can hold and the length it can be stored. It is also important to know that in order for information to move to long-term memory we must act on the information while it is in short-term/working memory (Figure 5). We will adjust our model to accommodate the use of the term working memory. In our next unit, we will discuss what happens when information moves from short-term memory to long-term memory.

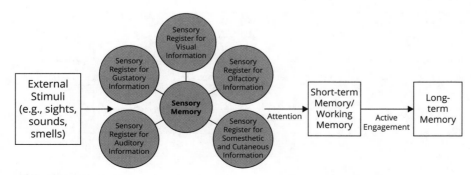

FIGURE 5 Modified stages of memory with inclusion of working memory.

Practice...

1. The average number of pieces of information that people can hold in their short-term/working memory at any one time is _____.
   a. three
   b. five
   c. seven
   d. twelve

2. Dr. McCaffery tells his class, "I am going to shine a stimulus up on the screen, and I'm only going to give you 3 seconds to memorize them. Go!" He shines a slide that has the following letters: "OVTCBBVTCCBC" on the screen. The student who wants to win the game by memorizing this most effective and most quickly will use what process to remember the 12 letters as "CBC-CTV-BBC–TVO"?
   a. Semantic grouping
   b. Clustering
   c. Chunking
   d. Affiliating

3. When we "cram" for a test we are more likely to remember the course material for a longer time compared to studying over several days.
   a. True
   b. False

4. Rote rehearsal is _____
   a. an effective strategy to transfer information to long term memory.
   b. decreases the amount of time information is stored in short term/working memory.
   c. Both (a) and (b) are correct.
   d. Neither (a) and (b) are correct.

5. Which of the following statements is correct?
   a. Short-term memory holds information for a longer time than sensory memory.
   b. Short-term memory has the largest storage capacity compared to sensory and long-term memory.
   c. Short-term memory is limited in capacity but not length of time it holds information.
   d. Short-term memory is limited in both capacity and length of time it holds information.

 # Apply...

1. **Short Term and Working Memory**

   Which hypothetical model of the relationship between short-term and working memory do you think is most accurate? Explain your choice.

   Note: You may have to do some research on this topic to formulate a strong rationale for your decision. You can use the internet, peer-reviewed journals, textbooks, etc. Remember to cite your sources.

   _____

   _____

   _____

   _____

   _____

   _____

   _____

to be continued

Apply...

continued

to be continued

Apply...

continued

2. **Chunking**

Come up with two examples of your use of chunking in your life. What are those examples?

Example 1:

_____

_____

_____

_____

_____

_____

Example 2:

_____

_____

_____

_____

_____

_____

Discuss your example with two of your classmates. Overall, do you and your classmates find chunking helpful? Please explain your answer.

_____

_____

_____

_____

_____

_____

_____

_____

_____

_____

_____

Long-Term Memory and Retrieval of Stored Information: Memories

LO4 Illustrate the key parts of each stage of memory

We have now arrived at the last stage of memory—long-term memory. Long-term memory is where information is stored indefinitely. So what do we need to know about long-term memory?

- Encoding into long-term memory can be conscious or unconscious.
- Memories that are stored unintentionally or unconsciously are referred to as **implicit memories** (also called nondeclarative memories).
  - ◊ An example of implicit memories is procedural memory (information about how to do something).
- Memories that are stored intentionally or consciously are referred to as **explicit memories** (also called declarative memories).
  - ◊ Examples of explicit memories are semantic (information that is factual information or conceptualizations that are not linked to our lives) and episodic memory (an entire sequence of events).
- Some information will bypass short-term memory/working memory and go directly into long-term memory; Flashbulb memories, which are highly emotional, are stored in this way (Baird & McCarthy, 2014).
- Our adjusted model for long-term memory would look like Figure 6.

As previously noted, information must be encoded or converted into a form that we can store. This happens when information moves from sensory memory to short-term/working memory and when it moves from short-term/working memory to long-term memory. We also know that if we do not pay attention then the information is lost or forgotten.

The last part of the process is **retrieval**. When we retrieve information, we are pulling it from long-term memory and sending it to short-term/working memory. Here are some key things to learn about the retrieval of memories:

- Retrieval from short-term/working memory is easier than retrieval from long-term memory.

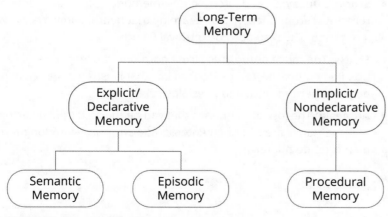

FIGURE 6 Components of long-term memory.

- We tend to have better retrieval of information that is recent because it is still in our short-term/working memory. This is called the recency effect.

- We tend to have better retrieval of information that is presented first because we have had more time to engage that information, through rehearsal for example. This is called the primacy effect.

- Our ability to recall (or not recall) items depending on their position in a list is known as the serial position effect.

- We can either recall information that is stored in our memory or we can recognize it.

  ◊ One way to remember the difference between recalling and recognizing stored information is to think of it in terms of a test in this course, or any course:

    ▪ Multiple choice tests can be considered "recognizing" because the correct answer is presented in the answer choices. Your job is to look at the answer choices and recognize which one is correct.

    ▪ Test questions that do not present the correct answer, such as short answer or essay can be considered "recall" because you must call up the information needed to answer the question.

- Our overall model would now look like Figure 7.

But, what happens when we cannot remember something? Why does this happen? When we cannot remember something, we have experienced a retrieval failure. This is often referred to as forgetting. Forgetting occurs because we are not able to access the information we have stored in our long-term memory (Baird & McCarthy, 2014). Why does this happen?

- **Interference:** When other information interferes, blocks, or makes it hard for us to retrieve other information. It can be proactive interference, which occurs when we cannot retrieve newly learned information because of interference by previously learned information. It can be retroactive interference, which occurs when we cannot retrieve previously learned information because of interference by newly learned information.

- **Storage Decay:** Stored information—memories—fade over time. You will remember from Chapter 7 on Learning that neural pathways will weaken if not used. The result can be retrieval failure.

- **Stress:** Too much or too little stress hormone can lead to retrieval failure. Remember the Yerkes-Dodson law that illustrates the relationship between performance and physiological arousal.

- **Amnesia:** The loss of memories that can be the result of: (i) Retrograde—past memories are lost or (ii) Anterograde amnesia—new long-term memories do not form.

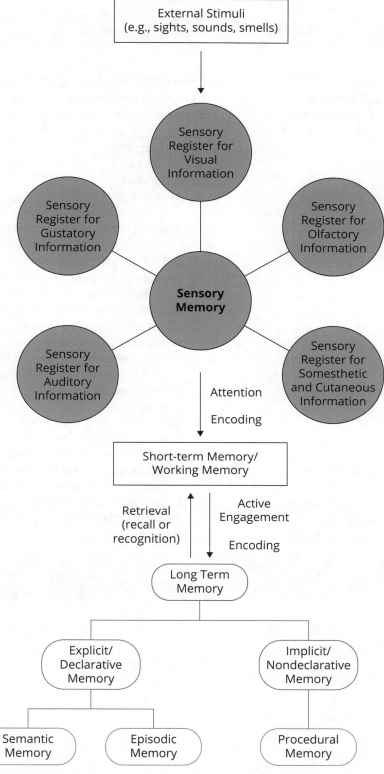

FIGURE 7 Modified stages of memory with expanded long-term memory stage: A more complete model.

Practice...

1. If you are given a list of information to remember, your memory of the items at/in the _____ of the list is going to be the worst.
   a. end
   b. beginning
   c. middle
   d. beginning and end

2. _____ are memories of which a person is consciously aware.
   a. Covert
   b. Overt
   c. Implicit
   d. Explicit

3. _____ memory and _____ memory are both considered types of explicit memory.
   a. Implicit; episodic
   b. Semantic; episodic
   c. Semantic; implicit
   d. Procedural; semantic

4. The movie "The Vow" is based on the true story of Krickett Carpenter who, after sustaining a head injury, was unable to recall her life before the accident. She did not even remember meeting or marrying her husband, Kim. Krickett has no difficulties encoding and storing new information. Based on this information, you would conclude that Krickett is suffering from _____ amnesia.
   a. anterograde
   b. retrograde
   c. retroactive
   d. proactive

5. Why does interference explain why we sometimes seem to forget information that is, in fact, still stored in our memories?
   a. Because although the capacity of our long-term memory is unlimited, the amount of information that can come in or out of that storage facility at any one moment is not unlimited.
   b. Because the more we remember the more it fundamentally alters the structure of the hippocampus, causing some memories to be lost.
   c. Because the memory system is easily confused by conflicting information, and thus we can only remember a specific amount before other facts become erased.
   d. Because the passage of time causes facts to get "melted together", making individual units of memory difficult to retrieve.

 **Apply...**

1. **Explicit versus Implicit Memories and the Brain**

   Research explicit and implicit memories. You can use the internet, peer-reviewed journals, textbooks, etc.

   Identify the parts of the brain that are involved in each type of memory.

   _____

   _____

   _____

   _____

   _____

   _____

   _____

   _____

   _____

   _____

   _____

   _____

2. **Memory Strategies**

   Research memory strategies. You can use the internet, peer-reviewed journals, textbooks, etc.

   Make a list of the top five strategies that you think would be most helpful to you in your life (school, work, relationships, etc.). Provide a brief explanation for each strategy and explain how you think it may help you.

   - Strategy:
     ◊ Explanation:

     _____

     _____

     _____

     ◊ How it may help:

     _____

     _____

     _____

   - Strategy:
     ◊ Explanation:

     _____

     _____

     _____

   to be continued

 # Apply...

continued

◊ How it may help:

_____

_____

_____

- Strategy:

  ◊ Explanation:

  _____

  _____

  _____

  ◊ How it may help:

  _____

  _____

  _____

- Strategy:

  ◊ Explanation:

  _____

  _____

  _____

  ◊ How it may help:

  _____

  _____

  _____

- Strategy:

  ◊ Explanation:

  _____

  _____

  _____

  ◊ How it may help:

  _____

  _____

  _____

  _____

to be continued

Apply...

continued

3. **Disorders of Memory**

    Most of us are familiar with Alzheimer's disease, but there are other disorders that impact memory.

    Research memory disorders. You can use the internet, peer-reviewed journals, textbooks, etc.

    Choose two disorders and write a brief summary of the disorder, including its impact on memory, how it is diagnosed, likely outcome, and treatment.

    - Disorder 1:

       Impact on memory:

       _____

       _____

       Method of diagnosis:

       _____

       _____

       Treatment:

       _____

       _____

       Likely outcome:

       _____

       _____

    - Disorder 2:

       Impact on memory:

       _____

       _____

       Method of diagnosis:

       _____

       _____

       Treatment:

       _____

       _____

       Likely outcome:

       _____

       _____

       _____

KNOW...

Learning Objectives

1. Basic stages of memory:
   - Sensory memory
   - Short-term memory
   - Long-term memory

2. Sensory registers and two examples of sensory registers:
   - Sensory registers form sensory memory
   - They hold sensory information
   - Each sense has its own register
   - Examples: iconic, echoic, haptic

3. Limitations of short-term memory and two ways of addressing these limitations:
   - Short-term memory (and working memory) is limited in the amount of information it can hold—seven plus or minus two pieces of information—and in how long information is stored—only 15–30 seconds
   - We can use chunking to help us store more information and rehearsal to help us hold on to information and move it to long-term memory

4. Key parts of each stage of memory:

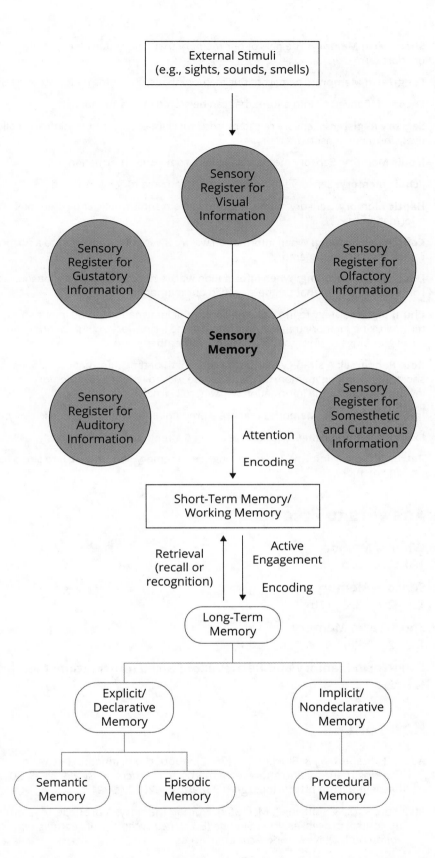

Key Terms

Memory: Brain's system for storing and retrieving information we have collected or learned.

Sensory Memory: The part of our memory that stores sensory information.

Short-Term Memory: The part of our memory that holds information for immediate or short-term use.

Long-Term Memory: The part of our memory that stores information indefinitely.

Encoded: Converted into a form that can be stored in our memory.

Sensory Registers: Sensory registers store specific sensory information and collectively form our sensory memory.

Iconic Memory: Sensory memories formed from visual information.

Echoic Memory: Sensory memories formed from auditory information.

Haptic Memory: Sensory memories formed from somesthetic and cutaneous information.

Conscious Encoding: When information we are aware of is converted to a form that can be stored in our memory.

Unconscious Encoding: When information we are not aware of (consciousness of) is converted to a form that can be stored in our memory.

Chunking: A strategy to increase the amount of information stored in our short-term/working memory that involves breaking up large pieces of information into small groupings or units that are easier to remember.

Rote Rehearsal: A strategy to increase the length of time information remains in short-term/working memory so that it can be moved to long-term memory, that involves repeating the information we want to learn.

Implicit Memories: Memories that are stored unintentionally or unconsciously.

Explicit Memories: Memories that are stored intentionally or consciously.

Retrieval: Pulling information from long-term memory and sending it to short-term/working memory.

Answers to Practice

What Is Memory?
1. d   2. c   3. b   4. a   5. d

Sensory Memory
1. c   2. d   3. c   4. b   5. a

Short-Term Memory
1. c   2. c   3. b   4. a   5. d

Long-Term Memory and Retrieval of Stored Information: Memories
1. c   2. d   3. b   4. b   5. a

References

Aben, B., Stapert, S., & Blokland, A. (2012). About the distinction between working memory and short-term memory. *Frontiers in Psychology*, *3*, 301. Retrieved from http://doi.org/10.3389/fpsyg.2012.00301.

Atkinson, R. C., & Shiffrin, R. M. (1968). Human memory: A proposed system and its control processes. In K. Spence (Ed.), *The Psychology of Learning and Motivation* (Vol. 2). New York: Academic Press.

Baird, A., & McCarthy, A. (2014). *THINK psychology* (2nd Canadian edition). Don Mills, ON: Pearson Education, Inc.; pp. 167–177.

Gordon, B. (2013). I developed what appears to be a photographic memory when I was 16 years old. Does this kind of memory truly exist, and, if so, how did I develop it? *Scientific American*. Retrieved from https://www.scientificamerican.com/article/i-developed-what-appears-to-be-a-ph/.

10 Personality

LEARNING OBJECTIVES

LO1 List five research methods used to study personality

LO2 List the trait theories of personality

LO3 Explain the key principles behind the personality theories proposed by Freud and Jung

LO4 Discuss the major biological and social-cognitive theories of personality

LEARN...

It is our personality that makes each of us unique. Personality, then, can be viewed as the distinctive and consistent way we think, feel, and interact with others and the world around us. If you had to describe yourself, you would include some of your personality characteristics. To understand personality, we must look at both the internal processes and external actions that are unique to each of us, and those that are common across groups and humans in general. An idiographic approach allows us to look at individual differences, while a nomothetic approach allows us to look at patterns that exist across individuals. In this chapter, we discuss some of the common methods used to assess personality. We also discuss some of the most influential and well-known theories of personality. We focus on trait, intrapsychic, biological, and social-cognitive perspectives. Trait theories propose that each of us has a usual way of thinking, feeling, and behaving and that personality is formed from these traits, which are measured on a continuum from low to high. The difficulty with assessing traits lies in the fact that they cannot be directly measured. While we discuss several trait theories, one of the most common ones is the Big Five, which proposes that our personality is composed of five traits: Neuroticism, Extraversion, Openness, Agreeableness, and Conscientiousness. In our discussions of intrapsychic theories of personality, we revisit Freud and Jung. We discuss the stages of Feud's Psychosexual Development, and his proposed structure of personality: Id, ego, and superego. In your activity for this unit, you will have the opportunity to determine your personality profile based on Jung's Theory. The biological theories propose that personality stems from the way various biological processes respond to stimuli. For example, in response to a stimuli, our Behavioural Inhibition System may be activated leading us to avoid the situation or event. In exploring social-cognitive theories of personality, we discuss the roles of perceived personal control, belief in our ability to complete a task, and the way we explain our life events. Through your activities for this chapter, you will have the opportunity to research additional theories of personality, to apply personality theories to your own life, and to assess which theory you think best explains personality.

What Is Personality?

L01 List five research methods used to study personality

We are all unique. There is no one that is exactly like us—not even an identical twin. But, what makes each of us unique? It is our **personality**. Personality can be thought of the distinctive and consistent way each of thinks, feels, and interacts with others and the world around us (Baird & McCarthy, 2014; American Psychological Association, 2017). In this chapter, we explore personality.

One of the challenges of understanding, studying, and determining personality is the fact that we must examine both the internal processes and external actions that are unique to individuals as well as those that are common across groups and humans in general. To do this, researchers who study personality do so using two approaches:

- **Idiographic Approach:** Focuses on differences across individuals, with the goal of understanding how all parts of our personality form our unique selves.

- **Nomothetic Approach:** Focuses on general themes, principles, and patterns that exist across individuals, with the goal of understanding relationships among common personality characteristics.

- An easy way to remember the difference between idiographic and nomothetic is to think of it as "I" = individual and "n" = normal = average.

So, what forms our personality? Think back to your previous chapters—what do you think forms our personality? Let's take a look:

If you look at Figure 1, you will notice that we have already discussed several of these factors in previous chapters. In this chapter, we will discuss these factors in terms of how they impact personality.

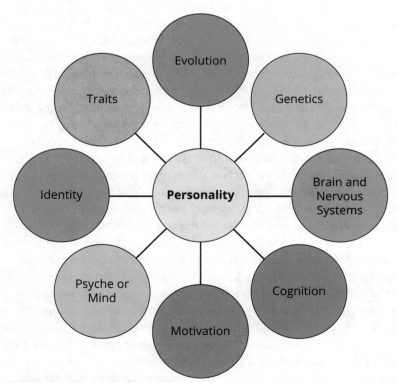

FIGURE 1 Factors that influence personality.

Adapted from Miserandino, M. & Porter, S. (2016). *Personality Psychology: Foundations and Findings*. Pearson Canada Inc.

So, how do researchers collect data on all these factors that make up our personality? Researchers who study personality use several diverse methods, such as:

- **Self-Report Tests:** It requires individuals to answer questions about themselves, most commonly used test, examples are the Big-Five Inventory.

- **Q-Sort Tests:** It requires individuals to sort a deck of cards based on how well each card describes them.

- **Judgments by Others:** It requires someone else (for example, parent, teacher, partner) to answer questions about an individual.

- **Biological Measures:** It requires specialized tests to examine physiology, such as electroencephalogram (EEG), positron emission tomography (PET) scan, magnetic resonance imagery (MRI), functional magnetic resonance imagery (fMRI), hormonal levels, and chromosomal analysis.

- **Behavioural Observations:** It requires someone to watch the behaviour of an individual.

- **Interviews:** It requires individuals to answer questions that are being asked verbally, can be unstructured (no predetermined set questions), or structured (set of predetermined questions).

- **Expressive Behaviour:** It requires the analysis of individuals' behaviours, such as posture, speech rate, and gestures.

- **Document Analysis:** It requires the analysis of individuals' written work.

- **Projective Tests:** It requires individuals to interpret or explain ambiguous stimuli, examples are Draw-a-person test, Rorschach Inkblot, and Thematic Apperception Test (TAT).

- **Demographics and Lifestyle:** It requires the analysis of individuals' demographics, such as age, family, and occupation (Baird & McCarthy, 2014; Miserandino & Porter, 2016).

The use of specific methods to examine personality will vary depending on a researcher's theoretical understanding or belief about how personality is formed. Figure 1 illustrates the different factors that play a role in personality and some of the ways personality can be viewed. We will look at some key theoretical models or conceptualizations of personality.

Practice...

1. _____ can be thought of the distinctive and consistent way each of us thinks, feels, and interacts with others and the world around us.
   a. Behaviour
   b. Personality
   c. Consciousness
   d. Learning

2. The Idiographic Approach focuses on the:
   a. individual and differences across individuals, with the goal of understanding how all parts of our personality form our unique selves.
   b. general themes, principles, and patterns that exist across individuals, with the goal of understanding relationships among common personality characteristics.
   c. specialized tests required to examine physiology.
   d. use of projective tests.

3. Personality is made up of which of the following factors?
   a. Cognition
   b. Motivation
   c. Identity
   d. All of the above are correct

4. Marley is asked to answer questions about her partner. This is an example of the use of _____ to understand personality.
   a. Q-sorts
   b. biological methods
   c. judgments of others
   d. interviews

5. _____ is the most common method used to study personality.
   a. Projective tests
   b. Q-sorts
   c. Self-Report tests
   d. Interviews

Apply...

1. **Your Personality**
   Describe your personality.

   _____

   _____

   _____

   _____

   _____

   _____

   _____

   _____

   _____

   _____

   _____

to be continued

Apply...

continued

_____

2. **Personality We Admire**

   • Describe the personality of someone you admire, look up to, or respect.

_____

to be continued

 **Apply...**

continued

- In what ways is your personality similar and different to the personality of the individual you described above.

_____
_____
_____
_____
_____
_____
_____
_____
_____
_____
_____
_____
_____
_____
_____
_____
_____
_____
_____
_____
_____
_____
_____
_____
_____
_____
_____
_____
_____

Trait Theories of Personality

L02 List the trait theories of personality

One of the most common perspectives on the formation of personality is the trait theory. **Traits** refer to our typical or usual way of thinking, feeling, and behaving. Traits are consistent and are measured on a continuum from low to high. The difficultly with assessing traits lies in the fact that they cannot be directly measured. There are several trait theories that attempt to explain personality. Let's look at some of them next (Baird & McCarthy, 2014; Miserandino & Porter, 2016).

Gordon Allport and H. S. Odbert (1936)

- First trait theory
- Identified almost 18 000 traits
- Allport proposed a three-tiered hierarchy of personality of traits (Figure 2):

  ◊ Cardinal: Single trait that completely dominates a personality

  ◊ Central: Influences behaviour, present in different levels or strengths in all people

  ◊ Secondary: Less important, less consistently displayed

Raymond Cattell (1965)

- Earliest well-known trait theory
- Condensed Alloport and Odbdert's 18 000 traits into 170 distinct adjectives
- Identified 16 distinct personality dimensions using statistical analyses (factor analysis):

  ◊ Warmth

  ◊ Reasoning

  ◊ Emotional Stability

  ◊ Dominance

  ◊ Liveliness

  ◊ Rule-Consciousness

  ◊ Social Boldness

  ◊ Sensitivity

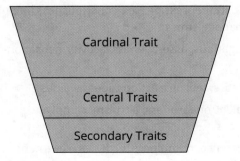

FIGURE 2 Allport's three-tiered hierarchy of personality of traits.

◊ Vigilance

◊ Abstractedness

◊ Privateness

◊ Apprehension

◊ Openness to Change

◊ Self-Reliance

◊ Perfectionism

◊ Tension

- Developed personality assessment called 16 PF (where PF stands for personality factors)

Hans Eysenck (1967)

- Initially, saw personality has two central dimensions:

  ◊ Emotional stability versus instability/neuroticism

  ◊ Extraversion versus introversion

- Later added a third dimension: socialization versus psychoticism

- Known as the PEN model of personality

- Focused on physiological and genetic evidence for his theory

- Where we landed on the continuums for these traits would determine our personality:

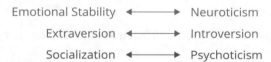

- Believed that physiology and genetics play major roles in personality

Robert McCrae and Paul Costa (1985)

- Simplified Cattell's 16 traits

- Five factors of personality = Big five or five factor model of Personality

  ◊ Neuroticism

  ◊ Extraversion

  ◊ Openness

  ◊ Agreeableness

  ◊ Conscientiousness

- Each trait has six facets:

  ◊ Neuroticism: Anxiety, hostility, depression, self-consciousness, impulsiveness, poor ability to manage stress

  ◊ Extraversion: Warmth, gregarious, assertiveness, activity, sensation-seeking, positive emotions

  ◊ Openness: Fantasy, aesthetics, feelings, actions, ideas, values

  ◊ Agreeableness: Trust, straightforwardness, altruism, compliance, modesty, tender-mindedness

  ◊ Conscientiousness: Competence, dutifulness, order, achievement-seeking, self-discipline, deliberation

- Traits reflect genetics and environmental factors

Auke Tellegen and Niels Waller (1987)

- Big Seven Model
- Similar to Big Five Model
- Addition of two factors represents how we evaluate ourselves
  - ◊ Negative Valence: Negative views of self
  - ◊ Positive Valence: Positive views of self
- Sees these valences as independent of Big five
- Reflects culture and language

Kibeom Lee and Michael Ashton (2004)

- Six factors of personality
- HEXACO Model:
  - ◊ Five factors similar to Five-Factor model
  - ◊ Sixth factor of Honesty/Humility added
- Reflects cultural or societal differences
- Believed to be redundant by some critics
- Several revisions to original model

Janek Musek (2007)

- Personality factors determined by Big five can be combined into a single super-factor—General Factor of Personality (GFP)
- High GFP indicates a person with high extraversion, openness, agreeableness, and conscientiousness, and low neuroticism
- Scoring high in GFP indicates an evolutionarily adaptive personality

Practice...

1. Gordon Allport became one of the first theorists to attempt to identify the basic human personality traits by creating a "trait dictionary". About how many trait descriptors were included in that dictionary?
   a. 246
   b. 1280
   c. 9700
   d. 18 000

2. Based on his research and his re-working of Allport's list of 18 000 personality descriptors, Raymond Cattell identified _____ different personality traits.
   a. 16
   b. 5
   c. 70
   d. 25

3. Which of the following personality traits is not contained in the five-factor model?
   a. Extraversion/introversion
   b. Conscientiousness/undirectedness
   c. Altruism/selfishness
   d. Openness to experience/non-openness

4. Marietta is always on-time for class, makes sure to do her reading the night before so that she will be ready for the class lectures and discussions, and writes her papers and assignments well ahead of the due dates so that she can bring them to the teacher's office hours to make sure that she has done a good job before submitting her work. Which of the following factors from the Big Five theory would Marietta be rated highly on?
   a. Agreeableness
   b. Emotional stability
   c. Extraversion
   d. Conscientiousness

5. All of the following can be viewed as revisions to the BIG five except _____.
   a. General Factor of Personality Model
   b. PEN Model
   c. Big Seven Model
   d. HEXACO Model

Apply...

1. **Big Five Traits**

   Define each of the traits that make up the BIG five and provide an example for each trait.

   _____

   _____

   _____

   _____

   _____

   _____

   _____

   _____

   to be continued

Apply...

continued

to be continued

 **Apply…**

continued

2. **Living Space and Personality**

    Watch the following video by Sam Gosling, "Snoop: The Secret Language of Stuff"
    http://library.fora.tv/2008/06/16/Sam_Gosling-Snoop_The_Secret_Language_of_Stuff

    Reflect on your current living space. What do you think your living space reveals about your personality traits?

    Source: Video by Sam Gosling, "Snoop: The Secret Language of Stuff" Fora TV.

_____

_____

_____

_____

_____

_____

_____

_____

_____

_____

_____

_____

_____

_____

_____

_____

_____

_____

_____

_____

_____

_____

to be continued

 **Apply...**

continued

Using two of the trait theories discussed, rate yourself as high or low on each trait based on what you have learned about the connection between living space and personality. Provide an explanation for your decisions.

_____

_____

_____

_____

_____

_____

_____

_____

_____

_____

_____

_____

_____

_____

_____

_____

_____

_____

_____

_____

_____

_____

_____

_____

Intrapsychic Theories of Personality

LO3 Explain the key principles behind the personality theories proposed by Freud and Jung

You will remember that we discussed the theories of Sigmund Freud and Carl Jung in Chapter 6 on Consciousness. Both Freud and Jung proposed **intrapsychic** models to explain personality. Intrapsychic refers to processes that occur in our mind, which is also referred to as our psyche. Both their theories noted processes that occur at different levels of our consciousness. In this unit, we will look again at the theories proposed by Freud and Jung in terms of how they attempt to explain personality.

Sigmund Freud

- Proposed a psychodynamic theory of personality
- Believed that that our past, especially our childhood, formed the basis of our personality
- He provided counselling to individuals and used that clinical information to formulate a stage theory of development.
- At each stage of development, we must successfully accomplish a goal:
  ◊ Our personality is influenced by the developmental goals we accomplish and by those that we do not meet.
  ◊ When we accomplish a developmental goal, we develop positive memories of that time in our lives and of that task. We move on to the next stage of development fully.
  ◊ If we are unable to accomplish or meet a goal at a given stage, or if the process of accomplishing the task is difficult, then we become **fixated,** or stuck in that stage. Our memories of that time in our lives and of that task are more negative. We do move on to the next developmental task, but still carry unresolved issues, challenges, etc. from the goal we did not meet or did not meet in a positive way. This is where terms like "orally fixated" or "anally fixated" came from. How do you think personality may be affected by being fixated or stuck in a stage of development? An example is a person who is rigid, overly neat, compulsive, uptight, etc.—he/she would be considered anally retentive or fixated at the anal stage. During this stage, we must develop control over our body. Failing to do so, could cause a person's psyche to remain in that stage leading a person to try to exercise control in other ways.
  ◊ Freud's theory of development is referred to a Theory of Psychosexual Development (Table 10.1):

TABLE 10.1 Freud's Theory of psychosexual development.

Stage	Age Range	Task
Oral	Birth to 18 months	Weaning
Anal	18 months to 3 years	Toilet training
Phallic	3–7 years	Sexual identity
Latency	7–12 years (or onset of puberty)	Gaining knowledge and skills
Genital	12 years to adult	Satisfying intimate relationships

- You will remember from Chapter 6 on Consciousness, that Freud believed our personality consisted of three parts: Id, ego, and superego

- As a reminder:

  ◊ Id = basic, biological needs and urges, more "animalistic" drives, driven by pleasure principle = immediate gratification

  ◊ Superego = moral, ethical guide

  ◊ Ego = the part the world sees, acts as a "referee" between Id and ego, driven by reality principle = delayed gratification until it is socially acceptable or appropriate

- The ego has a difficult job as it must meet the needs of the Id and super-ego. This puts a lot of stress and discomfort on the ego.

- Freud believed that we need to protect the ego. If we do not protect the ego then it will become damaged and mental illness will result.

- Freud believed that we protect the ego by developing **defence mechanisms**, which are unconscious strategies that protect the ego from the damage that can arise from the conflicts between the Id and superego. Defence mechanisms keep unconscious thoughts and motivations that are unpleasant or painful from entering our consciousness and potentially damaging our ego. Some defence mechanisms are:

  ◊ Denial

  ◊ Repression

  ◊ Projection

  ◊ Displacement

  ◊ Regression

  ◊ Sublimation

  ◊ Intellectualization

  ◊ Rationalization

  ◊ Reaction formation

  ◊ Suppression

- We are not always aware of our true motives or intentions because they are unconscious. But, when defence mechanisms breakdown, pieces of our unconscious motives, intentions, conflicts, desires, etc. may surface. Freud believed that this is what happens when we have a "slip-of-the-tongue" or when we dream (refer to your dream analysis from Chapter 6 on Consciousness)

- So, our personality is formed through our childhood and past experiences, our ability to meet developmental milestones, and our ego's ability to remain strong as it navigates through the conflicts between the Id and superego.

Carl Jung

- As a reminder:

  ◊ Supporter of Freud; unconscious plays a role in personality

  ◊ Our psyche is made of three main interacting parts:

    ■ Ego: Conscious part of who we are

    ■ Unconscious: Two parts: the personal unconscious, which is similar to what Freud believed along with containing complexes, which are beliefs and memories of specific concepts, derived from personal experience; and the collective unconscious, which consists of our innate, shared predispositions, beliefs, and memories that all humans have due to our common evolutionary experiences

- Key concepts:
  ◊ We engage in two processes:
    - Perceiving (P) = Taking in information from the world
      □ Done through senses (S) or through intuition (N)
    - Judging (J) = making sense, organizing, understanding, and making decisions about the information we take in from the world
      □ Done through thinking rationally (T) or by feelings (F)
  ◊ He believed that some of us do more perceiving than judging while others do more judging than perceiving; some do more sensing than intuiting; some do more thinking than feeling
  ◊ We get energy either by the external world, referred to as extraversion (E), or by our internal world, referred to as introversion (I). He believed that some of us prefer to get energy from the external world, while others prefer their internal world. This preference for extraversion or introversion forms the dominant part of our personality.
  ◊ These preferences combine to create our personality type:
    - Extraverted Sensing
    - Introverted Sensing
    - Extraverted Intuition
    - Introverted Intuition
    - Extraverted Thinking
    - Introverted Thinking
    - Extraverted Feeling
    - Introverted Feeling
- Katharine Cook Briggs and Isabel Briggs Myers created the Myers–Briggs Type Indicator (MBTI) based on Jung's theory
  ◊ Included all preferences: Extroverted versus Introverted, Sensing versus Intuition, Thinking versus Feeling, and Perceiving versus Judgment
  ◊ Now, 16 possible personality profiles
- One of your activities for this unit will be to complete a personality test to learn your four-letter personality type.
- Psychodynamic approaches to personality often use projective tests.

Practice...

1. _____ follows the _____ principle.
   a. Id, pleasure
   b. Id, reality
   c. Ego, pleasure
   d. Superego, reality

2. What is the purpose of a defence mechanism from the psychodynamic perspective?
   a. To make sure that we make rational decisions that are based on reason and logic.
   b. To make sure that people who are negative and can have a negative effect on our lives are kept outside of our consciousness.
   c. To keep unpleasant thoughts and motivations in our unconscious mind.
   d. To keep us from developing psychological pathologies that can cause problems in our lives.

3. If the Id acts like a child, then the _____ acts like a parent.
   a. ego
   b. superego
   c. defence mechanism
   d. unconscious

4. Jung believed that the dominant force in our personality is whether we _____.
   a. make decisions based on thinking or feeling
   b. rely on intuition to learn about the world
   c. prefer to perceive rather than judge the world
   d. get energized by others or by our internal self

5. Based on Jung's theory, how many personality profiles are possible?
   a. 8
   b. 12
   c. 16
   d. 20

 Apply...

1. **Defence Mechanisms**

- Choose three defence mechanisms. Write a definition of each and provide an example for each defence mechanism.

_____

_____

_____

_____

_____

_____

_____

_____

_____

_____

_____

_____

_____

- Reflect on your use of defence mechanisms. Which ones have you used? Did you find defence mechanisms helpful or harmful to your well-being? Explain your answer.

_____

_____

_____

_____

_____

_____

_____

_____

_____

_____

_____

_____

to be continued

 **Apply...**

continued

2. **Personality According to Freud**

For each stage of Freud's Psychosexual Development model, list the types of personality characteristics that may result if an individual (i) successfully accomplishes the task and (ii) fails to complete the task, or completes it with difficulty. You may have to do some research to answer fully.

Stage	Task	Personality Characteristics	
		Successfully Completed with little or no difficulty	Difficulty in completing or Does not complete
Oral	Weaning		
Anal	Toilet training		
Phallic	Sexual identity		
Latency	Gaining knowledge and skills		
Genital	Satisfying intimate relationships		

3. **The Four-Letter Personality Profile**

- Locate a free online personality test based on Jung and the Myers-Brigg (for example, "16 Personalities", "Jung personality test at 123 Test").

_____

_____

_____

_____

_____

_____

_____

_____

to be continued

 # Apply...

continued

- Take the test and determine your four-letter personality profile.

_____

_____

_____

_____

_____

_____

_____

_____

- What is your four-letter personality profile?

_____

_____

_____

_____

_____

_____

_____

_____

- What does your personality profile mean? You will need to look this up either on the website you used to complete the test, or by using other websites or resources.

_____

_____

_____

_____

_____

_____

_____

to be continued

Apply...

continued

- Based on your personality profile, what careers are you best suited for?

_____

_____

_____

_____

_____

_____

_____

_____

_____

_____

_____

_____

_____

- What does your personality profile say about your social relationships, such as friendships, parenting, and romantic relationships?

_____

_____

_____

_____

_____

_____

_____

_____

_____

_____

_____

_____

Biological and Social-Cognitive Theories of Personality

L04 Discuss the major biological and social-cognitive theories of personality

Now, we will look at some of the biological and social-cognitive theories of personality.

Biological Theories

As previously noted, Eysenck believed that difference across individuals in their level of physiological arousal, and specifically level of alertness, was the cause of differences in the reticular formation, across extroverts and introverts:

- Extroverts = less sensitive to stimuli, do not have level of arousal needed, so seek out or remain in stimulating situations to increase arousal
- Introverts = more sensitive to stimuli, have all arousal needed so minimize or even avoid stimuli so do not become over stimulated

Jeffery Gray

- Built on Eysenck's proposed explanation
- Proposed three personality dimensions:
  - GO System: Behavioural Activation System (BAS)
    - Responsible for "approach behaviour"
    - Leads us to engage in behaviours when we think there will be a reward
    - Responsible for positive emotions
    - High BAS leads to impulsivity
  - STOP System: Behavioural Inhibition System (BIS)
    - Responsible for inhibiting approach behaviour or avoiding behaviours
    - Leads us to engage in behaviours when we think there will be a punishment
    - Responsible for negative emotions
    - High BAS leads to anxiety
  - Fight-Flight-Freeze System (FFFS):
    - Responsible for reactions to conditioned and unconditioned (that is, learned or unlearned) stimuli that is aversive or fearful
    - Avoidance and escape behaviours
  - Do you remember what kind of learning is based on reward and punishment? If not, please review Chapter 7 on Learning.
  - Theory known as reinforcement sensitivity theory

Social-Cognitive Theories

1. **Julian Rotter (1954)**
   - Believed there was a connection between a person's sense of personal control and personality

- Our behaviour changes depending on how much control we think we have in a given situation = **locus of control**

    ◊ Internal locus of control: We control our own rewards, we are in control of our future

    ◊ External locus of control: Others, people and/or forces, control our rewards and our future

    ◊ An internal locus of control = Do better at school, more proactive in looking after their health, less anxious, more content with life

2. **Martin Seligman**

    - **Learned Helplessness**

        ◊ If we are consistently unable to control events in our life, we may eventually develop a sense of hopelessness and may "give up" because we believe our efforts will not change our circumstance.

        ◊ Tied to depression

        ◊ Think about how this would impact personality

    - **Explanatory Style** (how we view or explain things):

        ◊ Developed a questionnaire to examine how people explain negative events in their lives:

            ■ Optimistic explanatory style: Bad things are not my fault, unlikely to happen again, if something bad happens it just impacts one area of my life; cope better with negative events

            ■ Pessimistic explanatory style: Bad things are my fault and they will happen again, if something bad happens it impacts all areas of my life; poor coping with negative events

3. **Albert Bandura**

    - You will remember that we discussed Albert Bandura in Chapter 7 on Learning

    - Proposed the theory of Reciprocal Determinism (Figure 3)

    - Our personalities are made up of:

        ◊ Our cognitive processes, external environments, and behaviours

        ◊ All the interactions among our cognitive processes, external environments, and behaviours

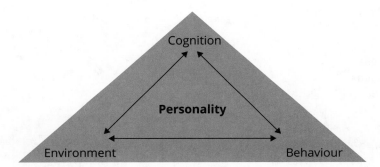

FIGURE 3 Bandura's theory of reciprocal determinism.

- Also proposed that **self-efficacy**, our belief in our ability to perform a task, influenced personality:
  - ◊ ↑ self-efficacy = ↑ belief we can do something
  - ◊ ↓ self-efficacy = ↓ belief we can do something

In this chapter, we discussed some of the most influential and well-known theories of personality (Baird & McCarthy, 2014; Miserandino & Porter, 2016). We focused on trait, intrapsychic, biological, and social-cognitive perspectives. There are other perspectives on personality. You will have a chance to research some of these in your activity for this unit.

 # Practice...

1. The _____ system is a part of the brain that stimulates approach behaviour in response to the anticipation of a reward.
   a. reticular activating
   b. cerebellar inhibition
   c. behavioural inhibition
   d. behavioural activating

2. While sitting in her class getting ready for her mid-term exam, Paris was full of anxiety. She whispered to her friend "I studied and studied, but I know I'm just going to fail this test." According to Julian Rotter, Paris has a(n) _____ locus of control.
   a. deficient
   b. unstable
   c. internal
   d. external

3. Perhaps you've read a difficult story about a person who was in an abusive relationship for an extended period of time. Perhaps you've also wondered, even momentarily, "Why did the person stay in such a relationship?" Which theory would do the best job of explaining why people stay in abusive relationships?
   a. The theory of Freudian defence mechanisms
   b. The theory of learned helplessness
   c. The theory of the hierarchy of needs
   d. The theory of the locus of control

4. Which of the following factors are not included in the theory of reciprocal determinism?
   a. Evolution
   b. Behaviour
   c. Environment
   d. Personal factors

5. _____ people tend to cope more effectively with negative events than do people who tend to be _____.
   a. internally oriented; externally oriented
   b. realistic; unrealistic
   c. optimistic; pessimistic
   d. ambitious; lazy

 **Apply...**

1. **Locus of Control**

   - Do you have an internal or external locus of control?

   _____

   _____

   _____

   _____

   _____

   _____

   _____

   _____

   _____

   - In what ways to do you think having this type of locus of control has been helpful in your life?

   _____

   _____

   _____

   _____

   _____

   _____

   _____

   _____

   _____

   - In what ways to do you think having this type of locus of control has been limiting or harmful in your life?

   _____

   _____

   _____

   _____

   _____

   _____

   _____

   _____

   _____

to be continued

Apply...

continued

2. **Other Theories of Personality**

   Research other theories of personality (for example, biochemical, humanistic approach, behavioural approach, self-determination approach, brain structures)

   Choose two of these theories and briefly summarize how they explain or conceptualize personality.

   _____

   _____

   _____

   _____

   _____

   _____

   _____

   _____

   _____

   _____

   _____

   _____

   _____

   _____

   _____

   _____

   _____

   _____

   _____

   _____

   _____

   _____

   _____

   _____

   _____

   _____

   _____

   _____

to be continued

 **Apply…**

continued

3. **Which theory is Best?**

   In this chapter, and in your activity above, you learned about some of the main theories that attempt to explain personality. Based on what you have learned, choose the one personality theory/model that you think best explains personality. Explain your choice.

   _____

   _____

   _____

   _____

   _____

   _____

   _____

   _____

   _____

   _____

   _____

   _____

   _____

   _____

   _____

   _____

KNOW…

Learning Objectives

1. Five research methods used to study personality:
You can list any five methods. Examples include:

- Self-Report Tests
- Judgments by Others
- Biological Measures
- Behavioural Observations
- Interviews
- Expressive Behaviour

2. Trait theories of personality:

Trait theories include:

- Allport and Odbert's three-tiered hierarchy of personality of traits
- Cattell's 16 PF
- Eysenck's PEN model of personality
- McCrae and Costa's Big Five
- Tellegen and Waller's Big Seven Model
- Lee and Ashton's: HEXACO Model
- Musek's General Factor of Personality (GFP)

3. Key principles behind the personality theories proposed by Freud and Jung:

- **Freud:** Personality made up of Id, Ego, and Superego. Our personality is formed through our childhood and past experiences, our ability to meet developmental milestones, and our ego's ability to remain strong as it navigates through the conflicts between the Id and superego.

- **Jung:** Our personality is created by how we get energy (external versus internal sources), how we take in information (through senses versus intuition), and how we make decisions (rational thinking versus feeling). This creates 8 possible personality types. With expansion from Myers-Briggs, it is now 16 personality profiles.

4. Major biological and social-cognitive theories of personality:

- Biological Theories

  ◊ **Eysenck's PEN Theory:** Believed that extroverts were less sensitive to stimuli and would seek out stimulating situations to increase arousal, whereas introverts were more sensitive to stimuli and would minimize stimuli so do not become over stimulated

  ◊ **Gray's Reinforcement Sensitivity Theory:** GO System (BAS: approach behaviour, reward driven, positive emotions, high BAS = impulsive), STOP System (BIS: inhibit approach behaviour, punishment avoidance, negative emotions, high BIS = anxious), and Fight-Flight-Freeze System (FFFS: reactions to fear, avoid or escape)

- Social-Cognitive Theories:

  ◊ **Rotter's Locus of Control Theory:** Internal locus of control (we control our own rewards, we are in control of our future) versus external locus of control (others, people and/or forces, control our rewards and our future) is foundation of personality.

  ◊ **Martin Seligman's Learning Helplessness and Explanatory Style Theories:** Having control over our life events and circumstances and how we view negative events (optimistically versus pessimistically) impacts personality.

  ◊ **Albert Bandura's Reciprocal Determinism and Self-Efficacy Theories:** Our personalities are made up of our cognitive processes, external environments, and behaviours, and all their reciprocal interactions, and our belief in our ability to perform a task (self-efficacy) influences our personality.

Key Terms

Personality: The distinctive and consistent way each of us thinks, feels, and interacts with others and the world around us.

Idiographic Approach: An approach to studying personality that focuses on the differences across individuals.

Nomothetic Approach: An approach to studying personality that focuses on general themes, principles, and patterns that exist across individuals.

Traits: Our typical or usual way of thinking, feeling, and behaving.

Intrapsychic: Processes that occur in our mind/psyche.

Fixated: Being stuck.

Defence Mechanisms: Unconscious strategies that protect the ego from damage that can occur if unpleasant or painful thoughts and motivations move into consciousness.

Locus of Control: How much control we think we have in a given situation.

Learned Helplessness: A belief that our efforts will not change our circumstance.

Explanatory Style: How we view or explain things.

Self-Efficacy: Our belief in our ability to perform a task.

Answers to Practice

What Is Personality?
1. b   2. a   3. d   4. c   5. c

Trait Theories of Personality
1. d   2. a   3. c   4. d   5. b

Intrapsychic Theories of Personality
1. a   2. c   3. b   4. d   5. a

Biological and Social-Cognitive Theories of Personality
1. d   2. d   3. b   4. a   5. c

References

American Psychological Association. (2017). *Personality*. Retrieved from http://www.apa.org/topics/personality/.

Baird, A., & McCarthy, A. (2014). *THINK psychology* (2nd Canadian edition). Don Mills, ON: Pearson Education, Inc.; pp. 217–227.

Miserandino, M. & Porter, S. (2016). *Personality psychology: foundations and findings*. Pearson Canada Inc.

Our Social World

LEARNING OBJECTIVES

LO1 List key principles of attachment

LO2 Identify two key developmental activities that occur in childhood, adolescence, and adulthood

LO3 Discuss two processes we use during social perception

LO4 Define conformity, compliance, and obedience and provide an example of each

LO5 Explain how stereotypes and discrimination can develop

LEARN...

Humans are social beings, and in this chapter we take a look at our social world. We look at some key aspects of our social development, how we understand and respond to others, and how we influence others. We begin by discussing the general processes of socialization through which we develop socially appropriate behaviour. Our first social experiences are usually with our caregivers, and we form attachments to them. The attachments that we form in infancy impact future relationships and interactions throughout our lives. As we move from infancy to childhood, we spend more time with peers and engage in play. Play is important in the development of language, imagination, physical abilities, and moral understanding. In adolescence, we are involved with cliques, our close-knit group of friends, and crowds, our larger social group, and we face challenges surrounding self-esteem, sexual activity, and drug use. In adulthood, we focus on committed relationships, having children, and career advancement. As we enter old age, we may strengthen our relationships or withdraw from our social world. In this chapter, we outline Erikson's theory of social development and Kholberg's theory of moral development. We then explore the way we perceive others and our social world, referred to as social perception. One key part of social perception is face recognition, which is so important that from birth we prefer to look at human faces over other stimuli. We also use non-verbal behaviours, such as eye contact when perceiving others. When making judgments about others, we attribute their behaviour either to internal dispositions (for example, personality, feelings) or to external situations (for example, work, family). However, we can fall victim to the fundamental attribution error, when we attribute someone's behaviour to internal dispositions even when we know that it is situationally caused. Conversely, the self-serving bias is our tendency to attribute our own negative behaviours to situational causes and our positive behaviours to internal causes. There are times in our social interactions when we try to influence others through conformity, compliance, or obedience. These strategies underlie the power of persuasion. In this chapter, we also revisit humans as emotional beings. For example, one reason negative social interactions occurs is because of another person's prejudice. Prejudice is a learned negative perception, belief, or attitude directed towards specific people or groups. We are not always aware of our prejudice. Prejudice can lead to aggression. However, most of our social interactions are positive, and we may engage in cooperation or altruism.

Social Development: Attachment and Erikson's Stage Theory

L01 List key principles of attachment

Humans are social beings. In previous chapters, we have discussed the many ways that we are social—learning, thinking, behaving, and so on. Social psychologists study the social world of humans and animals. In this chapter, we look at our social world a little closer. Let us start with how we develop into social beings—Social Development. We start the **socialization** process when we are born. It is through the process of socialization that we develop socially appropriate behaviour. You can see then that socialization would vary across cultures.

The first social experiences we have are usually with our caregivers. Through these interactions, we develop an emotional bond with our caregivers, which is called **attachment**. Our caregivers also develop an emotional bond to us, which is called **bonding**. The attachment that we form in infancy directly impacts the relationships and interactions we have throughout our lives. Let us take a look at the key principles of attachment.

Attachment

1. **John Bolby**
   - First proposed term "attachment"
   - Believed that instinct drove behaviours between infants and caregivers
   - Goal was survival
     ◊ Example: Stranger anxiety develops around 8 months of age to keep baby safe by creating fear or apprehension around people they do not recognize

2. **Harry Harlow**
   - Studied attachment using infant monkeys and their mothers
   - Found that infant monkeys seek out comfort from caregiver
   - Attachment forms based on comfort and not because caregiver provides food
   - Touch provides a way for infants and caregivers to communicate, to share, and respond to emotion

3. **Mary Ainsworth**
   - Developed the "strange situation" test
     ◊ Infant is briefly separated from mother and left to play in a new environment under a stranger's supervision.
     ◊ Look at how infant responds to mothers' return

- Based on the strange situation, Ainsworth found different types of attachment (Baird & McCarthy, 2014):
  ◊ **Secure Attachment:** Infant happy to play in new environment while mother was present, became upset when she left, but were soon comforted by parental contact upon mother's return; mother was warm, loving, and responsive to infant's needs; most infants develop secure attachment; this is the type of attachment we want.
  ◊ **Anxious-Ambivalent Attachment:** Infant not comfortable even with mother present, became distressed when she left, and were difficult to comfort even when she returned.
  ◊ **Anxious-Avoidant Attachment:** Infant not upset when mother left and actively ignored her when she returned.
  ◊ **Disorganized-Disoriented Attachment** (added by Mary Main and Erik Hesse): Infant was confused, wandered around, or froze when mother returned; lacked consistent pattern of coping.
- Mothers who were unresponsive or insensitive had anxious and insecure children (anxious-ambivalent or anxious-avoidant).
- Experiencing trauma, fear, or abuse can lead to disorganized-disoriented attachment.

Our attachment to our caregivers forms our first relationships. This stage in our social development corresponds well to the first stage in Erik Erikson's Theory of Social Development. According to Erikson, social development occurs through a series of stages. At each stage, we experience a crisis and we must accomplish a task in order to resolve the crisis.

4. **Erik Erikson's Theory of Social Development**
   - Stage 1:
     ◊ Crisis = TRUST versus MISTRUST
     ◊ Age = Birth to 1 year of age
     ◊ Task = Learn to develop trust
   - Stage 2:
     ◊ Crisis = AUTONOMY versus SHAME AND DOUBT
     ◊ Age = 1–2 years of age
     ◊ Task = Learn to be independent
   - Stage 3:
     ◊ Crisis = INITIATIVE versus GUILT
     ◊ Age = 3–5 years of age
     ◊ Task = Learn to be take responsibility for behaviour and to demonstrate initiative
   - Stage 4:
     ◊ Crisis = COMPENTENCE versus. INFERIORITY
     ◊ Age = 6 years of age to onset of puberty
     ◊ Task = Develop new skills and acquire knowledge
   - Stage 5:
     ◊ Crisis = IDENTITY versus ROLE CONFUSION
     ◊ Age = Adolescence to 20s
     ◊ Task = Develop a sense of identity

- Stage 6:
    - ◊ Crisis = INTIMACY versus ISOLATION
    - ◊ Age = 20s to early 40s
    - ◊ Task = Establish close, healthy relationships
- Stage 7:
    - ◊ Crisis = Generativity versus STAGNATION
    - ◊ Age = 40s to early 60s
    - ◊ Task = Develop a sense of purpose, look to mentor, and guide future generations
- Stage 8:
    - ◊ Crisis = EGO INTEGRITY versus DISPAIR
    - ◊ Age = 60s and older
    - ◊ Task = Develop a sense of satisfaction and contentment with your life

 # Practice...

1. As Enrique grows up from childhood to adolescence and then to adulthood, he is constantly receiving messages about how he should think, feel, and act. He gets these messages from his parents, siblings, friends, school, church, and from various media sources (television, radio, internet, etc). The way in which his behaviours are shaped by his surroundings is called _____.
   a. cognitization
   b. maturation
   c. socialization
   d. normalization

2. The emotional bond that an infant develops towards caregiver(s) is called _____.
   a. bonding
   b. paternity
   c. affective link
   d. attachment

3. John Bowlby believed that attachment between a child and caregiver develops out of _____.
   a. instinct
   b. love
   c. necessity
   d. fear

4. Young Finn is being observed as he plays in a room with his mother. Finn frequently goes to the toys in the room, but occasionally looks back at his mother to make sure she is there. After a quick smile is exchanged between mother and child, Finn goes back to the task of building with the toys. When Finn's mother leaves the room, he becomes moderately upset, but is easily soothed when she returns. Which type of attachment does Finn seem to have with his mother?
   a. Ambivalent
   b. Secure
   c. Interdependent
   d. Avoidant

5. Who is in Erikson's competence versus inferiority stage?
   a. Jing Mei, who is 4 years old and who always volunteers to turn the pages during storytime at her preschool.
   b. Thalia, who is 2 years old and who can reach her sippy cup on the counter without help from her mom or dad.
   c. Ashley, who is 7 years old and who is learning how to tie her shoelaces.
   d. Ethan, who is 20 years old and who desperately wants a partner.

Apply...

1. **The Power of Touch**

   Research the importance of touch in attachment. You may use the internet, peer-reviewed journals, textbooks, etc.

   Write a summary of what you learned.

   _____
   _____
   _____
   _____
   _____
   _____
   _____
   _____
   _____
   _____
   _____
   _____
   _____
   _____

   What are the implications for caregivers?

   _____
   _____
   _____
   _____
   _____
   _____
   _____
   _____
   _____
   _____
   _____
   _____

   to be continued

 Apply...

continued

2. **Culture and Attachment**

Research the relationship between culture and attachment. You may use the internet, peer-reviewed journals, textbooks, etc.

Write a summary of what you learned.

_____

_____

_____

_____

_____

_____

_____

_____

_____

_____

_____

_____

_____

_____

_____

_____

_____

_____

_____

_____

_____

_____

_____

_____

_____

_____

_____

_____

_____

to be continued

 **Apply...**

continued

3. **Erikson versus Freud**

    Now that you have learned about Freud and Erikson's theories of development, you may have noticed some similarities and differences across these theories.

    Please compare (how are the theories similar) and contrast (how are the theories different) these two influential theories of development.

    _____

    _____

    _____

    _____

    _____

    _____

    _____

    _____

    _____

    _____

    _____

    _____

    _____

    _____

    _____

    _____

    _____

    _____

    _____

    _____

    _____

    _____

    _____

    _____

    _____

    _____

    _____

    _____

Social Development: Some Key Activities from Childhood to Adulthood

 Identify two key developmental activities that occur in childhood, adolescence, and adulthood

To understand what aspects of social interaction are seen through our lifetime, it is helpful to have a general idea of development. Let us take a very quick look at some key aspects of social development.

Childhood

- We begin interacting with others around our own chronological age and developmental stage fairly early.
- Environments such as daycare, activity groups, and school provide opportunities for children to interact with peers.
- Early on we spend more time with peers than with our caregivers.
- Our early attachments to our caregivers and others will impact our relationships with peers.
- Erikson's stages 1–4.
- Play is most often with same-sex and same-aged children.
- Play helps children develop the skills they need later in life:
  - ◊ Language
  - ◊ Imagination
  - ◊ Physical abilities
  - ◊ Social rules
  - ◊ Self-regulation
  - ◊ Moral understanding
- Jean Piaget believed that unsupervised play with peers was key to moral development.
- Lawrence Kholberg developed a stage theory of moral development:
  - ◊ Preconventional Level: Punishment and Reward
    - ■ Stage 1: Obedience to authority
    - ■ Stage 2: Nice behaviour in exchange for future favours
    - ■ Children are at this level
  - ◊ Conventional Level: Social Norms
    - ■ Stage 3: Live up to other's expectations
    - ■ Stage 4: Follow rules to maintain social order
    - ■ Early adolescents and older individuals are at this level
  - ◊ Postconventional level: Moral Codes
    - ■ Stage 5: Adhere to a social contract when it is valid
    - ■ Stage 6: Personal moral system based on abstract principles
    - ■ Not everyone reaches this stage
    - ■ Cognitive development is tied closely to stages of moral development

Adolescence

- Remember from Erikson's model that this is the stage at which we are trying to develop an identity.
- Peers continue to play a key role:
  - ◊ Cliques: A small group of same-sex peers who have a close relationship and share details of their lives.
  - ◊ Crowds: A larger group of mixed-sex peers who participate in social activities together.
- Peer Pressure: The influence, positive or negative, of peers on our behaviour.
- Remember from past chapters that brain and cognitive development are rapid during adolescence.
- Issues of self-esteem are critical.
- Expressions of sexuality occur and sexual activity may begin.
- Drug use, mental health issues, rebellion, etc., may occur.

Adulthood

- Bernice Neugarten: There is a difference between chronological age and social age, which is based on our life experience
- Erikson's stages 6 and 7
- Infant attachment plays a role in our ability to form and maintain intimate relationships:
  - ◊ In adults, secure relationship is one in which both partners provide each other with comfort and security. Secure attachment in infancy helps with developing secure relationships in adulthood.
  - ◊ In adults, an anxious relationship is one in which there is concern about whether there is love from a partner.
  - ◊ In adults, an avoidant relationship is one in which there is ambivalence towards commitment and has little or no intimacy.
- Marriage, having children, and career development and stability often occurs in this stage of development.
- As we get older we may experience:
  - ◊ Increased health issues
  - ◊ Ageism: Bias against elderly
  - ◊ Social interactions can change:
    - Happiest when stay engaged and active, called the active theory of aging
    - Focus on present more than future
    - Marital satisfaction increases, relationships with children, grandchildren, and friends strengthen
    - Those who still work tend to maintain their social relationships from work
    - May disengage from social world in preparation for death, called the disengagement theory of aging (Baird & McCarthy, 2014)

Now that we have a general idea of some of the key developmental activities we engage in, we can look at other aspects of our social world, such as social perception, social influence, and social interaction.

Practice...

1. Jean Piaget argued that unsupervised play with peers is critical to the _____ development.
   a. cognitive
   b. moral
   c. social
   d. emotional

2. According to Erikson, which of the following persons would mostly likely be experiencing despair?
   a. 30-year-old Andy, who is convinced he is going to die a single man
   b. 45-year-old Andre, who feels he has not made a difference in the world
   c. 63-year-old Martina, who feels she has failed at everything her entire life
   d. 15-year-old Sloane, who cannot seem to decide who she really is

3. A _____ is a small, same-sex group of peers while a _____ is a large, mixed-sex group of peers.
   a. cohort; crowd
   b. clique; crowd
   c. cohort; clique
   d. crowd; clique

4. "Man, I cannot believe how smart David is! He is so much more intelligent than other kids his age, and he also seems to have a good head on his shoulders when it comes to making decisions. He is polite, doesn't get into trouble, and seems to naturally make good decisions. It is hard to believe he is only 13 years old!" According to Bernice Neugarten, David's _____ age appears to be well ahead of his _____ age.
   a. chronological; mental
   b. mental; social
   c. social; chronological
   d. chronological; social

5. Henry is 96 years old, and he remains very active. He still plays golf, although he only has the energy for 9 holes. He goes for walks every day, plays cards with others at the senior center, does his own shopping, and makes sure to get out to a movie at least once every few months. According to the _____ theory of aging, Henry will be happiest as long as he continues doing the things that he enjoys and is physically capable of doing.
   a. activity
   b. activation synthesis
   c. disengagement
   d. socioemotional selectivity

 **Apply...**

1. **Adolescence**

   Write a letter addressed to your teenage self. In your letter, tell your teenage self what you wish you had known, what you wish you had done and not done, and what you are proud of doing.

   In writing this letter, it will allow you to reflect on some of the key developmental milestones that you have achieved, and allow you to see how your experiences have helped to shape who you are today.

   _____
   _____
   _____
   _____
   _____
   _____
   _____
   _____
   _____
   _____
   _____
   _____
   _____
   _____
   _____
   _____
   _____
   _____
   _____
   _____
   _____
   _____
   _____
   _____
   _____
   _____

to be continued

 **Apply...**

continued

2. **Marriage**

How would you define a successful marriage?

_____
_____
_____
_____
_____
_____
_____
_____
_____
_____

What characteristics or qualities do you think a successful marriage has?

_____
_____
_____
_____
_____
_____
_____
_____

Discuss your answers with a classmate. How are your answers similar and different to those of your classmate?

_____
_____
_____
_____
_____
_____
_____
_____
_____

Social Perception

L03 Discuss two processes we use during social perception

Social perception refers to the way we see, understand, and interpret other people, our social interactions, and our social world. One key part of social perception is recognizing others—facial recognition. Face recognition is so important that from birth we prefer to look at human faces over other stimuli, and there are parts of the brain that have been identified as specializing in facial recognition (for example, fusiform face area). When we look at a face we are able to determine if it is a new face or one we have seen before. We are able to determine if the face we see is familiar or unfamiliar. This information influences our interactions with others, how we judge others, and how we act towards others.

We are also able to read the expressions that are presented on the face we see. Facial expression is one type of non-verbal behaviour. We use non-verbal behaviours, such as eye contact, facial expressions, and posture to perceive others. In Chapter 5 on Motivation and Emotion, we discussed facial expressions and the fact that some of these expressions are universal. We know that we are able to "read" these universal displays of emotion. But, what happens if those expressions do not actually match the presenter's true emotions or even their intentions? What if we smile when we are actually sad? This is called **masking**, which occurs when we show one emotion when we are actually feeling a different emotion. We can also exaggerate our expression so that the viewer thinks we are feeling a more intense feeling, a process called **intensification**, or we can do the opposite, called deintensification, to minimize the expression of our emotions. Finally, we can **neutralize** our expressions so that they do not demonstrate any emotion (Baird & McCarthy, 2014). Emotional expression and the perception of other's emotional expression is an important part of social perception. Emotional expression plays a key role in communication. For this reason, the better we are at accurately detecting and understanding emotional expressions, including deceptive ones, the better social perception we will have. It is also important to remember that the behaviour of others impacts our own behaviours!

There are other strategies that we use to help us understand others. Let us take a look at some of these.

Attribution Theory

- Proposed by Fritz Heider in the 1950s
- We attribute the behaviour of others either to their internal dispositions (for example, personality, feelings) or to their external situations (for example, work, family)
- We make attributions based on the covariation principle:
  ◊ Consensus: Would most people behave in the same way?
  ◊ Distinctiveness: Would the same person behave differently in other situations?
  ◊ Consistency: Does the individual respond in the same way to the same stimulus in different contexts? (Baird & McCarthy, 2014; Duff & Peace, 2013)
- **The Fundamental Attribution Error:**
  ◊ Our tendency to attribute someone's behaviour to internal dispositions even when we know that it is situationally caused

- We do not always have full information about a person, their behaviour, and the situations in which they occur. We rely on our previous knowledge, experiences, and beliefs in deciding attributions. However, this can lead to bias.
  - ◊ For example:
    - ■ **Attractiveness Bias** = We view physically attractive individuals more positively; we see them as being more honest, intelligent, competent, etc.
    - ■ **Beauty is Beastly Effect** = We negatively perceive attractive women; common in male-dominated professions and in political leadership (Baird & McCarthy, 2014).
- **Self-Serving Bias:**
  - ◊ The tendency to attribute our own negative behaviours to situational causes but our positive behaviours to internal causes
  - ◊ A way to keep our self-system: Self-esteem, self-concept, and self-efficacy positive (Baird and McCarthy, 2014; Duff & Peace, 2013).

It is clear that we are not always perfect in the ways we perceive others or ourselves.

 # Practice...

1. We do not always want our true emotions to show. All of the following are ways that we can modify our emotional expressions except _____.
   a. neutralize
   b. masking
   c. intensification
   d. all of the above are ways we can modify our emotional expressions

2. Wendy is walking down the street when she suddenly falls down and lands squarely on her backside. A group of girls standing about 50 feet away start laughing hysterically, telling each other what a klutz that Wendy is. The unsympathetic girls in this group are making a _____ attribution to explain why Wendy fell down.
   a. situational
   b. negative
   c. positive
   d. dispositional

3. A(n) _____ attribution is an attribution that is based on a person's surroundings or environment.
   a. environmental
   b. dispositional
   c. situational
   d. contextual

4. What is the basic underlying reason why we tend to make attributional mistakes?
   a. We generally do not pay enough attention to our surroundings, and thus miss essential information that would help us avoid attributional mistakes.
   b. We are generally quick to assume the worst of intents in other people, so this leads us to attributional mistakes.
   c. We don't have enough information to know why a person is behaving in a particular way, so we make rapid assumptions.
   d. We are more concerned with getting an attribution made quickly than getting it made correctly, and this causes us to make mistakes.

5. "Look at that guy, texting on his cell phone while he's driving. I can't believe how rude that is," Annabelle told her friend Mary. Mary was not in the car, however, and Annabelle was talking to her over a cell phone. This tendency to judge other people harshly but excuse ourselves for the same behaviour is an example of the _____.
   a. availability heuristic
   b. self-serving bias
   c. attractiveness bias
   d. fundamental attribution error

 **Apply...**

1. **Cues to Deception**

   - Do you think you can tell if someone is telling you a lie? Explain your answer.

   _____

   _____

   _____

   _____

   _____

   _____

   _____

   _____

   _____

   - Play two Truths and a Lie with a friend or classmate.

     Were you able to identify the lie you were told? Were they able to identify the lie you told?

   _____

   _____

   _____

   _____

   _____

   _____

   _____

   _____

     What strategies did you both use to identify the lie?

   _____

   _____

   _____

   _____

   _____

   _____

   _____

   _____

   _____

to be continued

 **Apply…**

continued

- Research cues to deception. You can use the internet, peer-reviewed journals, textbooks, etc. Remember to cite your sources.
  - ◊ List some cues to deception that have been identified.

  _____

  _____

  _____

  _____

  _____

  _____

  _____

  _____

  _____

  - ◊ What does the research tell us about our ability to detect lies?

  _____

  _____

  _____

  _____

  _____

  _____

  _____

2. **Attribution Theory and Culture**

   Research the connection between culture and attribution patterns. You can use the internet, peer-reviewed journals, textbooks, etc.

   - Provide a summary of your findings.

   _____

   _____

   _____

   _____

   _____

   _____

   _____

   _____

   _____

   _____

to be continued

Apply...

continued

- What do you think these findings tell us about the process of socialization?

_____
_____
_____
_____
_____
_____
_____
_____
_____
_____
_____
_____
_____
_____
_____

- Discuss your findings and thoughts with another classmate. Write the key points that arise from your discussion.

_____
_____
_____
_____
_____
_____
_____
_____
_____
_____
_____
_____
_____
_____
_____

Social Influence

LO4 Define conformity, compliance, and obedience and provide an example of each

So far, we have looked at our social development and our social perception. Next, we will look at the ways we can influence others. **Social influence** refers to the processes that occur when we attempt to change the behaviours, beliefs, attitudes, etc. of others. Social influence can lead to **social pressure**, which leads us to change our behaviour. What does this social pressure look like? Why are we motivated to change our behaviour, based on the influences of others? We may be influenced by an incentive for acting a certain way called the **hedonic motive,** or by a desire to be accepted by others, called the **approval motive,** or by a need to be correct, called the **accuracy motive**. In your activity for this unit, you will have an opportunity to reflect on these motives in your own life. So, we know that there are several motives that drive us to change based on the influence of others, but what is it that people are doing that lead us to believe that we need to change in the first place? Typically, we attempt to influence others through **conformity, compliance,** and **obedience**. Let's look at each of these a little closer.

Conformity

- A type of social influence in which behaviour change results from a need to adhere to or match social norms or expectations
  - ◊ Informational Social Influence: Driven by accuracy motive; look to others to get correct information
  - ◊ Normative Social Influence: Driven by approval motive; do what the group does so we will be accepted
- Solomon Asch's studies using the sizes of lines found that 1/3 of the time participants would change their answers to match the answers given by a group, showing that **suggestibility** (how susceptible we are to the opinions of others) is an effective social pressure that leads to conformity.
- Bystander effect:
  - ◊ We are less likely to help someone in need, if there are people around.
  - ◊ We look to the other people present and if they are not helping, then we do not help either—we conform to their inaction.
  - ◊ The bystander effect increases as the number of people present increases.
  - ◊ Why does this occur?
    - ■ When we are uncertain how to behave we look to our **reference group** (people we feel connected to) for guidance.
  - ◊ When we are in **total situations** where we are isolated from alternative viewpoints and given strict rewards and punishments from leaders, we tend to adhere to social norms.

Compliance

- A type of social influence in which behaviour change results from a direct request (verbal or non-verbal).
- Robert Cialdini proposed the following principles of compliance:
  - ◊ **Friendship or Liking:** Getting someone to like us so they comply with our request, called Ingratiation Technique

◇ **Commitment or Consistency:**

■ **Foot-in-the-Door Technique:** Start by making a small request to a person and when that person complies with the small request, you make a larger request.

■ **Lowball Technique:** Offer a person an attractive deal and when that person complies you change the terms of the deal later on; think: bait-and-switch

◇ **Scarcity:** Believing that something is rare, limited, or hard to get makes us want it more, and we are more likely to comply

◇ **Reciprocity:**

■ **Door-in-the-Face Technique:** Opposite of foot-in-the-door technique; start by making a large request to a person and when that person refuses the request you make a smaller request

■ **The That's-Not-All Technique:** We add something to an original offer which makes it seem more attractive

◇ **Social validation:** We are more likely to comply when requests come from others we view as similar to us.

◇ **Authority:** We are more likely to comply when requests come from people with authority, or who we view as having authority (Baird & McCarthy, 2014; Duff & Peace, 2013).

Obedience

- A type of social influence in which behaviour change results from following the requests of an authority figure.

- Stanley Milgram conducted research in this area. You will look at his famous experiment in detail in your activity for this unit.

- Factors affecting obedience (Baird & McCarthy, 2014):

  ◇ Proximity of person giving orders

  ◇ Person giving orders is a legitimate authority

  ◇ Depersonalization of victim (not treating them like a person, human, etc.)

  ◇ Absence of others who are not obeying

  ◇ Presence of a bystander

  ◇ Influence of informational and normative influence

  ◇ Requested behaviour is one that we already have

- Disrupting or changing any of these factors is a way to resist obedience

- Obedience has led to many negative things: cults (for example, Jim Jones), Abu Ghraib, Stanford prison experiment.

We have discussed several ways that we can influence the behaviours of others and how our behaviours are influenced by other people. These strategies underlie the power of **persuasion**. Persuasion is the process of deliberately trying to change another person's behaviour, beliefs, attitude, etc. There are two main strategies used to persuade us:

- **Central Route:** Attending to well-developed rational arguments or messages

- **Peripheral Route:** Attending to external cues, such as attractiveness of speaker, rather than to the argument or message

- **Elaboration-Likelihood Model:** We are persuaded through the central route when we are highly motivated and can understand the message, but we are persuaded by the peripheral route when our motivation is low or when we need to make a quick decision.

- **Perseverance Effect:** We form an initial impression and it is hard to change that.

- **Sleeper Effect:** We only remember the information we are told and not the fact that it came from an unreliable source (Baird & McCarthy, 2014; Duff & Peace, 2013).

 # Practice...

1. "If you all do well on the exam, I will let you skip one of the quizzes that I had planned for the rest of the semester", Professor Hollister tells his class. This sort of promise is an example of a(n) _____ motive, which gives a reward for acting in a certain way.
   a. hedonic
   b. influential
   c. approval
   d. affiliative

2. _____ is influence that draws on a person's desire for others' approval and his or her longing to be part of a group.
   a. External social influence
   b. Peer-induced social influence
   c. Informational social influence
   d. Normative social influence

3. One example of a _____ might be the prison camps of Nazi Germany, where guards were given strict instructions on how to behave, with the promise of rewards for compliance and punishment for disobedience.
   a. conformity situation
   b. coercive situation
   c. total situation
   d. bystander situation

4. The _____ technique encourages compliance by offering an attractive deal, only to change the terms of the deal at a later time.
   a. foot-in-the-door
   b. door-in-the-face
   c. lowball
   d. bait-and-switch

5. _____ is a direct and deliberate attempt to change a person's attitude or behaviour.
   a. Conformity
   b. Persuasion
   c. Influencing
   d. Pressure

 **Apply...**

1. **Factors Affecting Conformity**

   What factors do you think influence conformity? (Think about: when and why are we more likely to conform, when and why are we less likely to conform, what roles may group size, age, culture, gender, education, etc. play in conformity)

   _____

   _____

   _____

   _____

   _____

   _____

   _____

   _____

   _____

   _____

   _____

2. **Cognitive Dissonance**

   Research cognitive dissonance. You may use the internet, peer-reviewed journals, textbooks, etc.

   • How is cognitive dissonance defined?

   _____

   _____

   _____

   _____

   _____

   _____

   • How is cognitive dissonance connected to social influence?

   _____

   _____

   _____

   _____

   _____

   _____

   _____

to be continued

 **Apply...**

continued

3. **Milgram's Studies on Obedience**
    - Discuss Milgram's experiment with two classmates (Think about: what did you learn from this experiment, how did you feel watching the experiment, could this experiment be done today, what are the implications of Milgram's findings?)
    - Watch the video "The Milgram Experiment 1962 Full Documentary" at https://www.youtube.com/watch?v=ek4pWJ0_Xno

    - Provide a summary of your discussions.

Social Interactions

LO5 Explain how stereotypes and discrimination can develop

At the beginning of this chapter, it was noted that humans are social beings. We know from our chapter on Motivation and Emotion (Chapter 5) that humans are also emotional beings. The relationship between social interactions and emotions is reciprocal (Figure 1).

One example of this reciprocal relationship is **social pain**, which is the pain, feeling of rejection, and feeling of loss, we experience when we end a relationship. In addition, **self-conscious emotions**, which are feelings we have about ourselves and our behaviours, can help or hinder our social interactions:

- Guilt may help us to keep relationships.
- Embarrassment may lead us to behave differently in social situations.
- Shame may cause us to withdraw from social interactions.

The relationship between social interactions and emotions is the reason that we can identify both positive and negative interactions with others. For many, negative social interactions occur because of another person's **prejudice**. Prejudice is a learned perception, belief, or attitude that is negative and is directed towards specific people. Most people do not consider themselves to be prejudice, but we are not always aware of our prejudice. Prejudice can be implicit or indirect. They may, for example, develop from stereotypes.

Stereotypes

- General beliefs about a group of people
- Can be useful in social perception because they help us to make quick assessments about others
- They can, however, lead to false conclusions
- These false conclusions can lead to prejudice and discrimination
- Once we have a stereotype it is hard to disprove, thanks to the confirmation bias
- Negative stereotypes can be harmful even if not expressed or demonstrated
  - ◊ Just knowing that a negative stereotype about us exists changes our behaviour as we know we have to work against the stereotype.
- Mahzarin Banaji and Tony Greenwald developed "The Implicit Association Test" to access implicit attitudes (Baird & McCarthy, 2014; Duff & Peace, 2013).

You will have an opportunity to examine your implicit attitudes in your activity for this unit.

FIGURE 1 Reciprocal relationship between emotions and social interactions

Discrimination

- Negative behaviour directed towards specific people or groups.

- Directed to groups who are different from us in terms of skin colour, race, gender, sexual orientation, religion, etc.

- We form a concept of **ingroup** or our group, which is made up of members similar to us, and **outgroup** or other group, which is made of members that are not in our group, and who are different from us.

- This thinking of an "us" and "them" leads to prejudice and discrimination.

- When we feel angry or fearful of a group, it leads to prejudice and discrimination.

Unfortunately, prejudice can lead to **aggression**, which is behaviour intended to harm others, between ingroups and outgroups. We learned in our chapter on Genetics and Evolution that aggression serves to increase survival by protecting mate, offspring, territories, and food supplies. However, we have just learned that aggression to outgroups is founded not on justified threats to our well-being but on stereotypes, some of which we may not even be aware of. There are other factors that influence aggression, such as genetics, stress, drug use, prenatal exposure to drugs, frustration, previous abuse, unemployment, and hot weather. In addition, there are social norms that govern how much aggression is appropriate to show in any given social situation. Think about aggression on a children's playground, an adult only dance club, and a professional sports event—each has its own amount of socially appropriate aggression.

Up to this point, we have discussed what could be viewed as negative or harmful social interactions. But, we all know that most of our social interactions are in fact positive and enjoyable. We may even engage in cooperative acts or **cooperation**, which involve working together for the benefit of a specific group. Cooperation sometimes involves doing what is in the best interest of the group instead of what is in the best interest of an individual. Why do we cooperate? Some reasons include: personal accountability, reputation, reciprocity, and a shared social identity with a group.

In addition to cooperation, we also engage in the prosocial act of **altruism**, which is behaviour that we engage in because it benefits others with no concern for our interests. Why would we do this? Some reasons include:

- The Theory of Reciprocal Altruism: We are altruistic because we were the recipient of altruism in our past.

- We are altruistic towards our relatives.

- Altruism makes us more attractive to others (Baird & McCarthy, 2014).

Practice...

1. Explicit attitudes are held _____, while implicit attitudes are held _____.
   a. internally; externally
   b. unconsciously; consciously
   c. externally; internally
   d. consciously; unconsciously

2. A(n) _____ is a belief whereas _____ is an action.
   a. stereotype; discrimination
   b. stereotype; prejudice
   c. implicit stereotype; an explicit stereotype
   d. explicit stereotype; an implicit stereotype

3. Mary-Lou is a healthy living advocate. She tells you, "I believe that obese people are simply lazy." Mary-Lou is expressing a(n):
   a. explicit stereotype.
   b. implicit stereotype.
   c. prejudicial stereotype.
   d. discriminatory motive.

4. _____ refers to behaviour intended to harm others.
   a. Discrimination
   b. Aggression
   c. Violence
   d. Assertiveness

5. _____ is the act of working together for the good of the group.
   a. Group facilitation
   b. Teamwork
   c. Cooperation
   d. Social contracting

Apply...

1. **Implicit Attitudes**
   - Go to the website for "Project Implicit" (https://implicit.harvard.edu/implicit/).
   - Complete any two of the tests.
   - What did you learn about your implicit attitudes by completing these tests?

_____

_____

_____

_____

_____

_____

_____

_____

_____

to be continued

Apply...

continued

_____
_____
_____
_____
_____
_____
_____
_____
_____
_____
_____
_____
_____
_____
_____
_____
_____
_____
_____

- Do you see any limitations to tests like these?

_____
_____
_____
_____
_____
_____
_____
_____

to be continued

Apply...

continued

2. **Reducing Prejudice**

    Research ways to reduce or prevent prejudice. You may use the internet, peer-reviewed journals, textbooks, etc.

    - Make a list of the ways that have been shown to reduce or prevent prejudice.

    _____

    _____

    _____

    _____

    _____

    _____

    _____

    _____

    _____

    _____

    _____

    _____

    _____

    - Do you think it is possible to eliminate prejudice? Explain your answer.

    _____

    _____

    _____

    _____

    _____

    _____

    _____

    _____

    _____

    _____

    _____

    _____

to be continued

 **Apply...**

continued

3. **Morality and Prosocial Behaviour**

What do you think is the relationship between morality and prosocial behaviour?

_____

_____

_____

_____

_____

_____

_____

_____

_____

_____

_____

_____

KNOW...

Learning Objectives

1. Key principles of attachment:

Attachment is the emotional connection that an infant forms to caregivers. The type of attachment we develop in infancy will impact our future relationships. Bowlby first coined the term attachment and believed that it was formed instinctively. Harlow found that touch and comfort were important in forming attachment. Ainsworth developed the Strange Situation which can be used to determine the type of attachment an infant has to caregivers. She found that infants who had secure attachments had mothers who were warm, attentive, and sensitive to the needs of their infants. Secure attachments are the most common type of attachment. Mothers who were unresponsive or insensitive had anxious and insecure children (anxious-ambivalent or anxious-avoidant); while experiencing trauma, fear, or abuse can lead to disorganized-disoriented attachment.

2. Two key developmental activities that occur in childhood, adolescence, and adulthood:

    - Childhood: Increased interactions with peers, play, moral development is in Stage 1

    - Adolescence: Forming of an identity, involved with cliques and crowds, peer pressure

    - Adulthood: Marriage, having children, establishing career, attachment in infancy impacts future relationships

3. Two processes we use during social perception:

    You can choose any two processes. Here are two examples:

    1. We use facial recognition to determine whether we are seeing some-one we know or do not know. This recognition is important as it will influence our own behaviours, and our perception of the person we are seeing.

    2. We also use the non-verbal behaviours of others to gain information about their feelings and intentions. For example, we read their facial expressions to understand what they are feeling. This knowledge influences how we interact with others.

4. Conformity, compliance, and obedience and an example of each:

    - Conformity: A type of social influence in which behaviour change results from a need to adhere to or match social norms or expectations. For example, the bystander effect, in which people do not help others in need because when they look to their reference group for guidance they see that no one is helping, and so they do not help either.

    - Compliance: A type of social influence in which behaviour change results from a direct request (verbal or non-verbal). For example, low-ball-techniques that get us to purchase something greater than we originally wanted.

    - Obedience: A type of social influence in which behaviour change results from following the requests of an authority figure. For example, Milgram's experiment in which participants complied with demands of authority and presented electrical shocks to other people, even at dangerous voltages.

5. How stereotypes and discrimination can develop:

    We develop frameworks for understanding groups of people. When these frameworks are negative in nature or based on incorrect or inaccurate infor-mation, then we see certain people or groups in a negative way. These negative stereotypes are often implicit and we are not consciously aware of them, but they still impact the way that we interact with certain people or groups. In addi-tion, when we start to categorize or group people as being a part of our ingroup or as being part of our outgroup, we are more likely to behave differently towards them if they are in the outgroup. This is discrimination. Both stereo-types and discrimination are forms of prejudice.

Key Terms

Socialization: The process that shapes our socially appropriate behaviour.

Attachment: The emotional bond an infant forms with caregivers.

Bonding: The emotional bond a caregiver forms with an infant.

Cliques: A small group of same-sex peers who have a close relationship and share details of their lives.

Crowds: A large group of mixed-sex peers who participate in social activities together.

Social Perception: The way we see, understand, and interpret other people, our social interactions, and our social world.

Social Influence: The processes that occur when we attempt to change the behaviours, beliefs, or attitudes of others.

Conformity: A type of social influence in which behaviour change results from a need to adhere to or match social norms or expectations.

Compliance: A type of social influence in which behaviour change results from a direct request (verbal or non-verbal).

Obedience: A type of social influence in which behaviour change results from following the requests of an authority figure.

Persuasion: The process of deliberately trying to change another person's behaviour, beliefs, or attitude.

Social Pain: The pain, feeling of rejection, and feeling of loss, we experience when we end a relationship.

Prejudice: A learned negative perception, belief, or attitude directed towards specific people.

Stereotypes: General beliefs about a group of people.

Discrimination: Negative behaviour directed towards specific people or groups.

Aggression: Behaviour intended to harm others.

Cooperation: Working together for the benefit of a specific group.

Altruism: Behaviour we engage in because it benefits others with no concern for our interests.

Answers to Practice

Social Development: Attachment and Erikson's Stage Theory
1. c   2. d   3. a   4. b   5. c

Social Development: Some Key Activities from Childhood to Adulthood
1. b   2. c   3. b   4. c   5. a

Social Perception
1. d   2. d   3. c   4. c   5. b

Social Influence
1. a   2. d   3. c   4. c   5. b

Social Interactions
1. d   2. a   3. a   4. b   5. c

References

Baird, A., & McCarthy, A. (2014). *THINK psychology* (2nd Canadian edition). Don Mills, ON: Pearson Education, Inc.; pp. 95–105.

Baird, A., & McCarthy, A. (2014). *THINK Psychology* (2nd Canadian edition). Don Mills, ON: Pearson Education, Inc.; pp. 199–213.

Duff, K. & Peace, K. (2013). *THINK social psychology* (1st Canadian edition). Don Mills, ON: Pearson Education, Inc.

12 Health

LEARNING OBJECTIVES

LO1 List the dimensions of health

LO2 Discuss ways we can manage stress

LO3 List, in order, the top six leading causes of death among Canadians

LO4 Explain two ways that health promotion messages are presented

LEARN...

Health refers to our physical, mental, and social well-being. We can view health as encompassing multiple domains: physical, spiritual, intellectual, social, emotional, occupational, and environmental. If we achieve high levels of health on all the dimensions we are said to have wellness—a goal we should all strive to obtain. There are several models that attempt to explain health, such as the biomedical model (which proposes that illness is caused by disease) and the biopsychosocial model (which focuses on biological, psychological, and social factors). Health psychology is an area of psychology that focuses on the diagnosis and treatment of people who are ill, and on ways to improve and maintain health. We discuss motivational models, behavioural enaction model, stages of change model, and others that outline key principles of health psychology. We also look at the way stress impacts our health. The General Adaptation Syndrome (GAS) outlines what happens when we encounter something that we judge to be stressful: First, there is the alarm stage where we decide whether to stay and fight or to leave a situation, then there is the resistance stage, where we begin to use our resources to manage ongoing stress, and finally the last stage is exhaustion, where our resources are used up. It is important that we find ways to manage or cope with stress, as ongoing stress negatively impacts our health. Coping strategies include relaxation techniques, social support, and exercise. These coping strategies help us to develop a positive healthy lifestyle. But, for many of us the goal of a healthy lifestyle is yet to be achieved. In this chapter, we look at diseases that are negatively impacted by poor, unhealthy lifestyles. The top three leading causes of death among Canadians are cancer, heart disease, and stroke, which collectively contribute to 55% of deaths. These illnesses are impacted by unhealthy behaviours or factors, such as smoking, unsafe sexual behaviour, drug use, and obesity. Although most of us know that we should address these factors, change is not easy. The Canadian government has been engaged in health promotion since the 1700s. Since that time they have developed a framework for health promotion, and have actively presented Canadians with information geared towards improving our health. Often strategies such as message framing, repetition of message, and the use of credible and attractive sources are used. Through the activities for this chapter, you will reflect on your own health, the factors that impact it, and your strategies for managing stress. You will also have an opportunity to develop strategies to help people change their unhealthy behaviours.

What Is Health?

 L01 List the dimensions of health

The World Health Organization defines **health** as "a state of complete physical, mental and social well-being and not merely the absence of disease or infirmity" (WHO, 1946). More recently, health has been described as an ever-changing multi-dimensional process that allows us to adapt to life circumstances (Baird & McCarthy, 2014).

Dimensions of Health

- Physical
- Spiritual
- Intellectual
- Social
- Emotional
- Occupational
- Environmental

Each of these dimensions lies on a continuum from high to low. The dimensions interact to give us our overall health. If we achieve high levels of health on all the dimensions, we are said to have **wellness** (Poole, Matheson, & Cox, 2016).

We should all strive for wellness, because it is tied to better quality of life, longer life, stronger immune systems, more energy, better relationships, and greater ability to manage stress. But, how do we achieve and maintain good health? There are several models and approaches that attempt to explain health:

- **Biomedical Model:** Illness is caused by disease
- **Biopsychosocial Model:** Focus is on biological, psychological, and social factors
- **Wellness Model:** Focuses on the seven dimensions of health previously listed
- **Social Ecological Model:** Health determined by the individual, social, and physical environments, and health policies and systems
- **Behavioural Medicine:** Focuses on the relationship between medicine and behaviour
- **Health Psychology:**
  - ◊ An area of psychology that focuses on diagnosis and treatment of people who are ill, and on ways to improve and maintain health
  - ◊ Addresses the connection between our mind and our body
  - ◊ Applies psychological principles (for example, learning, motivation) to health

◊ Includes **psychoneuroimmunology**, which focuses on the connection between our immune system and our psychology states; work in psychoneuroimmunology provides support for mind-body connection

(Baird & McCarthy, 2014; Poole et al., 2016; Ragin, 2014).

Key Theories in Health Psychology

- **Motivational Models:**

  ◊ Look at intention as a driving force

  ◊ **Health Belief Model:** Assumes that if we believe a health risk is real then we will act to address it, if we think it will make a difference:

    ■ **Response Efficacy Belief:** The belief that a given strategy will reduce a health risk.

    ■ **Cost-Gain Belief:** A type of pro/con analysis that focuses on the costs associated with a given strategy versus the benefit of that strategy.

    ■ How much a person values good health is an important factor.

  ◊ **Theory of Reasoned Action:** Similar to Health belief model, but includes other people's beliefs as a factor

  ◊ **Theory of Planned Behaviour:** Similar to theory of reasoned action, but includes **perceived behavioural control**, which is our belief that we control a given behaviour

- **Behavioural Enaction Model:** Looks at ways to get us to act on an intended behaviour

- **Gollwitzer's Implementation Intentions Model:** Similar to motivational models, but includes the use of an implementation plan, like a "how-to" to achieve better health

- **Bagozzi's Goal Theory:** Similar to Gollwitzer's model but includes the impacts of perceived control and cost-gain beliefs

- **Multi-Stage Models:** A step-by-step guide to implementing behaviours to achieve better health

- **The Health Action Process Approach:** Two stages—motivational phase, in which we develop expectations and perceived control, and volitional phase, in which we plan and carry out a change in behaviour to achieve better health

- **The Stages of Change Model:** Similar to the health action process approach, but outlines steps in the process of change:

  ◊ Pre-contemplation

  ◊ Contemplation

  ◊ Action

  ◊ Maintenance

  ◊ Termination

  ◊ Relapse

One goal of health psychology is to identify factors that positively or negatively impact our health (Baird & McCarthy, 2014; Poole et al., 2016; Ragin, 2014). Next, we will look at stress and the ways it puts our well-being at risk.

Practice...

1. The application of psychological principles to the understanding of and improvement of health refers to the work of:
   a. behaviourists.
   b. clinical psychologists.
   c. counselling psychologists.
   d. health psychologists.

2. A branch of medicine concerned with the relationship between health and behaviour is:
   a. psychoneuroimmunology.
   b. rehabilitation.
   c. behavioural medicine.
   d. biomedicine.

3. The extent to which you think a course of action will actually work to reduce a threat is called:
   a. a response efficacy belief.
   b. a cost gain belief.
   c. a biomedical belief.
   d. risk reduction belief.

4. One important assumption of the Theory of Reasoned Action that is different from the Health Belief Model is:
   a. that health behaviours are explained by our health beliefs.
   b. a person's beliefs regarding the subjective norm.
   c. a person's belief that a health threat exists.
   d. the belief that a given course of action will affect a health threat.

5. The Stages of Change model identifies six stages. Which of the following is the correct order of these stages?
   a. Action, precontemplation, contemplation, termination, maintenance, relapse
   b. Precontemplation, contemplation, action, relapse, termination, maintenance
   c. Precontemplation, contemplation, action, termination, maintenance, relapse
   d. Relapse, precontemplation, contemplation, termination, maintenance

 # Apply...

1. **Health Puzzle**
   - Using the blank puzzle below fill in the factors that you think impact your health. You can use one puzzle piece per factor.
   - Colour code your puzzle so that factors that negatively impact your health are coloured red, factors that positively impact your health are coloured green, and factors that negatively and positively impact your health are coloured yellow.

to be continued

 **Apply...**

continued

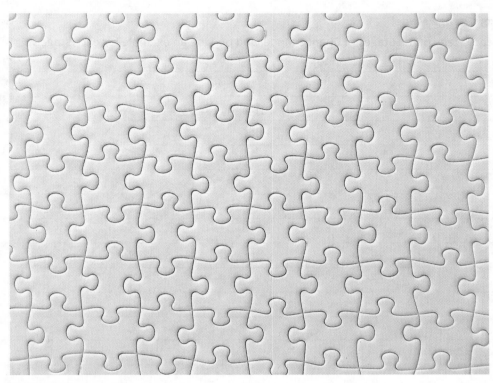

Nishihama/Shutterstock

- Look at your puzzle. What does your puzzle tell you about your health and the factors that impact your health? Think about the dimensions of health.

  _____

  _____

  _____

  _____

  _____

  _____

- Taylor Swift's song "Shake it off" suggests that we can simply ignore some negative factors in our lives. Look at your puzzle and identify the factors that you can "shake off."

  _____

  _____

  _____

  _____

  _____

  _____

to be continued

 **Apply...**

continued

2. **Stages of Change Model**

Define each stage of the Stages of Change Model and provide an example for each stage.

_____

_____

_____

_____

_____

_____

_____

_____

_____

_____

_____

_____

_____

_____

_____

Stress

 Discuss ways we can manage stress

"I am so stressed out!" Have you ever felt this way? Chances are you have. It is likely that you have experienced stress at some point in your life. When we discuss **stress**, we are referring to our physical or mental response to a demand.

Stress

- **Eustress:** A positive type of stress, usually helps us attain a goal
- **Distress:** When stress is ongoing and we are not able to adequately cope
- **Stressor:** Anything that causes us stress
- **Acute Stress:** Short-term stress that may be extreme

- **Chronic Stress:** Longer term stress can make a person feel overwhelmed

Responses to Stress

- **Physical Responses**
  - ◊ Activated when we perceive a demand (real or imagined)
  - ◊ Body responds in two ways:
    - Sympathetic adrenomedullary system (SAM): Initiates fight-or-flight response by releasing adrenaline and noradrenaline; rapid response
    - Hypothalamic-pituitary-adrenal Axis (HPA): Goal is to minimize impact of stress and regain homeostasis by release of cortisol; delayed response
    - Amount of cortisol in blood and saliva corresponds to stress level
  - ◊ **Limbic System:** An emotional response
  - ◊ **Reticular Formation:** Impacts what sensory information is processed (see Chapter 10 on Personality) (Poole et al., 2016)
- **General Adaptation Syndrome (GAS)**
  - ◊ Proposed by Hans Selye
  - ◊ Stages of response:
    - Alarm: Fight or flight
    - Resistance: Mobilization of resources; activated when stress is chronic
    - Exhaustion: If stress is prolonged, resources are used up, we cannot respond to subsequent stress, can lead to burnout
  - ◊ Diseases of adaptation: Diseases, like heart disease and high blood pressure, which result from the physiological changes that occur when we experience ongoing stress
- **Tend and Befriend Theory**
  - ◊ Proposed by Shelley Taylor
  - ◊ Tendency to seek and give support in response to stress
  - ◊ More effective way to manage stress
- Stress negatively impacts all aspects of our health

Stressors

- **Significant Life Changes:** New job, new relationship, loss of a loved one, moving, getting married, having a baby, etc.
- **Daily Hassle:** Most frequent and common stressor, a minor nuisance that can build and become just as stressful as other bigger stressors
- **Catastrophes:** Unpredictable, large-scale events; can lead to post-traumatic stress disorder

Ways to Manage Stress

- **Coping**
  - ◊ The strategies we use to help us deal with stress
  - ◊ Goal is to minimize the impact of stressors

◊ Usually, we use cognitive, emotional, and behavioural strategies

◊ **Problem-Focused Coping:** Goal is to solve the problem

◊ **Emotion-Focused Coping:** Goal is to manage emotions

◊ **Anticipatory Coping:** Goal is to develop an approach, based on past experience, for stressors that may happen in the future

- **Cognitive Strategies**

  ◊ We make **cognitive appraisals**, which are assessments about a situation or event, when we encounter a demand or threat to determine if it is stressful.

  ◊ Three processes

    ■ **Primary Appraisals:** This is our initial assessment; we determine if the situation is irrelevant (no effect on us), benign-positive (positive outcome for us), or stressful (negative outcome for us)

    ■ **Secondary Appraisals:** Focuses on our ability to cope with the stressful situation; works with primary assessment to produce an emotional reaction to the situation

    ■ **Reappraisals:** New information leads us to reassess

  ◊ Types of appraisals

    ■ **Rational Coping:** Deal with stress head-on; thoughtful, rational appraisal of stressor; effective strategy

    ■ **Repressive Coping:** Ignoring stressor, putting on a "happy" face; not effective strategy

    ■ **Reframing:** Think about stressor in a different, more positive way, effective strategy

- **Perceived Control:** People with high perceived control have better management of stressors (see Chapter 10 on Personality)

- **Explanatory Style:** Optimists have more perceived control which leads to better management of stress (see Chapter 10 on Personality)

- **Relaxation:** Decrease arousal and other physiological responses to stress; examples—progressive muscular relaxation (PMR), meditation, biofeedback

- **Cognitive-Behavioural Therapy:** The use of strategies to address the impact of stress on our cognitive and/or behavioural health; examples— systematic desensitization, modelling (see Chapter 7 on Learning), cognitive restructuring, stress inoculation training

- **Social Support:** Supportive relationships positively impact stress management

- **Exercise:** Aerobic exercise helps with stress management (Baird & McCarthy, 2014; Poole et al., 2016).

Practice...

1. The mental and physical response that we experience when exposed to threatening or challenging events is called _____.
   a. panic
   b. anxiety
   c. stress
   d. terror

2. A _____ is a stimulus—an event, a person, an object, a situation—that we perceive as threatening and/or challenging.
   a. stressor
   b. hurdle
   c. major life event
   d. hassle

3. Natalya has received phone call that her child is sick at school and needs to be picked up. Natalya is suddenly very flustered as she struggles to think of how she is going to get coverage at work, get to her child's school, and perhaps make an appointment with her doctor, all in just a few minutes. The stress that Natalya feels to this challenging set of circumstances could best be described as _____ stress.
   a. chronic
   b. intrinsic
   c. acute
   d. extrinsic

4. Stress can actually be good for you and serve positive functions. The stress that we experience in response to positive events is called _____.
   a. adaptive stress
   b. distress
   c. positive stress
   d. eustress

5. Which of the following is not one of the three stages of the general adaptation syndrome?
   a. Resistance
   b. Exhaustion
   c. Alarm
   d. Stabilization

Apply...

1. **Stress Index**

   Complete the Stress Index Test developed by the Canadian Mental Health Association http://www.cmha.ca/mental_health/whats-your-stress-index/#.WX89kVGQzIU

   What did you learn about your stress level?

   _____

   _____

   _____

   _____

   _____

   _____

   _____

   _____

to be continued

Apply...

continued

2. **Stress Management**

- List the strategies you use to manage your stress.

_____
_____
_____
_____
_____
_____
_____
_____
_____
_____
_____
_____
_____
_____

- Discuss stress management strategies with two of your classmates. Write a summary of what you have discussed.

_____
_____
_____
_____
_____
_____
_____
_____
_____
_____
_____
_____
_____

to be continued

 **Apply...**

continued

3. **Problem Focused Coping versus Emotion Focused Coping**

    • Which do you think is more effective—problem focused coping or emotion focused coping?

    _____

    _____

    _____

    _____

    _____

    • What does research tell us?

    _____

    _____

    _____

    _____

    _____

Lifestyle-Induced Health Concerns

L03 List, in order, the top six leading causes of death among Canadians

Over the last 100 years, the cause of death has moved from microbes to lifestyle. Thanks to the development of antibiotics, and other medical interventions, infections are no longer the main cause of death. Instead, it seems that we are the cause of our own ill health and shortened lifespan. Let us take a look at some of the lifestyle-induced health concerns that are prevalent today.

Leading Causes of Death for Canadians (Statistics Canada, 2017)

When we look at Figure 1 we see that cancer, heart disease, and stroke collectively contribute to 55% of deaths for Canadians. The Canadian Cancer Society (2017) estimates that almost one in two people will get cancer in their lifetime. The Heart and Stroke Foundation (2017) reports that over a million Canadians have heart disease and this is increasing every year—50 000 new

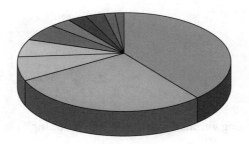

☐ Cancer   ☐ Heart disease

☐ Stroke   ☐ Chronic lower respiratory diseases

☐ Accidents   ☐ Diabetes mellitus

☐ Alzheimer's disease   ☐ Influenza and pneumonia

☐ Suicide   ☐ Kidney disease

FIGURE 1 Leading causes of death for Canadians.
Data from Statistics Canada (2017). Leading causes of death by sex (both sexes). Retrieved from http://www.statcan.gc.ca/tables-tableaux/sum-som/l01/cst01/hlth36a-eng.htm.

cases each year. About 100 000 Canadians die every year from stroke (Public Health Agency of Canada, 2016). Why should we care? Because people are dying of diseases which are influenced by lifestyle—this means we can do something about it!

There are several factors or behaviours that increase our risk of developing illness. Let's look at some of these factors.

- **Smoking:**
  - ◊ The number one preventable cause of death and disease in Canada
  - ◊ Can lead to cancer, heart disease, and chronic obstructive pulmonary diseases (fourth leading cause of death)
  - ◊ Smoking is an addiction that can form quickly and is very difficult to break
  - ◊ Second-hand smoke and residual chemicals on clothing, furniture, etc. are very damaging
- **Unsafe Sexual Behaviour:**
  - ◊ Increases risk of sexually transmitted illness (for example, HIV/AIDS, chlamydia, gonorrhoea)
  - ◊ Increases risk of developing certain kinds of cancer (for example, Human papillomavirus [HPV])
  - ◊ Some sexually transmitted illness are becoming more difficult to treat
- **Drug Use:**
  - ◊ Each drug has its own risks (refer to Chapter 6 on Consciousness)
  - ◊ Decision making may be impaired while taking a drug
  - ◊ Impacts prenatal development
- **Obesity:**
  - ◊ Measured using body mass index

◊ Rates increasing, even among children

   ■ Thirty-two percent of Canadian children are overweight or obese (Canadian Obesity Network, 2016)

◊ Can lead to hypertension (high blood pressure), type 2 diabetes, heart disease, depression, and cancer

- **Lack of Physical Activity:**

  ◊ Forty-five percent of Canadians (12 and older) are inactive (Canadian Obesity Network, 2016)

  ◊ Can lead to obesity, diabetes, heart disease, cancer, and osteoporosis

  ◊ May be as bad as smoking in terms of negative impact on health

- **Consuming Too Much Saturated Fat, Sugar, or Salt:**

  ◊ Can lead to obesity, tooth decay, liver disease, diabetes, heart disease, high blood pressure, kidney disease, stroke, and cancer

The information presented above on the factors that negatively impact our health is not new. Most of us already know this information, yet many of us continue to engage in these behaviours. Why? Because change is hard! In our final unit for this chapter, we will look at behavioural change again (see Chapter 7 on Learning) and the ways health promotion have been attempted.

 # Practice...

1. Historically, the greatest cause of death for humans was _____.
   a. infections
   b. lifestyle diseases
   c. suicide
   d. accidents

2. Currently, the greatest cause of death for humans is _____.
   a. infections
   b. lifestyle diseases
   c. suicide
   d. accidents

3. More Canadians die from _____ than any other diseases.
   a. suicide
   b. heart disease
   c. diabetes
   d. cancer

4. About _____ Canadians die every year from stroke.
   a. 10 000
   b. 100 000
   c. 5 000
   d. 50 000

5. All of the following are risk factors for cancer except _____.
   a. obesity
   b. smoking
   c. physical activity
   d. unsafe sexual behaviour

 **Apply...**

1. **Why do People Smoke?**

   • Why do you think people smoke even when they know how damaging it is to their health?

   _____

   _____

   _____

   _____

   _____

   _____

   • Discuss your thoughts and ideas with another classmate. Write a summary of your discussion.

   _____

   _____

   _____

   _____

   _____

   _____

   _____

2. **Body Mass Index**

   • Calculate your body mass index (BMI).
   • Do you think your BMI accurately reflects your health? Explain your answer.

   _____

   _____

   _____

   _____

   _____

   _____

   _____

   _____

   _____

   _____

to be continued

Apply...

continued

3. **Laughter and Health**

Research the impact of laughter on health. You may use the internet, peer-reviewed journals, textbooks, etc. Please cite your sources.

• Make a list of the ways laughter impacts health.

_____

_____

_____

_____

_____

_____

_____

_____

_____

_____

_____

_____

• What are the implications of your research findings to health care?

_____

_____

_____

_____

_____

_____

_____

_____

_____

_____

_____

_____

_____

Promoting Health

LO4 Explain two ways that health promotion messages are presented

One of the questions that arises when think about health is how can I be healthier? Most of us know the things we need to do to be healthier—exercise, eat right, limit saturated fat, sugar and salt, decrease stress, and so on. But for many of us this knowledge does not transfer to our behaviour. This challenge, of implementing positive change with the goal of improving health, is one that Canada has been actively engaged in since the 1700s. Since that time we have moved from promoting the benefits of proper sanitation to promoting the benefits of a healthy lifestyle. In 1974, Minister of Health and Welfare Marc LaLonde identified lifestyle as an important factor in health, and in 1986, Minister of Health and Welfare Jake Epp developed a framework for promoting strategies to establish, continue, and improve the health of Canadians, referred to as health promotion. Epp's framework places responsibility for health on the individual and the goal of health promotion was for every Canadian to achieve good health (Health and Welfare Canada, 1986).

Epp's Framework for Health Promotion

- **Health Challenges:**
  - ◊ Reducing inequities in the health of low- versus high-income groups in Canada
  - ◊ Develop prevention strategies for injuries and illnesses
  - ◊ Improve coping skills
- **Mechanisms:**
  - ◊ Self-care (our decisions and behaviours aimed at improving our health)
  - ◊ Mutual aid (things we do to help others):
    - ▪ Naturally occurring support: Support from one's own social network (for example, friends, family)
    - ▪ Agency-provided support: Support provided by agencies or organizations to address gaps in naturally occurring support (for example, community support group)
    - ▪ Can be practical, informational, or emotional
  - ◊ Healthy environments (creating surroundings that help us to establish and maintain good health)
- **Strategies:**
  - ◊ Encouraging public participation, we control the factors that impact our health
  - ◊ Strengthen community health services
  - ◊ Coordinate all policies that impact health (Health and Welfare Canada, 1986)

Community Oriented Health Promotion

- Developed by Ronald Labonte in 1987
- Three levels for successful health promotion
  1. Medical: Goal is disease treatment
  2. Public Health: Goal is disease prevention
  3. Socioenvironmental: Goal is social change and healthy public policy
- Levels 2 and 3 focus on social factors of health, such as income, social support, and education

Getting the Message Out

- You learned in Chapter 11 (on Our Social World) that we have the ability to influence the attitudes and behaviours of others.
- Health promotion uses strategies of persuasion in an attempt to get us to change our attitudes and behaviours so that they are more health focused.
- Remember: Elaboration Likelihood Model of Persuasion: Attitudes are influenced through two routes:
  ◊ Central Route: Use of logic, facts, and reason
  ◊ Peripheral Route: Appeals to emotion
- Health promotions often involve **fear appeals**, which present the negative outcomes of our behaviour, and attempt to influence us via emotions or the peripheral route.
  ◊ In order to be effective we must see the behaviour or lack of a behaviour as a threat that we are vulnerable to—is this a danger to me?
  ◊ It is ineffective if we are too scared to act, or if we do not think anything will change.
- **Message Framing:**
  ◊ What aspects, positive or negative, are presented
  ◊ **Loss Framed Messages:** = Bad things will happen if we do not engage in a healthy behaviour; effective for risky behaviour, and getting tests to detect abnormalities
  ◊ **Gain Framed Messages:** = Good things will happen if we engage in a healthy behaviour; effective for behaviours aimed at prevention
- Repetition of message
- Use credible sources (central route) and attractive sources (peripheral route)
- Address audience demographics such as language and literacy (Poole et al., 2016)

Now that you are aware of some of the strategies that are used to promote healthy behaviours, you will be able to detect them in the messages you are given.

Practice...

1. Epp's framework for health promotion includes all the following except _____.
   a. fostering public participation
   b. enhancing coping
   c. decreasing prevention
   d. reducing inequities

2. In Labonte's framework for successful community-oriented health promotion, the first level is _____ and the second level deals with _____.
   a. biopsychosocial, environmental
   b. medical; public health
   c. biomedical; socioenvironmental
   d. medical; socioenvironmental

3. Health promotion has been a focus of the Canadian government since _____.
   a. 1700s
   b. 1800s
   c. 1950s
   d. 1970s

4. Jax has just returned home after having knee surgery. His neighbour brought over groceries for him as he is not able to move around by himself. This is an example of _____ support.
   a. naturally occurring
   b. community occurring
   c. government occurring
   d. agency-provided

5. A message that highlights the facts and statistics about a disease is using the _____.
   a. peripheral route of persuasion
   b. fear route of persuasion
   c. central route of persuasion
   d. reasoned action theory

 # Apply...

1. **Stages of Prevention**

   Research the stages of prevention. You may use the internet, peer-reviewed journals, textbooks, etc. List, define, and give an example for each stage of prevention.

   _____
   _____
   _____
   _____
   _____
   _____
   _____
   _____
   _____
   _____
   _____
   _____

   to be continued

 **Apply…**

continued

2. **Strategies for Improving Health**

Use what you have learned about motivation, cognition, learning, personality, social interactions, and health promotion to develop four strategies/approaches that we can use to improve health among adults. You may need to review previous chapters.

Explain each of these strategies in a way that would clearly outline how we could implement them. It may help to choose one behaviour to change, or one illness to address.

Apply...

continued

KNOW...

Learning Objectives

1. The dimensions of health:
   - Physical
   - Spiritual
   - Intellectual
   - Social
   - Emotional
   - Occupational
   - Environmental

2. Ways we can manage stress:

   When we manage stress we are said to be coping, which means we have effective strategies to address stressors and minimize the effects of stress. For example, perceived control and explanatory style influence coping. Optimists have high perceived control and cope better with stress compared to pessimists. We can also engage in activities that will help us cope, such as relaxation techniques (for example, meditation, deep breathing), aerobic exercise, or talking with close friends or family.

3. Top six leading causes of death among Canadians, in order:
   1. Cancer
   2. Heart disease
   3. Stroke
   4. Chronic lower respiratory diseases
   5. Accidents
   6. Diabetes

4. Two ways that health promotion messages are presented

   You can choose any two strategies. An example is:

   Health promotion often presents information or messages that appeal to our emotions. This is a persuasion strategy called the peripheral route, and often takes the form of fear appeals, that highlight the negative effects of a behaviour, such as smoking. Another way that messages are presented is through framing. Loss framed messages may be used, which outline the negative outcomes of not engaging in a healthy behaviour, and is effective for risky behaviour, and for getting tests to detect abnormalities. Gain framed messages may also be used, which outline the benefits of engaging in a healthy behaviour, and is effective for behaviours aimed at prevention. Other key strategies involve using credible and attractive sources, and repeating the message.

Key Terms

Health: A state of complete physical, mental, and social well-being.

Wellness: High levels of health across dimensions.

Stress: Our physical or mental response to a demand.

Fear Appeals: A strategy that presents the negative outcomes of a behaviour with the goal of getting people to stop a behaviour.

Loss Framed Messages: A persuasion technique in which the negative outcomes of not engaging in a healthy behaviour is presented with the goal of getting people to engage in that behaviour.

Gain Framed Messages: A persuasion technique in which the positive outcomes of engaging in a healthy behaviour is presented with the goal of getting people to engage in that behaviour

Answers to Practice

What Is Health?
1. d   2. a   3. a   4. b   5. c

Stress
1. c   2. a   3. c   4. d   5. d

Lifestyle-Induced Health Concerns
1. a   2. b   3. d   4. b   5. c

Promoting Health
1. c   2. b   3. a   4. a   5. c

References

Baird, A., & McCarthy, A. (2014). *THINK psychology* (2nd Canadian edition). Don Mills, ON: Pearson Education, Inc.; pp. 265–277.

Canadian Cancer Society. (2017). *Nearly 1 in 2 Canadians expected to get cancer: Report*. Retrieved from http://www.cancer.ca/en/about-us/for-media/media-releases/national/2017/canadian-cancer-statistics/?region=on.

Canadian Obesity Network. (2016). *Preventing childhood obesity*. Retrieved from http://www.obesitynetwork.ca/understanding-obesity.

Health and Welfare Canada. (1986). *Achieving health for all: A framework for health promotion*. Retrieved from https://www.canada.ca/en/health-canada/services/health-care-system/reports-publications/health-care-system/achieving-health-framework-health-promotion.html.

Heart and Stroke Foundation. (2017). *2016 Report on the health of Canadians*. Retrieved from http://www.heartandstroke.ca/-/media/pdf-files/canada/2017-heart-month/heartandstroke-reportonhealth-2016.ashx?la=en.

Poole, G., Matheson, D., & Cox, D. (2016). *The psychology of health and health care: a canadian perspective* (5th edition). Don Mills, ON: Pearson Education Canada.

Public Health Agency of Canada. (2016). *Stroke*. Retrieved from http://www.phac-aspc.gc.ca/cd-mc/cvd-mcv/stroke-accident_vasculaire_cerebral/index-eng.php.

Ragin, D. (2014). *Health psychology: an interdisciplinary approach to health* (2nd edition). Upper Saddle River, NJ: Pearson Education, Inc.

Statistics Canada (2017). *Leading causes of death by sex (both sexes)*. Retrieved from http://www.statcan.gc.ca/tables-tableaux/sum-som/l01/cst01/hlth36a-eng.htm.

13 Psychopathology

LEARNING OBJECTIVES

LO1 Define mental disorder

LO2 Describe the essential features underlying anxiety disorders, obsessive-compulsive and related disorders, depressive disorders, bipolar and related disorders, and schizophrenia spectrum and other psychotic disorders

LO3 Provide an example for each of the following disorder categories: trauma- and stressor-related disorders, feeding and eating disorders, disruptive, impulse-control, and conduct disorders, substance-related and addictive disorders, and personality disorders

LO4 Discuss the general causes of mental disorders and how they are treated according to the biological, psychodynamic, behavioural, and cognitive approaches

LEARN...

One in five Canadians will develop a mental disorder during their lifetime, with 50% of the population developing a mental disorder by the age of 40. Given that mental health is one dimension of our overall health, we must identify and address the factors that put us at risk for mental health issues. In this chapter, we focus on key aspects of mental health. It is key for us to have a definition of mental disorder. Mental disorder is a syndrome characterized by clinically significant disturbance in an individual's cognition, emotion regulation, or behaviour that reflects a dysfunction in the psychological, biological, or developmental processes underlying mental functioning. We outline the key symptoms associated with several mental disorder categories. For example, (i) anxiety disorders are characterized by excessive fear and anxiety; (ii) obsessive-compulsive disorder involves recurring intrusive thoughts and repetitive behaviours; (iii) depressive disorders are identified by a sad or irritable mood; and (iv) bipolar disorders describe the cycling of manic and depressive episodes. In this chapter, we also look at some of the disorders that are found within different mental disorder categories, such as the feeding and eating disorder pica, where a person regularly eats non-food items, and the personality disorders of antisocial personality disorder and histrionic personality disorder. We discuss the fact that our view of the causes of mental disorders determines the way we approach treatment. The biological approach proposes causes such as genetics, personality traits, differences in brain functioning/structure or neurotransmitters, and treatment involves medication. The psychodynamic approach proposes causes such as unconscious conflict, damaged ego, or defence mechanisms, and treatment involves therapy to address unconscious conflicts. The behavioural approach proposes that learned and reinforced behaviours lead to mental disorders, and treatment aims to replace maladaptive behaviours with healthier ones. The cognitive approach proposes that faulty thinking, maladaptive thoughts, or hypersensitivity to body responses lead to mental disorders, and treatment aims to change our cognitions. Through your activities for this chapter, you will have an opportunity to examine cultural differences in mental disorders, the link between creativity and mental health, the role of social media in suicide prevention, and the reasons why many people with a mental disorder do not seek help.

Defining Mental Disorder

 Define mental disorder

One in five Canadians will develop a mental disorder during their lifetime, with 50% of the population developing a mental disorder by the age of 40 (Canadian Mental Health Association [CMHA], 2017). Given that mental health is one dimension of our overall health, it is critical for us, both collectively and individually, to identify and address the factors that put us at risk for mental health issues. In this chapter, we focus on key aspects of mental health.

Let us begin with some key definitions: **mental health** refers to a state of mental balance or homeostasis; **mental disorder or mental illness or psychological disorder** refers to a health condition characterized by altered thinking, feeling, or behaving that brings about distress and/or impaired functioning; **psychopathology or abnormal psychology** refers to the study of disorders of mind, mood, and behaviour (Baird & McCarthy, 2014; CMHA, 2017). These definitions are brief and simplistic. The current definition of mental disorder has been put forward in the fifth edition of the Diagnostic and Statistical Manual of Mental Disorders (DSM-5, 2013), which is the authoritative resource for classifying mental disorders. It includes key aspects such as:

- Significant problems in a person's cognitions, emotions, and/or behaviours
- Significant problems in daily life and activities

The DSM-5 contains 300 mental disorders that are discussed across 20 chapters. The DSM-5 is used by professionals in the mental health field, such as physicians, counsellors, psychologists, and psychotherapists (American Psychiatric Association [APA], 2013).

Why is it important for us to define, and to agree to a definition, of mental disorders? Simply, how we define mental disorders determines how we treat mental disorders. For example, in ancient times, mental disorders were defined as the possession of spirits or the devil. The treatment was exorcism or trephination, a method used to create a hole in the skull to release the evil spirits. In addition, how we organize mental disorders tells us which disorders are similar (found in same category) and which are different (found in different categories) in terms of key elements such as symptoms or treatment approaches. We will now take a brief look at the different theories, models, or approaches that attempt to explain mental disorders.

Views of Mental Disorders

- **Medical Model:** Mental disorders are diseases that, like biological diseases, have symptoms, causes, and cures.
- **Biological Approach:** Mental disorders are the result of physical problems.

- **Psychodynamic Approach:** Mental disorders are the result of unconscious conflicts.

- **Behavioural Approach:** Mental disorders are the result of dysfunctional behaviours and learned responses.

- **Cognitive Approach:** Mental disorders are the result of dysfunctional cognitive processes.

- **Biopsychosocial Approach:** An interdisciplinary approach that focuses on biological, psychological, and social factors, like what we discussed in Chapter 12 on Health (Baird & McCarthy, 2014; Beidel, Bulik, Stanley, & Taylor, 2017).

Remember that we have discussed these views in previous chapters—you may wish to review those discussions. We will discuss treatment options in our last unit for this chapter. At that time, you will see how treatment for mental disorders is derived from the view of mental disorders. Now, let's look at some of the common mental disorders affecting Canadians.

Practice...

1. _____ refers to the study of disorders of mind, mood, and behaviour.
   a. Mental illness
   b. Psychopathology
   c. Trephination
   d. Mental health

2. The DSM-5 _____.
   a. is a trusted resource for defining, classifying, and assessing mental disorders
   b. is only used by physicians
   c. does not classify mental disorders, but does define mental disorders
   d. Diagnostic and Standardized Manual for Mental Heath

3. The DSM-5 contains _____ mental disorders that are discussed across _____ chapters.
   a. 100; 10
   b. 200; 20
   c. 300; 20
   d. 400; 20

4. _____ proposed that mental disorders are the result of unconscious conflict.
   a. Medical model
   b. Neurocognitive model
   c. Cognitive approach
   d. Psychodynamic approach

5. How we define mental disorder _____.
   a. is not important
   b. determines treatment
   c. has always been the same
   d. is based on how we respond to stress

 **Apply...**

1. **Defining Mental Disorders Across Cultures**

   - Research cultural differences in defining and identifying mental disorders. You can use the internet, peer-reviewed journals, textbooks, etc. Please cite your sources.
   - What does your research tell us about defining mental disorders?

   _____

   _____

   _____

   _____

   _____

   _____

   _____

   _____

   _____

   _____

   _____

   _____

   _____

   _____

   _____

   _____

   - What does your research tell us about the use of the DSM-5 to define and categorize mental disorders?

   _____

   _____

   _____

   _____

   _____

   _____

   _____

   _____

to be continued

 **Apply...**

continued

2. **Creativity and Mental Health**
    - Research the relationship between creativity and mental health. You can use the internet, peer-reviewed journals, textbooks, etc. Please cite your sources.
    - What does your research tell us about the relationship between creativity and mental health?

_____

_____

_____

_____

_____

_____

_____

_____

_____

_____

_____

_____

_____

_____

_____

_____

_____

_____

_____

_____

_____

_____

_____

_____

_____

_____

Anxiety Disorders, Obsessive-Compulsive and Related Disorders, Depressive Disorders, Bipolar and Related Disorders, and Schizophrenia Spectrum and Other Psychotic Disorders

 Describe the essential features underlying anxiety disorders, obsessive-compulsive and related disorders, depressive disorders, bipolar and related disorders, and schizophrenia spectrum and other psychotic disorders

To learn about these mental disorders, along with others, we can use the DSM-5 (APA, 2013). Through Units 2 and 3, we will list key concepts (as discussed in the DSM-5) for some of the most common mental disorders.

Anxiety Disorders

- Most common mental disorder in Canada
- Characterized by excessive fear and anxiety:
  ◊ Fear is an appropriate response to a real threat, fight-or-flight response
  ◊ Anxiety is disproportionate fear; behaviour is focused on preparing for or avoiding danger
- **Types of Anxiety Disorders**
  ◊ **Separation Anxiety Disorder:** A person experiences fear when they are separated from home or people they are attached to; not developmentally appropriate
  ◊ **Selective Mutism:** No speech in social situations, but speech in other settings
  ◊ **Specific Phobia:** Fear directed towards a specific object or situation
  ◊ **Social Anxiety Disorder:** Fear about being negatively viewed in social situations
  ◊ **Panic Disorder:** Experience panic attacks, which are periods of intense fear; unexpected and reoccur
  ◊ **Agoraphobia:** Fear about two or more of the following situations— public transportation, open spaces, enclosed places, standing in line or being in a crowd, being outside of the home alone
  ◊ **Generalized Anxiety Disorder:** Overall fear and worry occurring most days for at least 6 months

Obsessive-Compulsive Disorder and Related Disorders

- New category of mental disorder in DSM-5; used to be placed under anxiety disorders; examples are:
  ◊ **Obsessive-Compulsive Disorder (OCD):** Characterized by **obsessions** (intrusive thoughts and urges that reoccur) and **compulsions** (engage in repetitive behaviours or mental acts in response to an obsession)
  ◊ **Body Dysmorphic Disorder:** Not seeing actual physical self; preoccupation with one or more perceived flaws
  ◊ **Hoarding Disorder:** Continual difficulty leaving or throwing out things

Depressive Disorders

- All depressive disorders are characterized by a sad or irritable mood; examples are:
  - ◊ **Disruptive Mood Dysregulation Disorder:** Disorder seen in children; ongoing irritability and tantrums; may lead to other types of depressive or anxiety disorder
  - ◊ **Major Depressive Disorder:** Depressed mood present for most of the day, nearly every day
  - ◊ **Persistent Depressive Disorder:** Depressed mood that occurs for most of the day, for more days than not, for at least 2 years, or at least 1 year for children and adolescents
  - ◊ **Premenstrual Dysphoric Disorder:** Depressed mood, irritability, and anxiety that occurs during the premenstrual phase of the cycle and ends when menstruation begins

Bipolar and Related Disorders

- New category of mental disorder in DSM-5; used to be placed under depressive disorders
- Now placed between depressive disorders and schizophrenia spectrum disorders to represent it being a bridge between these two groups of disorders in terms of symptoms, genetics, etc.; examples are:
  - ◊ **Bipolar I Disorder:** Used to be called manic-depression; cycling between episodes of mania (elevated mood, increased energy lasting almost all day for at least 1 week) and episodes of major depression
  - ◊ **Bipolar II Disorder:** Similar to Bipolar I, but manic episode lasts for at least 4 days (called hypomania)
  - ◊ **Cyclothymic Disorder:** Cycling of hypomanic symptoms and depressive symptoms that do not meet criteria for hypomania or a major depression; present 2 years for adults and 1 year for children/adolescents

Schizophrenia Spectrum and Other Psychotic Disorders

- Characterized by abnormalities in one or more of the following:
  - ◊ **Delusions:** Fixed beliefs that are held to be true despite evidence that they are not
  - ◊ **Hallucinations:** False sensory perception that occurs without external stimuli
  - ◊ **Disorganized Thinking:** Typically expressed through speech, which can be disjointed, random, lacking focus (for example, world salad, jumping around to different topics)
  - ◊ **Disorganized Motor Behaviour:** Behaviour that ranges from those found in childhood to agitation; catatonia—decreased responsiveness to external stimuli
  - ◊ **Negative Symptoms:** Decrease in normal functions such as emotional expression, motivation (avolition), speech (alogia), ability to experience pleasure (anhedonia), and interest in social interactions (asociality)

- Examples are:

  ◊ **Schizotypal (Personality) Disorder:**

  ◊ **Delusional Disorder:** One or more delusions that persist for at least 1 month

  ◊ **Brief Psychotic Disorder:** Sudden onset of at least one of the following—delusions, hallucinations, disorganized speech, abnormal motor behaviour

  ◊ **Schizophrenia:** Cognitive, behavioural, and motor dysfunction for minimum of 6 months; minimum of two of the following symptoms—delusion, hallucinations, disorganized thinking, disorganized motor behaviour, negative symptoms; one symptom must be delusion, hallu-cination, or disorganized thinking

  ◊ **Schizophreniform Disorder:** Same symptoms as schizophrenia but lasts shorter

  ◊ **Schizoaffective Disorder:** Symptoms seen in schizophrenia along with depressive symptoms (APA, 2013)

 Practice...

1. Gerald has a constant thought that he has germs on his hands, and the longer he thinks about this the more uncomfortable he gets. If he cannot get to a sink and wash with hot water and soap, he begins to feel that not only is he "dirty" but also that he is "contaminated". In this clinical example, the thoughts that invade Gerald's life are called _____.
   a. compulsions
   b. delusions
   c. obsessions
   d. fantasies

2. _____ is a period of euphoria characterized by elevated self-esteem, increased talkativeness, enhanced energy, and a decreased need for sleep.
   a. Hypomania
   b. Mania
   c. Dysthymia
   d. Rapid cycling

3. _____ is characterized by excessive fear.
   a. OCD
   b. Depressive disorders
   c. Bipolar II disorders
   d. Anxiety disorders

4. _____ are false beliefs, while _____ are false sensory perceptions.
   a. Hallucinations, delusions
   b. Delusions, hallucinations
   c. Obsessions, compulsions
   d. Compulsions, obsessions

5. Which of the following disorders is found only in children?
   a. Separation anxiety disorder
   b. Body dysmorphic disorder
   c. Disruptive mood dysregulation disorder
   d. Cyclothymic disorder

 **Apply...**

1. **How Common are Mental Disorders?**

   - What is the prevalence of the following categories/groups/classifications of mental disorders? (You will need to find this information online, in textbooks, etc.) Please cite your sources.

     ◊ Anxiety disorders

     _____

     _____

     _____

     ◊ Obsessive-compulsive disorders

     _____

     _____

     _____

     ◊ Depressive disorders

     _____

     _____

     _____

     ◊ Bipolar disorders

     _____

     _____

     _____

     ◊ Schizophrenia spectrum disorders

     _____

     _____

     _____

   - What does the prevalence rates of these mental disorders tell us about the health of Canadians?

     _____

     _____

     _____

     _____

   - What challenges did you experience while trying to locate the prevalence rates for these disorders?

     _____

     _____

     _____

     _____

to be continued

 **Apply...**

continued

2. **Delusions and Hallucinations**

   Complete the following table. You may use the internet, peer-reviewed journals, textbooks, etc. Please cite your sources.

	Delusions	Hallucinations
Definition		
Types		
Examples		
Sources used		

3. **Not guilty by reason of mental defect**

   Research the idea of "not guilty by reason of mental defect." You may use the internet, peer-reviewed journals, textbooks, etc. Please cite your sources.

   • What is the underlying premise of this legal concept?

   _____

   _____

   _____

   • How is this applied in Canada?

   _____

   _____

   _____

   • In small groups (three to five) discuss the pros and cons of this legal concept. What are the thoughts shared?

   _____

   _____

   _____

Trauma- and Stressor-Related Disorders, Feeding and Eating Disorders, Disruptive, Impulse-Control, and Conduct Disorders, Substance-Related and Addictive Disorders, and Personality Disorders

 Provide an example for each of the following disorder categories: trauma- and stressor-related disorders, feeding and eating disorders, disruptive, impulse-control, and conduct disorders, substance-related and addictive disorders, and personality disorders

As you have seen in our last unit, there are multiple disorders that fall under specific mental disorder classifications/categories. In addition to those outlined in Unit 2 of this chapter, you have already researched sleep disorders as one of your activities for Chapter 6 on Consciousness. We will outline a few more disorders in this unit, using the DSM-5 as our resource (APA, 2013).

Trauma- and Stressor-Related Disorders

- Exposure to a traumatic or stressful event is a criteria for diagnosis; some examples are:
  - ◊ **Reactive Attachment Disorder:** Child does not seek out or use attachment figure for comfort, support, protection, or nurturance
  - ◊ **Disinhibited Social Engagement Disorder:** Overly familiar behaviour with relative strangers
  - ◊ **Posttraumatic Stress Disorder (PTSD):** Development of characteristic symptoms, such as memories, dreams, flashbacks, changes in cognition, and avoidance, following exposure to one or more traumatic events
  - ◊ **Acute Stress Disorder:** Similar to PTSD, lasting between 3 days and 1 month
  - ◊ **Adjustment Disorders:** Excessive distress and/or significant impairment in life in response to an identifiable stressor, such as the end of a relationship

Feeding and Eating Disorders

- Disturbed eating behaviours resulting in impaired health; some examples are:
  - ◊ **Pica:** Eating non-food items for a minimum of 1 month
  - ◊ **Rumination Disorder:** Repeated regurgitation of food, minimum 1 month, regurgitated food may be re-chewed, re-swallowed, or spit out.
  - ◊ **Avoidant/Restrictive Food Intake Disorder:** Avoidance or restriction of food intake, due to lack of interest, or dislike of food texture or colour, etc., leading to significant weight loss, nutritional deficit
  - ◊ **Anorexia Nervosa:** Ongoing food restriction, intense fear of gaining weight, inaccurate perception of body weight or shape
  - ◊ **Bulimia Nervosa:** Recurrent binge eating followed by recurrent compensatory behaviours to prevent weight gain, such as vomiting
  - ◊ **Binge-Eating Disorder:** Recurrent episodes of binge eating, at least once per week for 3 months

Disruptive, Impulse-Control, and Conduct Disorders

- Problems in the self-control of emotions and behaviours; negative behaviours directed to others; some examples are:
  - ◊ **Oppositional Defiant Disorder:** Angry or irritable mood, and negative behaviour directed to at least one person (not a sibling); behaviour is argumentative or vindictive; ongoing for at least 6 months
  - ◊ **Intermittent Explosive Disorder:** Impulsive or aggressive outbursts that have a rapid onset and last for less than 30 minutes, in response to a minor provocation
  - ◊ **Conduct Disorder:** Ongoing behaviour which violates the rights of others; minimum of 6 months; behaviour may involve aggression to people and animals, destruction of property, deceitfulness, theft
  - ◊ **Pyromania:** Deliberately setting fires more than once
  - ◊ **Kleptomania:** Repeated stealing of objects not needed for personal use or their value

Substance-Related and Addictive Disorders

- Category encompasses 10 separate classes of drugs:
  - ◊ Alcohol
  - ◊ Caffeine
  - ◊ Cannabis
  - ◊ Hallucinogens
  - ◊ Inhalants
  - ◊ Opioids
  - ◊ Sedatives
  - ◊ Hypnotics and anxiolytics
  - ◊ Stimulants
  - ◊ Tobacco
  - ◊ Other (or unknown) substances
- All drugs activate the reward circuit (review chapters on the human brain [Chapter 2] and consciousness [Chapter 6])
- The substance-related disorders:
  - ◊ **Substance Use Disorders:** Continual use of a drug despite the problems it cause
  - ◊ **Substance-Induced Disorders:** Intoxication, withdrawal, and other substance/medication-induced mental disorders (psychotic disorders, bipolar and related disorders, depressive disorders, anxiety disorders, obsessive-compulsive and related disorders, sleep disorders, sexual dysfunctions, delirium, and neurocognitive disorders)
  - ◊ Specific disorders identified for each drug
- Also includes **gambling disorder:** Problematic gambling behaviour resulting in distress; gambling activates reward circuit like drugs do

Personality Disorders

- Disordered, faulty, dysfunctional, or maladaptive way of understanding and responding to the world; a personality that is inflexible and deviates greatly from social norms

- Some examples are:
  - ◊ **Paranoid Personality Disorder:** Distrust and suspicious of others' motives
  - ◊ **Schizoid Personality Disorder:** Detachment from social relationships, narrow range of emotional expression
  - ◊ **Schizotypal Personality Disorder:** Odd, eccentric, uncomfortable in social situations
  - ◊ **Antisocial Personality Disorder:** Disregard for, and violation of, the rights of others
  - ◊ **Borderline Personality Disorder:** Unstable relationships, self-image, and marked behaviours
  - ◊ **Histrionic Personality Disorder:** Overly emotional and attention seeking
  - ◊ **Narcissistic Personality Disorder:** Grandiosity, need for admiration, lack of empathy
  - ◊ **Avoidant Personality Disorder:** Social inhibition, feelings of inadequacy, hypersensitive to negative evaluation
  - ◊ **Dependent Personality Disorder:** Submissive and clingy behaviour
  - ◊ **Obsessive-Compulsive Personality:** Preoccupation with orderliness, perfectionism, control
  - ◊ **Personality Change Due to Another Medical Condition:** Personality disturbance due to the direct physiological effects of a medical condition, such as brain damage (APA, 2013)

Now that we have been introduced to some mental disorders, it is important to know that at any given time, we can be diagnosed with more than one mental disorder, which is referred to as **comorbidity**. For example, anxiety and depressive disorders often occur together.

 # Practice...

1. To be classified as a trauma/stress disorder, _____ is a criteria for diagnosis.
   a. exposure to a traumatic or stressful event
   b. recurring nightmares
   c. discomfort in social situations
   d. sadness

2. Diagnostic criteria for duration of symptoms is _____ in posttraumatic stress disorder compared to acute stress disorder.
   a. shorter
   b. longer
   c. the same
   d. they have different symptoms, so duration does not matter

3. Bulimia Nervosa and Binge-Eating Disorder are similar in that both _____.
   a. are subsets of anorexia
   b. involve eating non-food items
   c. involve periods of binging on food
   d. are forms of drug-induced illnesses

4. Gambling activates the reward circuit just as drugs do.
   a. True
   b. False

5. All of the following are personality disorders except _____.
   a. avoidant
   b. paranoid
   c. schizotypal
   d. kleptomania

1. **Neurodevelopmental Disorders**

   The DSM-5 identifies six classifications of neurodevelopmental disorders: intellectual disability, communication disorders, autism spectrum disorders, attention deficit hyperactive disorders, neurodevelopmental motor disorders, and specific learning disorder.

   - Choose two of these disorders. Research the disorders you have chosen and complete the following table. You may use the internet, peer-reviewed journals, textbooks, etc. Ensure that the resources you use reflect DSM-5 classifications and discussions of your chosen disorders.

   - Complete the table below.

	Disorder category #1:	**Disorder category #2:**
Definition of disorder, including symptoms		
Disorders found under category		
Causes of disorder		
Prevalence of disorder		

to be continued

Apply...

continued

- What challenges did you encounter as you attempted to complete the table?

_____
_____
_____
_____
_____
_____
_____
_____
_____
_____
_____
_____
_____
_____
_____
_____

2. **Substance Disorders**

   Choose one of the 10 drugs outlined in the DSM-5 under substance-related and addictive disorders.

   - Research that drug and describe the mental disorders associated with that drug.

   You may use the internet, peer-reviewed journals, textbooks, etc.

   - Share your findings with a classmate who has researched a different drug.

_____
_____
_____
_____
_____
_____
_____
_____
_____
_____
_____

Causes and Treatment of Mental Disorders

 Discuss the general causes of mental disorders and how they are treated according to the biological, psychodynamic, behavioural, and cognitive approaches

At this point you may be asking, "What causes mental disorders?" or even "How do we treat mental disorders?" In this unit, we discuss the **etiology** or causes of mental disorders. We can breakdown causes into:

- **Predisposing Cause:** Underlying factors that make us vulnerable to a mental disorder

- **Precipitating Cause:** An event that brings on, or is a catalyst for, a mental disorder

- **Perpetuating Cause:** Factors that keep mental disorder going after it develops (Baird & McCarthy, 2014)

The National Institute of Health (NIH) (2016) notes that predisposing factors interact with precipitating factors to create **risk** factors for mental disorders. Let's look at some of the risk factors NIH has identified for five of the mental disorders we have previously looked at.

Risk Factors for Anxiety Disorders:

- Childhood shyness
- Being female
- Divorced or widowed
- Stressful life events
- Family history of mental disorders
- Elevated afternoon cortisol levels in the saliva

Risk Factors for Obsessive-Compulsive Disorder:

- Differences in brain structures
- History of disorder in immediate family
- Trauma

Risk Factors for Depressive Disorders:

- Being an adult
- Family history of depression
- Major life changes, trauma, or stress
- Medical illness
- Some medications

Risk Factors for Bipolar Disorders:

- Family history of disorder
- Differences in brain structure

Risk Factors for Schizophrenia:

- Family history of disorder
- Neurotransmitter imbalances

TABLE 13.1 Mental disorders.

Theoretical Perspective/ Approach	Causes	Treatments
Biological	Genetics, personality traits, differences in brain functioning/ structure, neurotransmitters (for example, dopamine, serotonin, GABA)	Medication—selective serotonin reuptake inhibitors (SSRIs), benzodiazepines influence levels and activity of neurotransmitters
Psychodynamic	Unconscious conflict Damage to ego, weakened ego Defence mechanisms (repression and displacement)	Interpersonal psychotherapy (IPT) addresses unconscious conflicts
Behavioural	Learned through operant, classical, and observational learning; reinforced	Exposure therapy—disrupt learning, learn different associations, stop reinforcing behaviours; change behaviour
Cognitive	Faulty thinking, maladaptive thoughts, hypersensitive to body responses	Cognitive therapy—address faulty cognitions, change the way we perceive and think

- Viruses
- Prenatal malnutrition
- Birth complications

The **diathesis-stress model**—think "nature + nurture" model—is commonly used to explain the development of mental disorders. We know that how we view the cause of mental disorders will determine how we treat it. Let's take a look (APA, 2013; Baird & McCarthy, 2014; Beidel et al., 2017) (Table 13.1).

Now that we have looked at treatment approaches in general, we can focus on a few strategies to examine more fully.

Medications

Medications are used to treat many mental disorders. They work by impacting neural communication. Here are some examples:

- Antidepressant drugs (tricyclics, SSRIs, monoamine oxidase [MAO] inhibitors) for depressive disorders, bipolar disorders, anxiety disorders, OCD
- Antipsychotic drugs for schizophrenia and other psychotic disorders, bipolar disorders
- Antianxiety medications for anxiety disorders
- Stimulants, like Ritalin, for attention deficit hyperactive disorder
- Mood-stabilizers, like lithium, for bipolar disorder

Electroconvulsive Therapy

- Involves sending electric shocks to patients' brains
- Effective for treating severe depression when nothing else works
- Unilateral administration decreases memory loss

Psychosurgery

- Parts of patient's brain are surgically altered
- Highly localized to specific areas of brain
- Deep brain stimulation
- Effective for OCD when nothing else works

Therapy

Is therapy effective in treating mental disorders? Yes, it is! Here are some examples of common therapeutic approaches:

1. **Psychodynamic Therapies**

   - Psychoanalysis: Uses strategies like free association and dream analysis to access our unconscious conflicts, desires, motivations, fears, etc. and help us work out our issues; patient talks and therapist interprets
   - Interpersonal Psychotherapy: Focuses on helping us improve our relationships

2. **Humanistic Therapies**

   - Focus on achieving wellness; psychological problems are opportunities to reflect on our lives
   - Person-Centred Therapy: Therapeutic process focuses on the client's abilities and insights
   - Gestalt Therapy: Therapist attempts to make the client feel whole by helping the client feel aware of and responsible for his or her thoughts, behaviours, experiences, and feelings

3. **Cognitive and Behavioural Psychotherapy**

   - "Talk therapy"
   - Psychological problems are caused by faulty or irrational thinking, which in turn produces faulty or irrational behaviours
   - Identify and change the thinking and behaviour patterns that create problems
   - Combines cognitive approach and behavioural approach

There are many approaches to treating mental disorders, yet many people do not seek help. In your activity for this unit, you will examine the possible reasons why so many of us do not seek out the help necessary to improve our mental health.

Practice...

1. According to the National Institute of Health, all of the following are risk factors for depressive disorders except _____.
   a. family history of depression
   b. major life changes
   c. body mass index
   d. Medical illness

2. According to the behavioural approach, mental disorders are caused by _____.
   a. reinforced behaviours
   b. unconscious conflict
   c. faulty thinking patterns
   d. brain abnormalities

3. Modern electroconvulsive therapy is used to treat _____.
   a. bipolar II disorder
   b. paranoid schizophrenia
   c. severe depression
   d. anorexia nervosa

4. _____ is a treatment method in which parts of the brain are physically/medically altered to treat mental disorders.
   a. Psychotherapy
   b. Psychosurgery
   c. Electroconvulsive therapy
   d. The Luxembourg technique

5. _____ is a type of psychotherapy that relates closely to Freudian concepts like the influence of the unconscious. It requires patients to talk to a psychiatrist about their lives while the psychiatrist listens, analyzes, and interprets each word.
   a. Humanistic psychotherapy
   b. Person-centred therapy
   c. Cognitive-behavioural therapy
   d. Psychoanalysis

Apply...

1. **Social Media and Mental Health**

   • How do you think social media influences mental health?

   _____

   _____

   _____

   _____

   _____

   _____

   _____

   • What are the risk factors for suicide? (You will need to research this topic to answer these questions accurately and fully.)

   _____

   _____

to be continued

 **Apply…**

continued

_____
_____
_____
_____
_____

- How common is suicide?

_____
_____
_____
_____
_____
_____
_____
_____
_____

- How do you think we could use social media to prevent suicides?

_____
_____
_____
_____
_____
_____
_____
_____

- Discuss your answers in small groups (three to five members). Write a summary of your discussion.

_____
_____
_____
_____
_____
_____
_____

to be continued

 **Apply...**

continued

2. **Failing to Seek Help**

   Not everyone who has a mental disorder seeks help.

   • List the reasons why you think some people choose not to seek help for their mental health.

   _____

   _____

   _____

   _____

   _____

   _____

   _____

   _____

   _____

   _____

   _____

   _____

   _____

   _____

   • Would you seek help if you thought you had a mental disorder? Explain your answer.

   _____

   _____

   _____

   _____

   _____

   _____

   _____

   _____

   _____

   _____

   _____

   _____

   _____

   _____

   _____

KNOW...

Learning Objectives

1. Mental disorder:

Mental disorder is a syndrome characterized by clinically significant disturbance in an individual's cognition, emotion regulation, or behaviour that reflects a dysfunction in the psychological, biological, or developmental processes underlying mental functioning.

Taken From: *Diagnostic and Statistical Manual of Mental Disorders*, 5th edition, copyright: American Psychiatric Association.

2. Essential features underlying anxiety disorders, obsessive-compulsive and related disorders, depressive disorders, bipolar and related disorders, and schizophrenia spectrum and other psychotic disorders:

Anxiety disorders are characterized by excessive fear and anxiety. Obsessive-compulsive and related disorders have features of recurring intrusive thoughts, repetitive behaviours, or mental acts. Depressive disorders are identified by a sad or irritable mood. Bipolar and related disorders describe the cycling of episodes of mania and episodes of major depression. Schizophrenia spectrum and other psychotic disorders are characterized by the presence of delusions, hallucinations, disorganized thinking, disorganized motor behaviour, and negative symptoms.

3. Example of each of the following disorder categories: trauma- and stressor-related disorders, feeding and eating disorders, disruptive, impulse-control, and conduct disorders, substance-related and addictive disorders, and personality disorders:

You can choose the examples you want. Here is an example:

- Trauma- and stressor-related disorders: Post-traumatic stress disorder

- Feeding and eating disorders: Pica

- Disruptive, impulse-control, and conduct disorders: Oppositional defiant disorder

- Substance-related and addictive disorders: Gambling disorder

- Personality disorder: Antisocial personality disorder

4. General causes of mental disorders and how they are treated according to the biological, psychodynamic, behavioural, and cognitive approaches:

The biological approach proposes causes such as genetics, personality traits, differences in brain functioning/structure, or neurotransmitters and treatment involves medication. The psychodynamic approach proposes causes such as unconscious conflict, damaged ego, or defence mechanisms, and treatment involves therapy to address unconscious conflicts. The behavioural approach proposes that learned and reinforced behaviours lead to mental disorders, and treatment aims to replace maladaptive behaviour with healthier ones, through strategies like exposure therapy. The cognitive approach proposes that faulty thinking, maladaptive thoughts, or hypersensitivity to body responses lead to mental disorders, and treatment aims to change our cognitions.

Key Terms

Mental Health: A state of mental balance or homeostasis.

Mental Illness: A health condition characterized by altered thinking, feeling, or behaving that brings about distress and/or impaired functioning.

Psychopathology: The study of disorders of mind, mood, and behaviour; also referred to as abnormal psychology.

Comorbidity: Having more than one mental disorder at the same time.

Aetiology: Cause or causes of a disorder.

Answers to Practice

Defining Mental Disorder
1. b   2. a   3. c   4. d   5. b

Anxiety Disorders, Obsessive-Compulsive and Related Disorders, Depressive Disorders, Bipolar and Related Disorders, and Schizophrenia Spectrum and Other Psychotic Disorders
1. c   2. b   3. d   4. b   5. a

Trauma- and Stressor-Related Disorders, Feeding and Eating Disorders, Disruptive, Impulse-Control, and Conduct Disorders, Substance-Related and Addictive Disorders, and Personality Disorders
1. a   2. b   3. c   4. a   5. d

Causes and Treatment of Mental Disorders
1. c   2. a   3. c   4. b   5. d

References

American Psychiatric Association. (2013). *DSM-5.* Washington, DC: American Psychiatric Publishing.

Baird, A., & McCarthy, A. (2014). *THINK psychology* (2nd Canadian edition). Don Mills, ON: Pearson Education, Inc.; pp. 231–261.

Beidel., Deborah., Bulik, C., Stanley, M., & Taylor, S. (2017). *Abnormal psychology* (1st Canadian edition). Don Mills, ON: Pearson Education Canada.

Canadian Mental Health Association. (2017). *Fast facts about mental illness*. Retrieved from http://www.cmha.ca/media/fast-facts-about-mental-illness/#.WYEAsVGQzlU

National Institute of Health (NIH). (2016). *Mental health information*. Retrieved from https://www.nimh.nih.gov/health/topics/index.shtml.

Notes

Notes

Notes

Notes

Notes

Notes

Notes

Notes

Notes

Notes

Notes